I WAS ONE OF THE UNEMPLOYED

STUDIES IN
BRITISH LABOUR HISTORY

General Editor: Huw Beynon

I WAS ONE OF THE UNEMPLOYED

by

MAX COHEN

With a Foreword by
SIR WILLIAM BEVERIDGE

EP Publishing Limited
1978

First published by Victor Gollancz Ltd., London, 1945

Republished 1978 by
EP Publishing Limited
East Ardsley, Wakefield
West Yorkshire, England

by permission of the original publishers

ISBN 0 7158 1346 3

British Library Cataloguing in Publication Data
Cohen, Max
  I was one of the unemployed.
  – (Studies in British Labour History).
  1. Unemployed – England – History –
  20th century 2. England – Social life and
  customs – 20th century
  I. Title II. Series
  942.083'092'4   HD5766.A6
  ISBN 0-7158-1346-3

Please address all enquiries to EP Publishing Limited
(address as above)

Printed in Great Britain by
Redwood Burn Limited
Trowbridge & Esher

FOREWORD

By Sir William Beveridge

I AM HAPPY to write this foreword to Mr. Max Cohen's book, because the book shows vividly what unemployment has meant in the past, and thus provides one more demonstration of that which must not be allowed to recur.

"Statistics of unemployment," as I have written elsewhere,* "are not just statistics. Statistics of unemployment mean rows of men and women, not of figures only. The three million or so unemployed of 1932 means three million lives being wasted in idleness, growing despair and numbing indifference. Behind these three million individuals seeking an outlet for their energies and not finding it, are their wives and families making hopeless shift with want, losing their birthright of healthy development, wondering whether they should have been born. Beyond the men and women actually unemployed at any moment, are the millions more in work at that moment but never knowing how long that work or any work for them may last."

Mr. Cohen's book begins with the time about 1932. It sets out the experiences not simply of one of the unemployed, but of one of those whose unemployment was least excusable and most harmful, those who have been described as "Disinherited Youth" in a survey made for the Carnegie United Kingdom Trustees. The persons unemployed between the wars included in Britain and in America alike hundreds of thousands of young men and women just seeking to start their careers:

"The record of where youth stands in free democracies in times of peace is in poignant contrast to what is required of youth in war, and to the call to youth made by the German dictator in preparing war. By this judgment of uselessness that it passed so widely on adaptable youth, the unplanned market economy of the past in Britain and in America must itself be judged and stands condemned."

Mr. Cohen was just one of these many young men condemned to idleness. Of his native energy and ability no one who reads this account can have any doubt. It is fortunate that he had also the gift of words to recount his experience. He is able to describe at first hand what so many others have related at second hand of

* *Full Employment in a Free Society*, pp. 245 and 247.

the varied evils of unemployment. He shows, against the background of physical suffering, the gradual but certain loss of self-respect; the poisoning of family relations; the loss of privacy which poverty brings; the devastating effects of uncertainty as to how long a job may last even when one has a job, and finally, how meaningless is the term "liberty" for a starving man. Mr. Cohen's account of his first hunger when he came to see everything in terms of food is one of many striking passages in this remarkable book.

Liberty is not something negative: the absence of legal restraint, as so many self-styled apostles of liberty regard it. Liberty means effective choice of doing or not doing something. The greater the range of effective choice, the greater the liberty. It follows that a starving man, though he may be under no orders from the State as to how he shall act while starving, is not free, because he is a slave of his physical urgencies. Until he is fed, he has no effective choice of action; he is not a reasoning human being, but an animal needing to be fed. He cannot act as a human being until his physical urgencies are removed. It is this appreciation of liberty, as involving effective choice of action, that distinguishes those who understand liberty from many of those who merely talk about it. The man who, in order to satisfy his physical urgencies, is compelled for many hours to stand in a Labour Exchange queue to get the money for that purpose, and has no other choice open to him except starvation or theft, is not free.

As true, and even more important, is the fact that the main evil of unemployment is not physical but psychological. This also is illustrated by Mr. Cohen in many places, but particularly in a chapter headed "Nerves", dealing with the "multifarious sources of worry that can afflict an out-of-work", and rejecting the view that those who have no family responsibilities for that reason do not mind unemployment.

> "It may be thought that unemployed single men or women will not be so affected by worry as those unemployed who are married and have children. What must be kept clear, however, is that it is not the fact of marriage and children that is the basic cause of worry to the unemployed. The basic cause of worry is the fact of unemployment. Single men and women are just as much worried by unemployment as married people, with the additional fact that they are often living on their own and have no one with whom to share their more secret and agonising worries."

The evil of unemployment cannot be cured by improvement of the provision made for it through unemployment benefit or

assistance. The actual rates of benefit have in various wa
increased since the time to which Mr. Cohen's experiences
But all changes in the provision for unemployment lea
essential evil unchanged; mass-unemployment, involving id ...ss
in the individual case, for months and years together, is an evil
which cannot be alleviated. The only thing to do with mass-
unemployment is to abolish it. That is why the publication of
Mr. Cohen's book at the moment of our second passage from total
war to peace is so timely. It should be read widely, lest we forget
the past. It should be read above all by those, if any still exist, who
wonder whether we can afford to abolish unemployment.

We know now by repeated experience that by making total war
it is possible to abolish mass-unemployment. We know that this
happens because in war the nation has a common accepted purpose which it is determined to pursue at any cost in terms of
money, up to the physical limit set by its man-power. We have to
apply this knowledge to the conditions of peace.

The economic distinction between war and peace is that in war
commodities are scarce and men have value, while in peace commodities are abundant for those who have money to buy them,
and men suffer mass-unemployment. In war we have queues of
those who wish to buy things. In peace we have queues of those
who wish to sell their service. Mr. Cohen's vivid picture of the
Labour Exchanges in the depression raises acutely the question:
How can we abolish queues at the shops without re-establishing
queues at the Labour Exchanges?

It is not the purpose of Mr. Cohen's book to answer that
question. Nor, of course, can the answer be set out in this brief
foreword. But the direction in which the answer has to be sought
is clear.

The economic distinction between war and peace reflects a
political distinction. The political distinction between war and
peace hitherto in Britain has been that in war the nation has had
a common purpose, while in peace it has had no common purpose.
It has accepted the pursuit of individual self-interest as the guiding
and driving force in society. Experience has shown that this leads
to want and unemployment, to needless suffering and unjustified
inequality.

In war, because of the urgency of our national desire to win
victory or escape defeat, everything else is sacrificed to the arming
of men to fight. We are busy because we have a common national
purpose, and because we are busy. We have in war the dignity of
feeling useful. To enjoy the same dignity in peace, we must equally
have a common national purpose. We must replace the pursuit of
self-interest as a driving and guiding force in economic life, by the

pursuit of some common purpose, which some will describe as social justice, and others as putting first things first, seeing that there are bread, and health, and houses for all, before there are cake, and cars, and circuses for anyone.

Happiness, as Aristotle said, is an activity: idleness is misery. Activity for a nation, as for an individual, depends on purpose, on desire to do things.

Whether we can get full employment in any country depends on whether those who, in the last resort, control the money power—the spending—on which employment depends, wish sufficiently to get things done. We shall not get full employment by trusting to self-interest. "Experience in peace has shown that the desire of men who are already above want, to increase their profits by investment, is not a strong enough motive or sufficiently persistent in its action to produce a demand for labour which is strong enough and steady enough."* We shall get full employment only by pursuing a common purpose; by using for that purpose the organised power of the State, by the action of Government.

But employment is not an end in itself. Whether the employment will be harmful, or the reverse, whether it will be secured without sacrifice of things even more important, depends upon the kind of things which those who govern desire to get done.

It is possible to get full employment in making war and in preparing for war. It is possible to get full employment and in the process to destroy essential liberties. To get full employment in a free society we must have economic planning, but it must be directed by men who understand and value liberty. It must be directed by men who have imagination to see the infinite possibilities of human nature and the infinite variety of human needs. It must be directed by men filled with "large and liberal discontent".

The present moment of the ending of the second total war is a crisis in human affairs. It is as certain that we must find the means of abolishing mass unemployment as it has become certain, since the invention of the atomic bomb, that we must find a means of abolishing war. The desire of ordinary people of all nations to be rid of both war and of unemployment can be taken for granted. Whether this desire shall be satisfied or whether through defeat of it we shall plunge back into a world far worse than any that our fathers knew, depends in the last resort on the imagination and the courage of those who in the free countries of the world, by the choice of their fellows, are called to government. Their opportunity to-day is immense.

* *Full Employment in a Free Society*, p. 274.

CONTENTS

BOOK FOUR

Some Encounters

BOOK FIVE

Journeyings in the Wilderness

BOOK ONE

APPRENTICE TO POVERTY

CHAPTER I

A DRAMATIC MOMENT

One evening we were told to finish work at six o'clock. We were also told to come to work the next day, not in the morning but in the afternoon.

Everyone was rather taken aback, for till then we had been working full speed ahead, with as much overtime as it was possible for us to cope with. But, then, Christmas was drawing near. During the season immediately before, and for some time after Christmas, the cabinet-making trade endures an annual period of sleeping sickness. Christmas was drawing near. It was clear that the busy season was at an end.

It was one of Forgeton's black days when we reassembled the next afternoon outside the small, tumbledown factory where we worked. A heavy pall of soot turned the day into night, so that even at midday lights were blazing everywhere. The gloomy weather seemed a fit background for the occasion. Although we made many jokes about the luxury of beginning work in the afternoon, most of us were oppressed by the realisation that "the sack" was near.

We were a workshop of about a score of young fellows. All of us save the foreman were under twenty-one years old, and we began work that afternoon in a somewhat skittish mood.

Then at five o'clock the blow fell, and in a far more drastic fashion than any of us had anticipated. For the past two or three days our employer had been running about in the most distracted way, dashing into the workshop, mopping his brow and dashing out again. Now he suddenly bellowed:

"Everybody—stop work! Stop workin', boys!"

"Everybody stop work!" the boss's son reiterated.

It was a dramatic moment. On a sudden hands ceased moving. The noise of planes, saws and hammers abruptly gave way to silence. Wondering faces turned towards the boss.

The boss mopped his brow and moistened his lips. His melon-like face bore signs of acute emotion.

"Boys," he wheezed mournfully, "I got bad news for yer.

I'm sorry to 'ave ter tell yer, boys, but yer'll 'ave ter take an hour's notice—all of yer."

He paused. There was a deathly silence. The boss's face became more distressed than ever.

"Ye see 'ow it is, boys. There's no work about—none at all. I been running about all over the place trying ter get some for yer. But I can't get it. So yer'll all 'ave to finish wi' me, boys. It can't be 'elped, boys. As soon as there's any work knockin' about, yer can all come back an' start wi' me again."

Another pause.

"Well, start up again, boys; an' I'll 'ave yer money ready for yer when yer finish."

His fat, sympathetic face now bore signs of anguish. No doubt it was quite genuine. Our boss was one of those stout, apparently soft-hearted men who seem to be continually oppressed by the woes of others. Nevertheless, he was enough of what is euphemistically termed "a business man" not to allow his preoccupation with the troubles of mankind in general to blind him to his own interests in particular.

However, we were not very concerned with such questions at the moment. We resumed work in silence. Strangely enough, force of habit kept us working as intensely as if we had never heard that within an hour we would no longer be under the sway of our employer.

At six o'clock the boss's son blew his tin whistle. Work ceased again. With subdued airs we packed our tools away. The boss came into the workshop. In his hand he held our badges of unemployment—our cards. He seemed now in no mood for mournful oratory. In a quick and practical fashion he called out our names one by one, gave to each worker the Unemployment and Health Insurance cards that belonged to him, paid him what money was due, and then passed on to the next in the line.

I found myself out in the black street, a heavy toolbox in one hand, my other hand still clutching my cards and my wage-packet. For a few moments I joked uneasily with the group that had gathered outside the workshop. Then I went on my way.

CHAPTER II

SIGNING-ON

THE NEXT MORNING I went to sign-on at the Labour Exchange. In accordance with the necessary routine I went first to that part of the Exchange which is reserved for "fresh claims".

2

The inside of the Exchange was dingy and repellant to the eye. There appeared to be a large number of notices forbidding one to do this and warning one of the penalties incurred by doing that. A counter, behind which stood or sat various clerks, ran the length of the Exchange. Ever and again there was a discordant clang when a clerk shut one of the uncompromising steel cabinets. Men standing in front of the counter appeared to be engaged in confidential discussion with the clerks.

At intervals along the counter were attached notices bearing cryptic letters and numbers: "Box 1", "Box 2", "Box 3". Before each of these notices were queues of men, gradually moving up to the counter. These, then, were the "boxes", or sub-divisions, at which unemployed signed their names to the testimony that they were unemployed, and capable of, and available for, work.

My eye roved farther. Ah, there it was. "Fresh claims." I went to the clerk at the "Fresh Claims" counter. He was a small man in early middle-age, who appeared to be weary unto death of doing the same thing over and over again. He asked me for my Unemployment Book, and then told me to sit down and wait till I was called.

There were a few rows of chairs facing the "Fresh Claims" counter, and on them men sat waiting with an air of dumb resignation. I sat down.

At first I glanced round the Exchange, reading what notices I could. Then I engaged in wondering what was the business of various men who stood about in groups of two or three. I saw the clerk who had taken my Unemployment Book search for my claim in a filing-cabinet, ever and again referring to my Unemployment Book to see if he had found the right claim. Then I studied my fellow-unemployed seated around me, and tried to guess from their appearance their trades and status in life. Then I observed the clerks, their varying degrees of friendliness or officiousness. After that I began to feel bored; ennui descended upon me.

I looked at the clock. It was nearly five to ten. I had been here twenty minutes. Nothing seemed to have happened in the "Fresh Claims". Life appeared to be sunk in a peculiar Labour Exchange trance. Clerks seated behind the counter went on scribbling. Officials picked their way to and fro between desks and clerks. Men standing before the counter conversed in low, serious tones with clerks standing behind the counter.

I extracted a cigarette and prepared to light it. Someone tapped me on the shoulder. I glanced round. He was a tall, bony man dressed in the apparel of a navvy.

"You can't smoke in 'ere, mate," he whispered huskily. He pointed to a notice:

NO SMOKING.

I smiled in feeble apology to the navvy that I should have been so foolhardy as to attempt to smoke in these precincts.

It is ten o'clock . . . a quarter-past ten . . . half-past. . . . At every quarter of an hour, as though actuated by some weird mechanism, a horde of ill-shaved, shabby and hungry-looking men surges into the Exchange. Their boots sound like thunder on the wooden floor. They scramble hurriedly to their place in front of their "box". Like long twin snakes their double lines uncoil themselves before the clerks. The men scribble something. Then they push their way out through the crowd. For some reason they all look as though they have performed an unpleasant duty.

But with us scarcely anything happens. At rare intervals the clerk calls out a name. A man starts up, goes to the counter and engages in confidential talk with the clerks.

I understand now the reason for those men standing about in twos and threes. They have merely got fed up with sitting and waiting in silence. They are standing up to stretch their legs and have a low-voiced chat.

At a quarter to eleven I find it difficult to believe that I have been in here only a little over an hour. At eleven o'clock I feel that I have sat here all my life; everything else is merely something I dreamt on these chairs. At a quarter-past eleven I don't care any more.

Suddenly the clerk calls my name. I start up incredulously. I strive to look as though there is nothing wonderful in the fact that it is my turn at last. I go to the counter.

An unemployed man "makes a claim" for unemployment benefit. The various documents relating to the case are known as the "claim". The clerk had my "claim" before him. It appeared to consist of pages of stiff paper held together by an elastic band. On the various pages was recorded my Labour Exchange history.

The clerk proceeded to bring this history up to date. Who had I been working for? How long had I been working? Why had I been dismissed? What kind of work had I been doing?

When these and other questions had been disposed of, the clerk opened that section of the claim that was a kind of register for the number of days of unemployment. Obliterating those days of that week on which I had been working, he pointed to the day I was to sign for, and uttered those words which have

4

been heard millions of times in the Labour Exchanges of the country:

"Sign for to-day," he said.

I signed.

The clerk then filled up a yellow postcard, writing on it the information as to when and at which "Box" I was to sign-on in the future. I pocketed the card and went out.

I had signed-on.

CHAPTER III

THE LABOUR EXCHANGE

THE LONG, NARROW street appears to be suffused with portentous activity. Crowds of men stand about on the pavements and in the roadway. The crowds are steadily reinforced by a stream of men flowing towards one end of the street. A low hum of voices rises on the morning air.

Bicycles stagger uncertainly among the groups in the roadway. The riders of the rusty and decrepit machines are handicapped because of the fact that every unessential feature has long since been stripped from their vehicles. The bicycles are without mudguards, without brakes, without pumps, without bells.

As you make your way down the mean street, it occurs to you that the street, the men in it and the bicycles are alike, in that all are equally poverty-stricken. The same air of having descended gradually but surely to the ultimate depths of indigence stamps them all.

Down towards the end of the street is the reason for the crowds —the Labour Exchange. It is a building that gives the impression of having been built for an emergency—an emergency that has extended until it has long since become a commonplace of everyday life. Whether the authorities hoped, wished or believed that large-scale unemployment was merely a passing phenomenon; or whether they desired to be economical; or whether they were simply callous to the inconvenience and actual suffering caused to the unemployed and the Exchange clerks—whatever the reason, the "temporary" building has remained, despite the fact that it has long since become too small for its purpose.

It is something like a large green wooden shanty. Two stairways, each accommodating about two people abreast, lead into the building.

As you approach the Exchange there is a rattle of bolts. The doors open. There is a sudden furious rush of the crowd. Some of those who have waited, patient and orderly, in the queue, find themselves pushed aside by some who have been hanging about on the pavements opposite.

Everybody loathes the Exchange. Crowds struggle to get up the narrow stairs into the building and out again as soon as possible. The stairs are blocked. Men become wedged in inextricable positions. There is no shouting or horseplay. It is merely a mad, passionate determination to avoid waiting in the hated queue a moment longer than is essential.

The queues stretch out of the wooden shanty and into the street. Behind the nine o'clock queue is the nine-fifteen queue. Behind the nine-fifteen queue is the half-formed nine-thirty queue, to which I belong. Men wander up and down the queues questioning anxiously, "Are you nine o'clock?" "Are you nine-fifteen?" "Are you nine-thirty?"

We in the nine-thirty queue wait in apathetic boredom for the time to pass. It is only nearly a quarter-past nine, but most of the nine-thirty queue are already in position. Indeed, in a short time the nine-forty-five queue begins to form. Such anxiety to be early may seem rather foolish, but it is not as foolish as it may seem. There are already far more unemployed signing on in each quarter of an hour at each box than can be accommodated in that time. The clerks, sweating away at their task, can barely manage to sign-on each quarter-hour section in twenty minutes or so. The result is that as the morning passes, the time we unemployed actually sign-on lags more and more behind the quarter-hour we should have signed.

This has the rather paradoxical effect of making some men come to the Exchange earlier than they need. They prefer to queue up for some time outside, and be the first of their queue to go inside, than to come at their right time and have to queue up inside the building.

The Labour Exchange in the centre of the town caters for many people who are seasonally unemployed. Here also there are many who have been unemployed for a long time, but they are outnumbered by the seasonal workers. Poverty one sees, and shabbiness, and all the other signs of unemployment.

Nevertheless, at that Central Exchange one can notice a certain liveliness. Hope has not died in those who are signing-on. They are going through hard times now, but soon, they hope, the busy season will come along. They anticipate knowing again, sooner or later, the good feeling of having a job and taking home wages at the end of the week. And so lively discussions are carried on in the queues, jokes and witty remarks are bandied about.

But here, at this suburban Labour Exchange, the atmosphere

is different. A ghostly silence has stolen out from the deserted factories. It has crept up to the men in the queues, and is haunting them. For them unemployment is not seasonal; it is eternal and without end. Years and years have gone by since they last passed through the factory gates. They depend on the local factories for life and hope, and life and hope are eternally withheld from them. And so they are gaunt and silent in the queues.

I had never before seen faces so gaunt and white as these; not white—grey. And I came to recognise this gaunt grey pallor as the true hall-mark of the chronically unemployed; the hall-mark of those who have undergone years of underfeeding, of feeding on cheap imitations of food, of never knowing what it is to have a full stomach. Many of the faces were covered with angry-red blotches. This, too, was because the food they ate lacked vitamins and nourishment, was without the power to stave off rust and decay.

But I was as much impressed by the men's bicycles as I was by the men themselves. I had never before seen bicycles like these. I had imagined that long before they reached this stage they were thrown on to the scrap-heap. Nevertheless, here men still used them to look for jobs, and to ride to the Labour Exchange.

And I saw the men and I saw the bicycles, and a chill uneasiness gripped me. . . .

My thoughts were interrupted by a sudden lunge forward of the queue. The nine-thirty queue is surging into the Labour Exchange to sign on. Boots slur on the pavement, and men gasp for breath. Soon I am in the maelstrom struggling up the narrow stairway into the building. Our boots are thundering on the wooden floor.

In the gloom of the Exchange the queues creep forward towards the clerks. I watch each man in turn present his "U.I.40" card (the yellow postcard we were given when we first signed-on), scribble his name in his claim, wait for his Health Insurance card to be franked, and then turn away.

One by one those in front of me are disposed of. Now it is my turn. The clerk glances hurriedly at my U.I.40, fumbles for my claim, tosses it towards me, stamps my Health Insurance card, takes back my claim, and whilst he is replacing it calls out irritably, "Now then! Next one, please!"

I shoulder my way out through the pressing crowd. Well, that's over, thank goodness.

CHAPTER IV

PAY DAY

On Thursdays and Fridays chaos reigned at the Exchange. On these days we were paid our Unemployment Benefit. It was necessary for us to line up for our usual lengthy wait to sign-on, and then, when we had received our pay-check, to go to the end of an enormous queue that stretched out of the Exchange, down the street, doubled back again, and possibly redoubled again, according to circumstances.

Because the signing-on clerks had more unemployed than they could cope with, there were more and more unemployed waiting to sign-on as time passed. Presumably the only way all the unemployed were eventually signed-on was by the clerks working on into such time as they would normally have reserved for other purposes.

On Thursdays and Fridays, however, the position was worse than on other days. The already crowded Exchange was packed to suffocation by the queue to the pay-box. There was only one pay-box to deal with all the unemployed, and so the pay-clerks could cope even less with this crowd than the box-clerks could with theirs. The result was that as time passed, even more men accumulated in the pay-queue than in all the rest of the queues put together.

With the lengthy waiting that took place, it was quite common for men signing-on at nine-forty-five to arrive at the pay-box after twelve o'clock, and to be then told, "Come back this afternoon for your money." I had been told that this sometimes occurred even with the nine-thirty queue. And so, added to the boredom, discomfort, irritation and fatigue, was the anxiety: Would we, after waiting all morning, have to come back again in the afternoon?

On the third or fourth Friday that I signed-on matters seemed worse than ever. Inside the Exchange queues crossed and re-crossed in the most ramified way. Everyone was more than usually reluctant to wait outside, for there was a stinging downpour of rain.

When I had signed-on and received my pay-check, it was necessary for me to go to the rear of the queue to the pay-box. In the queue outside I realised that I was fortunate, in that I possessed an overcoat and shoes, which, whilst they were more utilitarian than beautiful, were sound. There were many in the queue who possessed neither. There was much shivering and writhing and low muttered cursing as the queues shuffled forward a step or two, stopped, waited, waited and waited, shuffled, stopped, waited and waited.

The entrance to the Exchange, the entrance to warmth and shelter, mocked and taunted us. It was so near, so far. Half a minute's walking, an hour's waiting. But gradually we approached it, one shuffle at a time. We had reached the stairway. We were climbing one stair every five minutes.

Now we were insinuating ourselves into the packed building. Endless waiting, and we were in the midst of a chaos of men. I became doubtful whether I was really in the queue for the pay-box or for a signing-on box. Nobody seemed to know which was which. Those of us who belonged to the queue for the pay-box kept in a close group, on the principle that unity is strength. Our group was constantly broken up by men frantically pushing their way from one part of the Exchange to another.

We were packed tight, one against the other. It was acutely uncomfortable to stand thus pressed tensely from all sides, to have to remain in the one position for long periods of time. To move away from those in front of you was to lose your place hopelessly. At times it seemed to become impossible to breathe in this close, warm atmosphere, and one was seized with a panic palpitation of the heart. Despite the cold outside, here inside everyone's face was damp with perspiration. An unhealthily fat man in front of me breathed rapidly, with an effort that was noticeable in the rise and fall of his shoulders.

I kept my elbows pressed sharply outwards in order to secure some breathing space, and a fierce but impotent anger filled me at the thought that all this was borne in silence, and no one made any attempt to secure at any rate some alleviation of this appalling state of affairs.

Time passed. It was half-past eleven. The pressure of men in the Exchange was somewhat relieved. There were spaces here and there. It had become obvious that those who signed-on at later times would never be paid in the morning, and so they had been sent home, to come for their pay in the afternoon. It was now possible for those who remained to stand at their ease.

The fingers of the clock moved round towards midday. It was now certain that some of us who remained in the pay-queue would not be paid before twelve o'clock. All our waiting in the rain and in the tightly packed Exchange would have been futile unless the clerks, seeing how few of us remained, paid all of us off.

In those days at the beginning of 1931 it was still the popular fashion to regard unemployed men as lazy good-for-nothings. Clerks, many of them yielding to this facile emotion, often used

9

their positions to behave arrogantly and unreasonably towards the men who signed-on. It was quite possible that the pay-clerk would send the remaining few of us away, telling us to come back at two o'clock.

In our eagerness to avoid this (for it had become almost an obsession with us to have as little to do with the hated Exchange as we would with the plague) we broke our ranks of two and gathered in small groups that edged eagerly towards the counter.

The counter had become to us the symbol of getting paid and going home. The nearer we got to it, even though the number of men before us was in no way diminished, the nearer we seemed to be to getting paid and going home. There was no disputing of right of place. Every man was in his place in the queue, and none had any intention of trying the somewhat dangerous trick of attempting to take priority over someone else. It was simply that our eagerness to get finished with the intolerable ordeal of waiting in the queue made us strive unconsciously to get at any rate nearer to the pay-box. And so we broke the slow-moving rank and gathered in small groups that strained nearer to the counter.

Suddenly the clerk who was paying out the money became aware of what was taking place.

"Hey, what's all this?" he called out. "Get back into the queue!"

Everyone glared sullenly and resentfully at him. Tempers were ragged. There was probably not one of us in the queue who had not been going extra short of food and been without tobacco for at least the previous day, if not for a longer period. The weekly dole payment was our temporary deliverance from either the threat of starvation or starvation itself. And we were tantalised and tortured by the morning-long wait for our deliverance. Everyone was sick to death of waiting in the creeping queue. We wanted acutely to be paid now, at once, without any further delays. And this clerk began kicking up a fuss about the shape of the queue! We made a reluctant attempt to re-form into ranks of two.

The clerk, however, not sensing the strained feelings of the waiting unemployed, heaped fuel on the fire.

"Now then!" he snapped. "I said get back into the queue!" He slammed down the lid of the pay-box. "Now then!" he went on, with truculent self-confidence. "I don't open this lid— don't pay another man—until you're all lined up properly!"

Suddenly resentment—goaded by my anxiety about the passing time—burst into flame within me. What the hell did it matter to him, anyway? The Exchange was empty now, except for us. Wasn't there plenty of room for us to stand as we liked? Were we causing any disorder, any confusion? He was just trying to be officious—that was all. The resentment at waiting these hours in the rain and in the packed Exchange—and now this!—exploded within me. I started forward.

"You open that bloody till!" I shouted. "Don't you start any nonsense now! Get on with the job!"

As though for an eternity, I waited to see what would happen. Would they think I had gone mad? I was soon reassured. The effect of my outburst was electrifying. The crowd surged forward. Passivity had vanished. Faces were distorted with rage.

"Open that —— till!" they roared. "We'll smash the bloody place up!" "Who the hell d'you think you are!" "Open the bloody till!"

The clerk went chalky white. He stood staring horrified at the explosion he had evoked.

"Well, get in the queue, then," he murmured, in a voice that could scarcely be heard. He opened the pay-till without waiting to see whether the queue were re-formed or not. The clerk who was working with him said in an abashed tone:

"Twenty-three, twelve, pay seventeen shillings."

Money passed over the counter once again. In a few minutes I was paid, and emerged into the open air.

CHAPTER V

AN UNCOMMERCIAL TRAVELLER

ONE DAY AS I was walking about, engaged in the never-ending search for work, I saw a notice stuck on the door of a shabby warehouse on the corner of a side street and the main road. The notice read: "Canvassers wanted".

Ordinarily I would not have paid much attention to this notice, but because of the fact that I urgently needed a job, and this was the first job I had seen advertised for some time, I paused to think the matter over.

It might be possible to divide mankind into two categories: those who are salesmen and those who are not. I was definitely one of the latter.

Nevertheless, I could not afford to allow this circumstance to prevent me from applying for the job.

During my period of unemployment, relatively short though it had been hitherto, I had learnt the meaning of the word hunger. I knew what it was to have to count my pennies carefully and to spend them with hesitation and misgiving. I knew the dull finality of having no money at all.

I came within the Labour Exchange category of a "Young Man (18–21 yrs.)." Therefore I was receiving fourteen shillings per week. On this sum I had to maintain myself in food, clothing, shelter and whatever luxuries and dissipations I could manage to indulge in on the balance.

Apparently it is assumed by the authorities that a "Young Man (18–21 yrs.)" can in some mysterious way support himself on a smaller sum than a "Man (21–65 yrs.)". At any rate, although I was living in lodgings and supporting myself, I was receiving three shillings less than I would have received had I been twenty months older.

After paying six shillings and sixpence a week rent, I was able, as a general rule, with much care and discrimination, to exist in a more or less normal fashion during the first half of the week. Of course, I could spend nothing on replacing any of my clothes, or on minor luxuries of any kind, no matter how trifling.

From the Tuesday onwards came bankruptcy. I lived on whatever may have been left of those things I had bought at the beginning of the week—on dry bread and bits of tasteless cheese.

Life ceased to flow smoothly. It became divided into more or less rigid periods. There was the Friday, the beginning and end of the week; the day that was the be-all and end-all of existence; the day when, after feverish waiting at the Labour Exchange, I received the life-giving fourteen shillings.

The illusion of wealth that this fourteen shillings gave was soon dispelled after I had paid the rent. There would follow the three or four days during which I carefully doled out my pence on this or that article of food. Then all that was left of the fourteen shillings was a few coppers with which to replenish my supply of bread or some other wholesome but unexciting item of diet. Followed inevitably, on Wednesday or Thursday, the time when I knew, with a kind of desperate relief, that I had no money at all, and so, in a sense, had nothing more to worry about. All that was necessary was to pull my belt tighter, ignore the empty ache in my stomach and hang on till Friday and deliverance came round again.

In circumstances such as these one is not excessively particular about the type of occupation that comes his way, so long as it will rescue him from such difficulties.

I went into the warehouse to try my luck at getting a job at something at which I had never had any experience. The warehouse proved to be a dirty, gloomy den in which a number of scruffy-looking lads were idling about. On a table and some chairs were a number of attaché cases which I assumed to be filled with the product to be canvassed.

A tall, lanky youth with a bored and sophisticated air directed me towards the office.

This proved to be a little cubby-hole which was sufficiently large to contain a man, a table, a chair, and, with difficulty, myself.

The man in the office was not of a type warranted to inspire confidence in the observer. He was of untidy appearance, with ruffled hair and flabby, unshaven face. His attire was of a homely nature, consisting as it did mainly of slippers, trousers and shirt. Portions of his underwear, not of a very salubrious character, peeped from the top of his trousers and from the extremities of his shirt-sleeves.

When I entered the room he assumed an exaggerated air of bluff honesty that matched ill with his shifty eyes and rather furtive expression. When I told him that I had come about a job as a canvasser, his manner became affectionate in the extreme. An onlooker might have been forgiven the assumption that I was his long-lost brother.

He hinted that whilst my mere appearance had given him the most favourable impression of my character, and whilst it was obvious to anyone that I was a person of sterling worth and goodwill, the fact that I wanted to enrol in the noble calling of canvasser added verisimilitude to what might otherwise have been mere illusion.

Moreover, my desire to become one of his staff of canvassers showed my resolute determination to get on in the world, and also, by the same token, that I possessed the necessary qualifications to succeed in this same project.

In inspiring words he pictured his staff of canvassers as a band of brothers toiling selflessly (though at the same time not altogether without very liberal reward), in order that a waiting world might receive the commodity disseminated by his establishment—a commodity that was at once cheap, lasting and of the utmost utility.

"What is it you sell?" I asked.

"Scouring powder," he replied solemnly.

I was at first pleasantly startled by the cordiality with which I was received. I had expected a somewhat harrowing interview in which I attempted, somewhat unsuccessfully, to pretend that I was an experienced canvasser, whilst all the time my pretence was slowly but surely riddled with doubt by keen and searching questions from the man who interviewed me. I had not anticipated a fraternal interview of this character.

Nevertheless, my relief began to give way more and more to suspicion. I waited patiently for this employer to give some information on the question I was most interested in—that is, how much I could earn.

As he seemed in no way eager to enlighten me on this point, and in fact appeared to be waiting for me to say something on the matter, I finally blurted out:

"Well, and how much will I get a week on this job?"

My interviewer cleared his throat. I felt that he was preparing for conversation of a diplomatic character.

"Well, now," he began, looking at me rather narrowly, and speaking in a low tone. "Are you on the dole?"

"Yes," I replied.

"Are you living with your people?"

"No."

"How much are you getting on the Labour?"

"Fourteen shillings," I answered reluctantly.

"Well, now," he said persuasively, "you can't manage on that, can you?"

"No."

"And, on the other hand," he went on, his tone becoming more confidential at every moment, "I can't afford—at least, not yet, you understand, not while the business is just beginning —I can't afford to pay a man a salary. What you earn here you earn on commission, see?"

He paused, and I waited for him to speak further, and come to what would be the main point of the argument.

"Now," he went on, and his voice had sunk to a whisper, "why don't you work for me and still sign-on at the Labour? I won't say nothing," he added kindly.

I remained silent. I wanted acutely to achieve some means of increasing my income to at least a bare subsistence level. An opportunity had presented itself, and it appeared that it was not the kind of opportunity I **had** anticipated. But it was an opportunity, the only opportunity.

"You see those lads out there," he went on in the same whisper. "They're all getting the dole and working for me at the same time. They're making good money, too. Why, there's that tall, thin lad, if you noticed him when you came in. He earns a good thirty shillings a week, and gets the dole as well. You could do the same. What about it?"

I still found it hard to make up my mind. I did not like the idea of this man exploiting the fact that I was hard up and was getting the dole. If he was not paying any wages, and the commission to be earned was so small that it had to be supplemented by the dole, then the job might prove more trouble than it was worth. It was probable that his statement that one of the lads earned thirty shillings a week was an exaggeration. Such statements always were. One of the first things one learnt when applying for jobs was that, in the absence of any definite hourly or weekly wage, the statements made by employers as to how much you "could earn" were nearly always highly exaggerated. Nevertheless, even a few shillings in addition to my dole would make all the difference.

There were two choices before me: either to go on in the same unbearable fashion of the past few weeks, or else grab this opportunity, such as it was, that appeared to be able to give me at least some means by which I could live in a state other than one of chronic semi-starvation. I made my decision.

"Alright," I said, "I'll take it on. What do I have to sell?"

He took me to the room where the other lads were, and opened one of the attaché cases. Like the other cases, it was rather large, and it was filled with canisters of scouring powder—or maybe I ought to say canisters purporting to contain scouring powder.

"Now you see these," he said. "Each of these is a sixpenny canister of Cleansing Powder. But," he went on gleefully, as one explaining a marvellously ingenious idea, "you sells them for sixpence, and *then*"—it appeared that this was the great, the devastating point of the whole thing—"you *give* one *away* as well."

I wondered why he did not just sell each canister for three-pence and have done with it. Moreover, I wondered where my commission came in after this somewhat sweeping concession.

"How much do I earn on these?" I asked.

Here again it appeared that his system was one of childlike simplicity.

"For every *two* lots you sell, you keep the money for *one*!" he said triumphantly.

I carried my calculations still farther. If I got half of all the cash I received, then he received, equally with me, three half-pence for each canister. Out of this three halfpence he had to pay for the canister, the cost of packing, the stuff inside the canister—whatever that might be—his rent, other overhead charges, and still make a profit. It was therefore highly probable that the stuff inside the canister was not of very great value, to put it mildly.

Nevertheless, I decided to go ahead with the scheme and give it a trial. I pronounced myself agreeable to canvass the product on his terms. Indeed, they began to seem highly attractive to me after he had made several eloquent if somewhat ungrammatical orations on the enormous profits I could make if I went into the job with true earnestness and enthusiasm, together with the requisite amount of pep, go, pull, shove and push, and similar commendable commercial qualities.

The next morning I went to receive the goods I was to canvass. I was given one of the big attaché cases filled to capacity with canisters, and informed that I ought to sell them within a few hours. I was also instructed as to my "territory", which was in some obscure district composed mainly of squalid slums.

I set off, eager for the prospect of knowing what it would be like to have some money in my pocket—even if it would not be all my own money—without having to wait another two endless days for Friday.

By the time I had reached my territory the case of canisters had assumed the weight of a block of reinforced concrete. I was used to carrying heavy weights, but this morning my stomach was empty, and I certainly found it a strain to carry this heavy load.

Taking two of the canisters out of the case, I began to "do" my first street, which was a typically broken-down slum street. I had some misgivings as to whether I would be able to sell anything at all in such a poverty-stricken area, and if I could, whether it was strictly ethical of me to do so.

Plucking up courage, I knocked at the first house. There was no answer. I knocked at several houses and either got no reply, or else the door was opened and then shut immediately it was perceived that someone was trying to sell something.

Then I came to a fish-and-chip shop. To my astonishment, the proprietor bought four canisters with great celerity, and with the air of one who knows when he is on a good thing. He invited me to call again in a week's time. I made a mental note to be careful not to do so.

In the rest of the street I sold another one and sixpennyworth of canisters. Those who bought them from me seemed glad of the opportunity of buying something that was above all cheap and plentiful. I did not have to engage in any sales talk, even had I been prepared to do so, which I was not. I merely showed the canisters when I got the opportunity and explained that although they were marked sixpence, an additional one was being given as a sample. I made no attempt to persuade people who were doubtful about the quality of the goods.

It was in the next street that trouble started. At the first door that opened to me, a withered old hag looked at me with venom and said:

"You been round with that stuff before, an' a lot of rubbish it is, an' all!"

I was made somewhat uneasy by this declaration, but I proceeded to canvass other houses. I sold one or two more lots of canisters, and then with regularity people began to tell me, with various degrees of indignation, that they had bought the stuff before and found it worthless. Moreover, they seemed to regard me as being responsible for the worthlessness of the product.

Finally I became involved in an interminable argument at another fish-and-chip shop, wherein the proprietor, with great vehemence, persistence and vocal power, demanded his money back, and I would not give it to him, because I had not sold him the cartons in question.

After this I decided that it would be advisable for me to bring my commercial career to an end.

I therefore returned to the dingy warehouse with the attaché case and the remaining canisters, paid what money I had to pay, and generally liquidated and wound up my business affairs.

Thus ended the one opportunity of employment I was able to discover at the time in a large city, representative of the highest stage of civilisation that mankind has yet reached.

CHAPTER VI

THE UNEMPLOYED PROTEST

I WAS OUT of work for about three months before I succeeded in getting a job. This job lasted till the autumn; then I found myself out of work again.

I imagined that I would get another job fairly quickly, for the autumn is the busy season in my trade. It soon became clear, however, that trade was very bad. Unemployment stalked the land, and the figures mounted every day.

The newly formed National Government announced its intention of economising by reducing standard unemployment benefits by one tenth, and by introducing a Means Test to determine how much benefit should be given to those who had been out of work for more than six months.

These were serious blows to the unemployed. It was hard enough to exist now. How would we be able to manage with only nine shillings where we had before received ten? In my own case, my benefit would be reduced from fourteen shillings to twelve shillings and sixpence a week.

As for those who had been out of work for more than six months, they were the least able to bear any reduction inflicted on them by a Means Test. In fact, the unemployed as a whole were that section of the population that could least afford to suffer any reduction in their income.

One afternoon I had to attend the Labour Exchange to make what is known as a "change-over" claim. After a certain amount of time has elapsed a claim expires, and a new one has to be made. The routine of this consists mainly in re-stating to the clerk all the details concerning your claim which he already possesses.

When on my way to the Exchange I was rather surprised to notice large crowds of men gathered round one of the streets. The street itself appeared already filled with people. It was obvious that most or all of these men were unemployed, and I wondered why such a large crowd of unemployed should have assembled.

I asked one of the men what the crowd was waiting for. He looked at me in surprise, as at one who asks a peculiar question. "They're waiting to start the demonstration," he told me. "There's a big demonstration going on this afternoon," he added. "They're going to march right round the town against this 'ere Means Test."

His answer filled me with surprise, and at the same time with hope. Here was the way to get the Government to abandon its intention of reducing unemployment benefit. By himself an individual might be pretty helpless against such attacks, but by combining with his fellows he might hope to achieve something.

"What time does it start?" I asked.

"At three o'clock."

It was only a little after two o'clock now, and it was possible that I might get back from the Labour Exchange in time to take part in the demonstration. The presence of such large crowds nearly an hour before the demonstration was due to begin promised an impressive affair.

At the Labour Exchange I had to wait for some time. There were two or three change-over claims to be made at two-thirty, and the other claims were dealt with before mine.

By the time I left the Exchange it was after three o'clock. However, it was only about ten minutes' walk to the starting point of the demonstration, and I did not doubt but that I should get there before it had actually begun.

Nevertheless, when I arrived at the street from which the demonstration had started, I discovered it almost entirely bereft of people. I was rather disappointed. I had been keen to take part.

I turned to a passer-by and asked him if he knew where the demonstration had gone. He waved vaguely in the direction of the centre of the town.

"A think they went down that road," he answered. "A'm not sure."

As it was obvious that by walking I would never catch up with the demonstration, I decided, somewhat recklessly, to spend one of my last pennies on a tram ticket. Accordingly I boarded the next tram going to the centre of the town, and went on top, in order to secure a better view of the demonstration, if we should approach it.

The tram reached the centre of the town. There had been no sign of the marchers. The tram proceeded down the main street, and suddenly I beheld a spectacle which electrified me. It seemed as though a mighty flood of people stretched down the street, into the distance, as far as the eye could see. I had never seen such a large crowd. The black flood surged impetuously towards the direction from which the tram was coming. It was a blacked flood flecked with red—red banners on which were slogans in white letters.

Everybody on top of the tram-car was standing up, craning eagerly in the direction of the demonstrators, gazing with wonderment and incredulity.

Suddenly, more astonishing than the pouring stream of people, a vast elemental roar smote the sky, re-echoed and vibrated from the tall buildings:

"Not—a—penny—off—the—d-o-ole!"

"Not—a man—off—benefit!"

"Down—with—the—Means—Test!"

I got off the tram-car just before the demonstration reached it. For a moment I hesitated on the pavement as the river of people swept past me, and then I plunged into it.

It was not without a certain feeling of strangeness that I slipped into the ranks of the demonstrators and found myself marching with people I had never seen before.

The demonstration surged irresistibly through the heart of the city. Crowds of well-dressed people, of the type who spend their afternoons shopping or visiting places of amusement, stood on the pavement and gaped at this unprecedented spectacle.

We turned to march through the commercial and business section of the town. There were large, high blocks of offices in these streets, and as we marched along, every window up to the highest storey was crowded with office-workers gazing down in astonishment. Accompanying the marchers were a number of collectors of funds for the National Unemployed Workers' Movement, which had arranged the march. As the collectors rattled their boxes, showers of coins descended from even the highest windows, and the collectors were kept busy hunting for them.

By now I had recovered from my first strangeness in taking part in the demonstration and began to look about me. I saw many of the marchers carrying posters nailed to short sticks. On the posters were various slogans:

Work or full maintenance!
Not a penny off the dole!
Not a man off benefit!
Down with the Means Test!

The tramp of thousands of feet seemed to make the very roadway tremble and vibrate. The roar of shouted slogans crashed against the walls of the office buildings and thundered against the sky.

The police and inspectors who accompanied us were politeness and courtesy personified. They held up the traffic to allow us to proceed without difficulty and without pausing. Press photographers, perched high on the tops of buildings, photographed the march as it passed by. Wherever the march passed, there the life of the town seemed to be held up whilst thousands thronged the pavements and crowded to windows to see the demonstration.

Finally we reached the conclusion of the march, and the demonstration wound up as a protest meeting against the new Unemployment Act and the Means Test. A vast sea of people listened to the speakers, who appeared tiny, puppet-like, by comparison with their enormous audience.

We dispersed from the meeting with the confident feeling that such an enormous demonstration could not but have the effect of bringing our case before the public and the Government in no uncertain manner. We dispersed with optimism, sure of victory.

CHAPTER VII

STREET FIGHTS

THE UNEMPLOYED DEMONSTRATION aroused a good deal of comment in Forgeton, and much discussion in the Labour Exchange queues. The news spread about that a further demonstration was to be held. Expectations were that it would be an even larger one than the first.

I went along to participate in the second demonstration, and found that the expectations of a larger crowd were fully realised. The whole of the neighbourhood from which the march was starting was a dense mass of people.

From a technical point of view also the march seemed far

better organised than the first. Marshals with red bands round their arm were allocated to various sections of the demonstration. There was a Ex-Servicemen's band, as well as many banners with white lettering bearing the popular slogans of the day. Numerous slogans painted on cardboard were affixed to sticks, so that they could be easily carried. Everywhere one went amongst the crowd the slogans repeated themselves persistently:

> We refuse to starve in silence!
> Not a penny off the dole!
> Down with the Means Test!

There was a good deal of bustle everywhere. Marshals walked amongst the crowds, attempting to create order out of what seemed a huge amorphous mass.

"Now then, missis, join in the ranks."

"Six abreast, please."

"Form up into line, will you, comrades?"

"One behind the other, mates."

The drummer of the band was banging his drum idly, and the boom, boom, boom, heard like faint thunder, gave the preparations a martial air.

At last the demonstration started. The crowds cheered.

" Come on, join in!" those in the ranks shouted to friends they recognised on the pavement, and every moment it was necessary to effect minor re-organisations of the ranks in order to make room for the newcomers. Many of the men taking part in the march wore medals and ribbons from their service in the Great War. The demonstration was so big that even after those at the head of it had been marching for quite a considerable time, a large part of the ranks still waited till they could proceed.

The starting point was at the top of a slight hill. I could see the mass of people pouring down the hill, like a swollen, turbulent river bearing on its surface banners and slogan-boards. There was a continual roar of voices, shouting slogans.

Scores of police and inspectors marched with the demonstration, or lined the street. The Ex-Servicemen's band struck up a brisk tune, and the blare of trumpet and thud of drums sounded cheerfully from the front rank. Banners floated up and down with the rhythm of the march.

Soon the whole of the road leading to the centre of the town was a thick mass of people, a moving mass that seemed without end.

We marched along filled with that exultation which is felt by all who are part of a large crowd and who feel at one with the crowd.

Suddenly the demonstration began to slow up. Then it stopped. Soon our section had also halted.

Everyone expected that this was probably a temporary halt of the kind which would be bound to mark the course of a large and rather unwieldy march such as this one.

Nevertheless, time passed, and still the demonstration remained at a standstill. Crowds upon crowds began to pile up in the rear. Uneasiness and curiosity began to manifest themselves. Everyone began to push towards the front, despite appeals that were made to keep in the ranks. Onlookers and passers-by began to crowd the pavements. Soon the whole length of the thoroughfare was massed with tens of thousands of people, piling back to the starting point of the march.

Filled with the contagious, eager curiosity, I tried to push my way to the front to catch a glimpse of what was taking place. However, I could make little headway, for the crowd was packed tightly together and was absolutely impenetrable.

At first I could see nothing, because of the crowd in front of me. Then I pushed my way to the pavement, which was the only direction in which I could move, and edged as near to the wall as possible. Then, by stretching on my heels as far as I could and at the same time holding on to some fixture on the wall, I managed to crane my neck sufficiently to catch a glimpse of what was taking place.

That which I saw filled me with astonishment and dismay. The whole of the road to the centre of the town seemed to have been put in a state of siege. Motor-cars and other vehicles had been converted into a kind of barricade, having been crowded directly across our route. Behind the motor-cars were some fire-engines, and these, for some reason which was later to become apparent, had their hoses trained on to the wall of the nearby Goods Station, on which columns of water were playing.

But more than the motor-cars and the fire-engines, that which astonished and dismayed me was the concentration of police. It was as though the town was facing the imminent threat of invasion and the authorities had taken measures for its defence.

Row upon row of foot-police were lined across the road. Behind them were rows of mounted police. A number of inspectors conferred with a fine air of unconcern.

A silence descended on the vast crowd—a heavy, oppressive silence that seemed to weigh down on us all. It was as though a door had been closed, shutting us out from the world of sound.

It was like the meeting of two opposing armies, though the armies were of diametrically opposite character. We were tense and disconcerted, though not prepared to yield to this sudden, altogether unanticipated show of force. They seemed calm and relaxed, brooding on thoughts utterly apart from the issue at hand. They stood inactive, as though waiting to be inspected on parade. The mounted police looked like sculptured figures as they sat their horses with careless ease, apparently oblivious of everything save their horse's neck. Their calm was the calm of strength and discipline, and reliance on a preconceived plan.

The silence appeared to last a long time. Suddenly it was ended by a shout, thin, elfin, clear in the still air. Before the shout died away a thousand-throated roar exploded, shattering the silence to fragments. Soon a never-ending, reverberating noise rose to the skies. The air was filled with clamour and discordant sound:

"What the hell's up?"

"Get the march going!"

"Down with the police!"

"Forward to the City Hall!"

The clamour to proceed rose to such a pitch that I found, to my surprise, that I, too, had been shouting, though what I had shouted I could not have said. I had fallen victim to the peculiar effect on the individual of being part of a large crowd.

At the head of the demonstration a small group could be seen. It was the committee responsible for organising the march. Their arms waved and faces strained with the effort of shouting. They seemed to wave and shout for an eternity before there was the slightest abatement in the torrent of noise. Gradually those at the front became quiet and the cloud of silence began to spread more and more to the rear.

Then one of the leaders was lifted on the shoulders of two men. His voice floated towards us, weak and vitiated, its virility sapped from it by the enormous crowd whose physical mass absorbed it as a sponge absorbs water. Faint scraps of words floated towards us:

". . . Impossible . . . this road . . . City Hall . . . other route . . ."

To those at the front of the crowd it was obvious that it would be impossible for us, unarmed as we were, to batter our way past the police and through the barricades of vehicles that barred the road. The best thing to do in the circumstances was to take the alternative route to the City Hall, which was our goal.

Nevertheless, no sooner had the unemployed leader ceased speaking than isolated voices, now here and now there, began to shout:

"Smash up the bloody police!"

"Down with the bastards!"

and other such incitements to the unarmed crowd to attack the well-prepared police. The incitement had its effect, for the crowd was in angry mood. Exhortations for a fight with the police sounded louder and louder.

Suddenly the foot police, with batons drawn, began to move forward towards the demonstration. Those at the head of the crowd moved towards the police. I saw men closing with the police, and police slashing out with their batons. A furore of noise raged over the crowd—boos, yells and shouts of rage. Soon a pitched battle was raging. Unemployed and police fought desperately together. Men lay unconscious on the ground. Sloganboards flew through the air, the sticks to which they were nailed cracked like rifles.

Then on a sudden there was an altogether unforeseen happening. From nowhere, or so it appeared, enormous powerful streams of water smashed on to the crowd.

There was a sudden gasp. Everyone realised that the fire-hoses, hitherto playing so innocuously on the walls of the Goods Station, had been turned on to the crowd.

There was a brief attempt to withstand the impetuous streams of water. Then the crowd surged back. It surged back so powerfully that though I faced the fire-hose, I was swept backwards a full twenty yards without any effort on my part, and in spite of attempts I made to keep control over my movements.

After a time the hoses ceased. Then the police rushed madly upon us, uttering wild, beast-like noises. They appeared to be demented with fear, but iron discipline compelled them to obey their superiors.

They slashed out incontinently with their batons, and the tumult within them forced them to give vent to guttural howls, animal bayings, and all the noises of the jungle. Immediately they found it possible to arrest anyone, three or four, or as many as half a dozen of the police rushed upon their victim, belabouring him with their batons, and almost sobbing aloud in their relief at a reason to get away from the furious fighting.

With the attack from the fire-hose and the penetration by the foot-police, the demonstrators retreated. The solid, packed mass at the front of the crowd was considerably diluted.

Now came the mounted police. With their long swordsticks they slashed expertly, with nicety, at the demonstrators. In groups they galloped forward. The horses' hoofs scrabbled on the cobbles. Step by step they drove us back.

Then suddenly a number of mounted police dashed towards the group of which I was part. We turned, and rushed down a side-street. And ever behind us was the staccato clatter of horses' hoofs, gaining on us.

I heard a shout, "Ooh! Stones, lads!" It was true. There

24

was a dray full of bricks and stones. Eagerly a dozen men clambered on the vehicle. Quickly they tumbled the bricks into the waiting hands of men below. Those with ammunition dashed off towards the end of the street.

The police galloped into the street. A voice shouted, "Now—give it to 'em, lads!" Stones hurtled through the air. Thud! A policeman's helmet bounded on the cobbles; the policeman slumped sideways over his horse. Horses reared terrifyingly up in the air, whinnying, striving madly to turn about. The police tried to ride forward, but a relentless volley of stones and bricks flew upon them.

Then they suddenly turned tail. They clattered out of the street. We surged forward, routing them utterly. A policeman slid off his horse, and lay still on the cobbles. It was strange to see that policeman lying there, curiously helmetless, no longer concerned with what was afoot. But we ignored him. There were enough unemployed lying about unconscious on various pavements. We rushed forward, filled with the mad, exultant joy of victorious battle.

We rushed out into the main road. In front of us was a motor-coach, held up by the street battle. It was filled with well-fed, well-clothed people. Enough! *Strike newly-found terror into the hearts of these who are well-fed, complacent, indifferent!* A brick smashed a window of the coach. The women inside it screamed, screams of dire terror and hysteria. They tumbled out of the coach and ran whither they could. *O ye who are hungry, shabby, needy—join with us now!* A brick plopped dully through a plate-glass shop window. There was an appalling cra-a-ash! like the harsh shriek of a thousand old women.

Wild scenes ensued everywhere. Groups of police fought with groups of unemployed. Bodies lay on the pavement and on the roadway. I noticed the instruments of the Ex-Servicemen's band scattered over the road, the big drum lying burst and shattered. What had been a busy road in a large town was transformed into a battlefield.

Gradually, with slow reluctance, like one of those thunderstorms that seem stubbornly reluctant to disperse and give way to fine weather, the battle died down. Neither force appeared to have won a decisive victory; neither had inflicted a crushing defeat on the other. The fighting ceased as if by tacit consent on both sides.

Once again the ranks were re-formed. I was struck, somehow, by the attitude of both the police and the unemployed. It seemed as though both sides, with true British gentlemanliness, were trying to pretend that nothing had happened. The police formed up, and we formed up, and everything was done in a quiet, orderly fashion. There was no apparent rancour or ill-feeling on either side.

The demonstration now proceeded down a side-street, to reach the City Hall by another route. There were not so many marching now. Nevertheless, it was still a formidable demonstration.

Once on the move, most marchers gave way to a sudden mood of rather inexplicable high spirits—a reaction, no doubt, from the nervous tension of the preceding hour. Everyone laughed and joked and sang. The slightest incident was sufficient to send a wave of joviality rippling through the ranks.

In order to reach the City Hall, one turned right at the end of the street through which we were passing. I noticed, however, that the marchers did not turn to the right, but, on the contrary, were turning to the left. Moreover, there appeared to be considerable excitement at the end of the street.

Hurrying to the front of the demonstration, I beheld a man in the early thirties, crimson-faced with effort, shouting from a speaker's platform. He was shouting hoarsely (and in fact appeared to be shouting little else), "Turn left! Don't turn right!" The air was tense with excitement. Making my way into the main street, I saw the reason for the man's directions to the marchers. What seemed to be a whole army of mounted police were lined up across the road, implacably barring the way to the City Hall.

I got the impression that nobody knew who the individual at the street-corner, shouting directions, really was. Nevertheless, the marchers obeyed him, though not without strong protest from a large section of the crowd. It seemed impossible for us, unarmed as we were, to batter our way through the solid ranks of mounted police.

The use of such colossal force to prevent us from reaching the City Hall—particularly after we had been given the impression that if we took the alternative route we would be allowed to march there—raised a strong spirit of protest in the marchers.

Once again the popular slogans reverberated to the sky. Once again people stared from all the storeys of high office buildings. Once again traffic came to a standstill. Once again passers-by stared in astonishment as the demonstration marched past.

We had got about half-way down the street when on a sudden came the rapid clatter of horses' hoofs. The next moment commotion reigned. The police were attacking us from the rear.

So sudden was the attack that we were taken by surprise. We had our backs to the mounted police, and it has to be said that they took full advantage of this position. They galloped down on us, reducing the rough order of our ranks to utter confusion.

One instant I was aware of the clatter of horses' hoofs. The next moment a baton descended on my shoulder. Another landed with a sickening thud on the head of a man in front of me. Police were everywhere: on the pavements, on the roadway, slashing indiscriminately with baton and swordstick at everyone. I felt, not for the first time that afternoon, a surge of hatred for these mounted, weaponed warriors who slashed so bravely at unarmed unemployed who were so contrary as to want to protest against a reduction in unemployment benefit.

The struggle was a comparatively short one. After a time the police retired to their previous position. Once again we formed our ranks, this time sadly thinned by comparison with the swollen mass which had flocked out at the beginning of the march. Nevertheless, though the actual demonstration was relatively small, the pavements were crowded with people who accompanied it.

However, we did not proceed very far, even this time. Once again there was the clatter and scrabble of horses' hoofs on the cobbles, once again the swift attack from mounted and foot police, slashing where they could.

The scenes at the other fights were repeated, and still the unemployed gave back as good as they received, and the papers were to report as many injured amongst the police as amongst the unemployed.

This proved to be the last baton charge of the afternoon. We went on our way without further struggle. Presumably the authorities saw that it was becoming obvious to the thousands of onlookers that the police had no grounds for these repeated and persistent attacks; that it was becoming obvious that the authorities had only one real aim in view—not the "protection of property" (baton-charges nearly always mean the destruction of property by the more uncontrollable element in a crowd), but plainly and simply the brutal beating-up and arrest of men who wanted to voice their protest against the cuts in the dole, and who were protesting in the traditional manner of the British people.

We proceeded to our revised destination, and here we held a mass meeting, not merely against the dole-cuts, but also against the vicious brutality of the authorities.

CHAPTER VIII

THE BUSY SEASON—1931 VERSION

Two or three further demonstrations took place. The unemployed, by using more mobile tactics and preserving greater discipline, managed to avoid further clashes with the police, whilst getting to where they wanted to go, and making the most effective protest in the circumstances.

Nevertheless, after a time the demonstrations died down in our locality, as in the country as a whole. The Government was able to ignore the nation-wide protest of the unemployed—precisely because it was almost entirely a protest from the unemployed only. The majority of people failed to realise how closely their own interests and their own security were bound up with the living standards of the unemployed. No strong bond was forged between those with jobs and those without jobs. And so the demonstrations of the unemployed remained the protest of a more or less isolated section of the community.

So life resumed that particular course which is termed normal—that is, those who had jobs were thankful that they had them, and afraid lest the jobs might not last very long; those who did not have jobs endured a worsening of their lives under the Means Test and a reduced rate of benefit, in order that the money-bags might not become unduly worried by the financial situation.

As for me, I found it a harassing and nerve-wracking ordeal to accommodate myself to the reduced rate of benefit. When, after paying rent, one is left with a mere seven shillings and sixpence on which to live, the situation is far from idyllic. To be then faced with the loss of one shilling and sixpence from this amount is a severe blow.

I lived in dread of those empty, boring, monotonous days of walking about searching for a job that was never there, and returning to a lodging bereft of warmth and stimulating food. The emptiness of the belly, and the accompanying tension and worry, produced an emptiness of the brain and of the spirit. I walked about looking for work as much to distract myself as to find work.

In the past I had often wondered how I would fare if I were out of work. I had come to the conclusion that in any case, even if one found life on the dole very difficult, all he had to do was to pull in as many holes in his belt as was necessary for a certain grim comfort, and then stoically await the day when things would change for the better.

In my actual experience of living on the dole, however, I had to revise nearly all my preconceived ideas on the question.

For one thing, I was soon made aware of the large proportion of one's money which is taken up by "overhead" charges—rent, bread, tea, sugar, and so on—before anything is available for food in its more general aspect.

Bread, it might be protested, is a food, and an important one. Yes, but when it is of necessity the main article of diet, how dreary and insipid it becomes! I became sick of the taste of bread, a loathing I have not quite overcome to this day. Bread became to me the emblem of indigence, the last defence against utter starvation. I found literal truth in the saying: "Man does not live by bread alone."

Most people are aware that the unemployed cannot afford sufficient food. However, it is true to say that the unemployed suffer as much, if not more, through the deprivation of the small comforts and luxuries of life as by lack of food.

I soon discovered that the price of such a commodity as tea could prove formidable in a microscopically small budget; that lack of money for amusements could soon prove rather wearing, and that the inability to satisfy the desire for a minor luxury such as cigarettes could be a form of refined torture.

However, if experience had taught me to revise my former notions about life on the dole, then possibly I was correct in my previous fancy that even if I were going short, all I had to do was to be sternly stoical in the best tradition of grim, heroic figures of romance. Nevertheless, even here I had to revise my ideas. I found that a man getting a sufficiency of food, and a man not getting enough food, could be two very different persons.

It may be possible for a sufficiently fed man to be stoical about various matters; it may need very great self-control for a hungry man to be stoical about the same things. Similarly, a man who spends the greater part of his waking hours occupied by his work, and then by those amusements and recreations he can afford, will often ignore matters which appear of mountainous significance to one who has long, empty days in which to brood.

I discovered also that the symptoms of hunger are not quite so easy to ignore as is imagined by those who have not experienced that enervating sensation. Hunger is not merely a feeling localised and static. The hunger itself appears to be a hungry, voracious animal, a beast of prey, steadfastly pursuing its course of swallowing its victim whole.

It was when I was out looking for a job that I found hunger most unendurable. Setting out in the morning not feeling very

29

hungry (I soon became accustomed to going without breakfast), I generally found that by the time I decided to return to my lodging the effort involved seemed quite beyond me. The aching hollow in my belly was a magnet attracting to it all the energy that should have inhabited my limbs. It was a drain, a sump, down which poured all those vital impulses which make exercise effortless to the young. It was an insidious weakening poison that left me physically weak and mentally irresolute.

This period of unemployment lasted for about two months. Then, when I was about to abandon all hope of getting a job that season, for it was only some six or seven weeks to Christmas, I secured a fairly decent job on the outskirts of Forgeton. I soon discovered that my employer had vague Socialist leanings, and this no doubt was the reason why we worked such "clerk's hours" as eight to five-thirty, a somewhat rare phenomenon in the cabinet-making trade. For the rest, the work was congenial, and the pay the highest I had yet earned.

Christmas drew near, and I was made more than usually uneasy at the prospect of the sack. It would be bad enough to lose an ordinary job, but it would be worse to lose a job with reasonable hours and good pay.

However, a week before Christmas I was still working, and there appeared to be a brisk supply of work. I began to hope, somewhat daringly, that we would continue to work right over Christmas and well into the New Year, possibly carrying me through the slack season.

It was about this time that I received a letter from my elder sister and her husband in London, inviting me to pay them a visit for Christmas.

My family consisted of my two sisters and my mother. Four years previously my elder sister had married, and shortly afterwards her husband had been transferred by his firm to London. Subsequently my younger sister visited them in London and became acquainted with a young man whom she later married. My mother now began to find existence in Forgeton somewhat lonely, and when my younger sister gave birth to a child, my mother decided to move to London. She therefore gave up the small shop which theoretically provided her with a livelihood, and moved to London with plans to set up for herself in a shop, if this was at all possible.

It was taken for granted that I would go with my mother, but actually there were a number of obstacles to this plan. I had, after all, got a job in Forgeton, which it was not altogether certain that I could replace if I went to London. This was an important consideration, as my mother's funds were very small, and it was necessary that I should be able to assist her whilst I was working.

In addition to this, there was the question of accommodation. My mother could, for the time being, stay with my younger sister, but the small house could not accommodate me, which meant that I would have to take lodgings, which would be an additional expense. My elder sister had no room for me, as at that time her husband and herself were occupying two small rooms.

Lastly was my own predilection. I found a certain glamour in the idea of independence, in living "on my own", in being the affectionate son earning his living from afar, sending regular weekly letters containing a postal order, and occasionally travelling gloriously down to London to visit his family.

Matters did not work out quite as we had expected them to do, however. For one thing, my mother soon discovered that in London the rents of even small shops, with no living accommodation attached, could be quite fantastically high by her provincial standards. Then, her health, which had been poor in recent years, declined to a state in which she was little more than a semi-invalid. The result was that nothing came of her plan to set up a shop.

As for me, the job which had been such an important factor in deciding me to remain in Forgeton lasted barely three months after my mother went to London.

Nevertheless, that which originally had been merely a matter of expediency became somehow transformed into a matter of principle.

During the first few weeks I was living "on my own" I wrote to my mother hearty letters in which I extolled independence and gave it as my firm belief that all young people should learn to support themselves. Having said this when I was working and relatively well off, how could I alter my attitude when I was out of work and hard up? For the first week or two I hid from my mother the fact that I was unemployed, continuing to send her the allowance I had sent when I was working. Later, I broke the news of my unemployment, but insisted that I was managing well, and that there was no need for her to worry on my behalf.

Thus it was that by the Christmas of 1931 I had lived for fourteen months "on my own", assisting my mother when I could. I had not yet visited my family in London, and the letter from my elder sister came as a great temptation, bidding me throw aside careful calculations about the future and make the journey south.

However, I still found it difficult to make up my mind. On the one hand I was very keen to go to London for Christmas.

On the other hand, it seemed highly probable that I would get the sack before Christmas. If this happened it would be impossible for me to make the trip, for I would be spending money I ought to save for the two or three months I might expect to be unemployed at the beginning of the New Year.

I waited from day to day to see whether or not I would get the sack, and thus have my mind made up for me. But the days passed with no untoward event. It was three days to Christmas, and I was still working.

Then I received a further letter from my sister asking me to let her know when I would be coming. They had moved to a larger flat, and, though they had more room than in their previous place, they had not very much furniture. If I were coming she would have to make preparations, such as borrowing one of those articles of furniture that look like a couch during the day and like a bed during the night, and are neither very satisfactorily.

There also came a letter from my mother, who had heard of my sister's invitation to me, asking me if I were really coming.

These letters decided me. I waited one further day, and as I was still working, wrote a hasty letter to my mother and sister telling them that I would be coming to London and asking for directions to get to their addresses.

I little knew what was to be the outcome of this decision.

END OF BOOK ONE

BOOK TWO

SLINGS AND ARROWS

CHAPTER I

NIGHT RIDE

It was Christmas Eve, and I was still the possessor of a job.
I therefore spent what money I could spare on replacing the
more worn of my clothes, and as one undergoing a high adventure, set out for the railway station at eleven o'clock.

Like most inexperienced travellers, I arrived at the station
long before my train was due to start. At first I was rather relieved in that the clerk at the booking-office did not inform me
that all seats for the train were already taken, but my relief
soon gave way to boredom at having to wait over half-an-hour
(so early had I come) till the train should start. It was something
of an anti-climax to have to wait thirty-five minutes, when I had
rushed so quickly to the station.

I paced up and down the platform and gazed at old advertisements of seaside resorts, and wondered why it was necessary that
all pictorial advertisements for seaside resorts must feature young
women in bathing costumes, complete with prominent busts,
inviting smiles and acrobatic attitudes. Being unable to discover
any satisfactory answer to this passing problem, I got into a
carriage of the waiting train and sat down in a corner seat.

The station began to resound with the noises of the impending
departure of midnight trains. A desultory hiss filled the air.
My train began to fill up. In the corridor, leaning through the
window, a young man was being loudly and self-consciously
witty to his two loud and self-consciously witty friends on the
platform. A young couple walked alongside the train, nervously
scrutinising the interiors of the carriages. Apparently my
appearance was one of encouragement to young lovers, for, after
glancing at the next carriage, they returned and entered the one
I was in.

A muscular, heavy-limbed young man in the early twenties
was the next to be added to our company. He had no luggage,
not even a small attaché case such as I carried. He was dressed
in a shabby brown suit and a cap, but had no overcoat. I got the
impression that he was going to London not for any definite

33

employment, but to look for a job. But if he was in that position, why did he spend all that money on a railway ticket to London? Possibly some cautious Samaritan had annoyingly responded to his hard-up tale by giving him, not money, but a railway ticket. However, it was possible that I was entirely wrong about it all.

A business-man, complete with brief-case, stared uncompromisingly through the window, came in, and assertively plumped himself down opposite me. (H'm, rather strange for Christmas Eve.) A young man, very upright and grave, opened the door neatly, entered the carriage neatly, closed the door neatly and sat down opposite the young out-of-work. A middle-aged woman of benevolent aspect then came in, and kindly but insistently upset the carriage in her determination to fill both luggage-racks with a large assortment of paper parcels.

The thirty-five minutes had passed quickly. A sudden excitement thrilled me when, without any preliminary fuss or last-minute waitings, the train began to glide from the station. With feelings of relief I settled myself in my corner. Everyone settled in their places, even the persistent and benevolent middle-aged.

Tat-tat. . . . Tat-tat. . . . The train swings along easily, now making a sudden swerve to the right or to the left as its wheels are guided by the points.

Tat-tattat. . . . *Tat*-tattat. . . . *Tat*-tattat. . . . We are gliding past many parallel lines of gleaming steel rails. Signals glow with vari-coloured lights—red, green, yellow. Unhurriedly, at leisure, we rumble through a deserted suburban station.

Tat-tattat. . . . *Tat*-tattat. . . . *Tat*-tattat. . . . In the carriage we yield ourselves to the train. Take us where we want to go, train. We have confidence in you. We will go to sleep. The young couple, greatly daring, enfold one another, lean against each other and close their eyes. Their faces are not happy, but engraved with yearning and abnegation. I feel that in London they must part, and for some considerable time. The business man takes off his hat, grasps his brief-case tightly, and haughtily closes his eyes. The grave and erect young man is still grave and erect, though his eyes are closed, and he has prepared himself to sleep as neatly as possible. The young out-of-work is bending forward, his chin resting on his hand. He is gazing intently out of the window. The benevolent middle-aged lady (by now I am certain she is a widow visiting her children) is leaning backwards, eyes closed, and is swaying with the movements of the train. As for me, I am awake, agreeable to let sleep come when it may, gazing at my fellow-passengers, enjoying the feeling of night and of sleeping humanity, and listening to the rhythm of the train.

34

Tat-tatta-*TAT*. . . . *Tat*-tatta-*TAT*. . . . *Tat*-tatta-*TAT*. . . .
I have a desire to hear the train surging ahead swifter, swifter.
It seems to be merely ambling along now. It seems rather incredible that in five hours or less this ambling, jogging train will
have reached London—London, 240 miles in a diagonal line
south-east across the broad back of England. . . .

Tat-tatt*ATat*. . . . *Tat*-tatt*ATat*. . . . *Tat*-tatt*ATat*. . . . The
train is warming to its work. But swifter, swifter yet. It is a long
way, and every yard of the track must be covered, 240 miles of it.

TAtatatAT. . . . *TAtatatAT*. . . . *TAtatatAT*. . . . The train
moves more quickly, rapping out the beat of its rhythm sternly,
smartly. I thought of the long lines of steel rail, stretching ahead,
stretching on for over 200 miles.

TAtataTAtat. . . . *TAtataTAtat*. . . . *TAtataTAtat*. . . .
Good! it is moving quickly. There is *élan*, tempo, in its rhythm.
Now at every moment it travels more swiftly. . . .

Tatatat. . . . *Tatatat*. . . . *Tatatat*. . . . *Tatatat*. . . . *Tatatat*.
. . . Now it is hurrying, now it is flashing, smashing through
the night.

Tat*AT*-Tat*AT*-Tat*AT*-Tat*AT*-Tat*AT*-Tat*AT*-Tat*AT*. . . . It
is thundering over bridges, howling through the tunnels, roaring
through deserted stations. . . .

I open my eyes. Could I have been asleep? Yes, I felt as
though I had slept satisfyingly for some length of time. The
train, unsleeping, was battering its way steadily and unflaggingly
through the night. I had a picture of the engine as some flying
steed of romance, a horse wild-eyed and wide-nostrilled, bringing
the news from Ghent to Aix.

The business man opposite me now looked very uncom-
mercial. His head had dropped back against the upholstery
and his mouth hung relaxed and open. He snored long and
voluptuously, in strange contrast to the weary indifference of his
face. The young couple still enfolded one another, and in sleep
they seemed pathetic, two babes in the wood. Their heads lolled
away from each other in curiously decapitated attitudes. The
neat young man in the corner was sleeping neatly and gravely,
as though conforming rigidly to certain rules that had been laid
down in connection with sleeping in railway carriages. As I
looked at him he disconcertingly opened his eyes, gazed at me
sadly, and then closed them again. The other young man had
fallen asleep with his chin cupped in his palm, his elbow on
his knee. He looked like Rodin's "Thinker", modernised and
fallen asleep, wearied with overmuch thought. The widow
slept placidly, not without a certain enjoyment written on her
features.

For a long time, endlessly, the train rushed clamouring through the night. It seemed that there was no other existence than this. Then suddenly there was a new note in the titanic song of the train. The taut urgency of the rhythm slackened, the key descended an octave. At first one could not be sure of the difference, or whether, indeed, there was any difference. Then came a further slackening of rhythm, a further descent in the key of the train's harmony. Now it was only jogging ahead. It seemed as though it were determined yet, but had suddenly discovered that it was very tired.

The windows of the carriage were blurred with moisture from within and frost from without. Through them, startlingly, could be detected the hazy lights of a town. That which before had been an oblong of blackness glimmered now with many lights that stretched before us and swung behind.

The train dawdled slowly, more slowly. It staggered wearily into a station. With an asthmatic wheeze and a death-rattle of brakes it jerked to a shuddering standstill. A vast and empty silence descended on the night.

With the startling and overwhelming quiet, sleep disappeared. One by one, with varying degrees of surprise and bewilderment, those in the carriage awoke. People passed to and fro along the corridor. Voices could be heard seeking and vouchsafing information. It appeared that we had paused at a London suburb, so that ticket-collectors might board the train. The train, then, had nearly fulfilled its task. Everyone started making preparations for the end of the journey.

The train began again to move, this time with a leisurely and contented air, as of one who knows that the end of long labour is very near. A ticket-collector moved long the corridor, his progress marked by the sound, drawing ever nearer, of the sliding to and fro of the carriage doors.

Through many empty suburban stations we jolted. The business man, with a serious and profound air, was putting on his coat. The neat young man was waiting with quiet discipline until the train would stop definitely, before he moved from his seat. The middle-aged lady had gathered all her parcels to her, like a hen her chickens, and was insistently making sure that she would leave nothing behind; to the discomfort of the rest of us. The two young lovers, no longer enfolding one another, but correctly and prosaically apart, sat with an air of dazed and gloomy disillusion. The out-of-work still sat with his elbow on his knee. His eyes were bleary and he yawned endlessly. I felt extremely reluctant to leave the warm train for the dark, chilly world.

The train was grinding to a standstill. We were at Euston. There was an opening and closing of doors, a busy murmur of voices, a hurrying to and fro, and over it all the leisurely hiss of the train, its journey done. I stumbled out into the biting, penetrating cold of the early morning, and wondered why I had undertaken the trip at this time, when I could have done it at a warmer time of the year.

As it was Christmas morning, London had yielded itself in utter abandonment to rest. There were no trams, buses or tubes. The earliest tube would not be running for two or three hours yet, and trams and buses would also not be running for some considerable time. I set out to walk to my mother's.

Inquiring the direction now from some solitary passer-by and now from a policeman, I made my way towards the East End. As I did not want to arrive too early, I strolled along casually, glancing into many shop windows and admiring the wide street devoid of people.

A slow and tardy light was beginning to struggle into the sky, and the dome of St. Paul's swam with heavy majesty towards me as I walked up Ludgate Hill. As I passed through Aldgate, life was beginning to reassert itself. In the pale blue dawn people were opening sweetshops, tobacco shops and such-like enterprises. But along Commercial Road and the streets that flanked it silence still reigned. Those who were abroad wore the moody and reluctant aspect of those whom circumstances force to go about their business whilst the rest of the world is on holiday.

CHAPTER II

AFTER THE FEAST

Christmas was on the Friday, and I returned to Forgeton by the Sunday midnight train. The time in between I spent at the dwellings of my younger and elder sisters and in a number of excursions about London. I left London with the satisfying feeling of having spent two or three days of friendly companionship with those who were near to me.

After my all-night journey back from London, I was not in a very keen mood for work on the Monday morning. At my bench I eagerly anticipated the time when work would be finished for the day. This acute desire of mine was gratified most unexpectedly. At half-past eleven my employer approached me and said:

"I'm sorry, but I'll have to give you an hour's notice."

Shock as this would have been to me in ordinary circumstances, it was doubly a shock because of the fact that I had practically no money left. In addition to the amount I had spent on fares and on replacing my clothes, I had given my mother a few shillings, and, precisely because I had thought my job secure for at least another week or so, had placed no great restraint on myself in spending a few coppers here and there. I had practically no money at all, and anticipated managing for the rest of the week by securing a "sub" from my boss. After this week was over I would be alright, I had thought. And now he had given me the sack. What was I going to do?

My perturbed thoughts were interrupted by my employer.

"Actually," he said, "there wasn't any work for a day or two before Christmas, but I didn't want to give you the sack before Christmas and spoil your holiday."

He smiled in what appeared to me at that moment to be the most idiotic, foolish and fatuous manner.

"Didn't want to spoil my holiday!" I fumed inwardly. "Just the sort of brain-wave a sentimental philanthropist would have. Couldn't he have guessed that if I thought my job was secure I'd spend money I would have saved if he'd given me the sack before Christmas? Now I'm in a real mess. But it's true. He didn't spoil my holiday. . . ."

I packed my tools and was paid the money that was due to me. Another aspect of my employer's naïve desire not to spoil my holiday was that although I had only worked for four and a half hours, it was still necessary to take one shilling and sixpence off my earnings for insurance stamps, so that for that morning's work I received the princely sum of three shillings and fourpence halfpenny.

My position struck me as being so desperate that I did not even ride home with my tools. I carried them all the way back to my lodgings. This is the kind of fantastic economy one carries out at the first impact of the knowledge that one is going to be very hard up.

Back in my lodgings, I considered the position seriously and gravely, and yet strangely without uneasiness. I counted up my money, and discovered that I had nearly five shillings. I had no food at all, though I had the last remains of a pound of sugar, a few spoonsful of tea and a tin of condensed mild. These items were the credit side of my account.

The debit side consisted of the various facts that I was out of work, would probably have the greatest difficulty in finding work for at least a number of weeks, and would have no source of income for the next eleven or twelve days.

A sum amounting to less than five shillings is not a large one on which to exist for eleven days, particularly when at the end of that period you will receive only a few days' unemployment benefit.

Many people assume that an unemployed man receives a full week's benefit at the end of the first week of unemployment. This, however, is not the case. In actual fact, an out-of-work may have to wait nearly three weeks before he receives a full week's unemployment pay.

Assuming that a man is discharged from work on Saturday dinner-time, he will go to sign-on the following Monday morning. The whole of the following six days* are his "waiting days"— *i.e.*, days for which he receives no benefit. Presumably the reason for this peculiar practice is that it is assumed by those in authority that people who have difficulty enough in managing when they are working (and these constitute the majority of working people) are sufficiently wealthy to be able to live on their savings during the first period of unemployment.

It is only from the second Monday that the days are counted for unemployment benefit. If benefit is paid on the Friday, the days for which it will be paid are reckoned until the Wednesday night. If benefit is paid on the Thursday, then the days are reckoned until the Tuesday night. So that after being out of work for close on a fortnight, the unemployed receives three days' benefit on the Friday, or two on the Thursday. It is only by the time that the third Thursday or Friday comes along that he receives a full week's benefit.

I, however, had no waiting days to endure, as I had not been working for the full ten weeks which are required before the "waiting days" can be reckoned. Therefore the amount I would receive in twelve days would be (at the rates prevalent at the time) sixteen shillings and eightpence. If I got paid on the Thursday I would get fourteen shillings and sevenpence. I was thankful I did not have to "wait" six days.

I wondered what I could do in the meantime. I realised, in a vague, theoretical way, that if I did nothing I would starve before I got the dole. Even when I became the possessor of an income of twelve shilling and sixpence a week my position would not be very rosy, to put it mildly. But what was I going to do in the meantime, before I got the dole?

There was only one thing to do. That was, to try to get another job. If I did not succeed (which was highly probable), well, I was going to have a very uncomfortable time during the next two or three weeks.

I bought some food, and after I had had a meal, went to sign-on

* Reduced to three days in 1937.

at the Labour Exchange. I spent the day searching mechanically and fruitlessly for work.

By the following Friday I was penniless and without food. I had taken great care to spend my money as wisely as possible, and it seemed to me that on the whole I had done fairly well. Nevertheless, there were seven more implacable days before I would receive any money—seven days stretching into eternity; 168 hours that each had to be lived through with its full quota of 60 minutes, 3,600 seconds.

Strangely enough, I was intimidated most by the fact that I would not be able to pay the rent at the week-end, and would have the somewhat formidable task of informing my landlady to that effect.

By the Friday night I was perversely feeling far more hungry than I imagined I would have felt in ordinary circumstances, and was enduring mild tortures by reason of my desire for a cigarette.

When unemployed in the past, and at the end of my resources, I had known that the next day, or the day after that, I would get some unemployment benefit. But now there was no benefit waiting for me the next day, or the day after that, or the day after that. There were seven more such nights as these (hungry nights are worse than hungry days) to go through before I would get any money. Maybe I was pessimistic, thinking in this way, but it did not occur to me to think of the matter in abstract terms of pessimism or optimism. The facts were there; they were gloomy, and they made me feel gloomy. My experience of life hitherto had dispersed within me any notions of the type others might have had of providential, last-minute escapes from hard facts.

An innate, morbid sensitiveness of my position had been growing within me during the past few days. I had been brought up in what is known as the proud, independent working-class spirit—that is to say, in that social code that bids a man allow himself to be starved to death rather than beg the means of subsistence from others, whether from private people or public bodies. And so, though it might perhaps have been possible for me to have received help from one or two acquaintances, I knew that I would not be able to let anyone know the full seriousness of my position.

I found it impossible to write to my mother and younger sister asking for help. I wrote my usual weekly letter, though I had to post it without any stamp on the envelope. Similarly, I could not bring myself to apply for help to my elder sister and her husband. It seemed to me, in the somewhat peculiar way I was beginning to view the whole problem, that they would assume that I was trying to hold them responsible in some way for my present plight. I somehow failed to compose a letter that did not seem to contain an implication that I was demanding help from them because my present difficulties could, from one aspect, be traced to their invitation to me to visit London.

The irony of it was that this morbid and unwholesome attitude of mine towards asking for assistance was made all the more acute by the very acuteness of my need. Had my need not been so great I would no doubt have found it fairly easy to ask for help.

In addition to this, there was the physical aspect of the matter. Asking for money and help is, to those unaccustomed to it, a somewhat harassing ordeal. The more their stamina is undermined by lack of food and the stimulants to which they are accustomed—tea and cigarettes in my case—the more difficult the matter becomes. Anyone who is deprived of a stimulant to which he has become accustomed suffers, in the early stages, at any rate, a weakening of the faculties. There is also a tendency for any innate characteristics of an inhibiting kind (such as shyness and lack of confidence) to manifest themselves in an exaggerated form. The lack of food also acts in a similar way on an individual.

These circumstances make the overcoming of inhibitions more difficult, and requiring more nervous energy than usual. The store of nervous energy is, however, lower than usual. And so the whole matter turns in a vicious circle.

This was the case with me at the time, unaware though I was of this fact, and under the impression that my attitude on the question of asking for assistance was perfectly normal. The lack of food, tea and cigarettes brought to full flower all tendencies within me of a kind that would make the task of asking for aid an impossible one.

The result was that the very circumstances which demanded that I should not suffer from morbid sensitivity were in themselves responsible for the fact that I did harbour such feelings. So I found it impossible to apply to others for assistance.

CHAPTER III

A FAIR PRICE

As I walked aimlessly through the streets on the Saturday morning, I was attracted by a notice in a shop window. This notice read: "We pay cash for gents' cast-off clothing".

I had seen such notices before, but they had rarely penetrated to my consciousness. But if there was one word now that could stimulate my flow of ideas, it was the word "cash". I had, after all, been concentrating my thoughts for the past week on ways and means by which I could raise money. Here was a way—a delightfully easy way! All I had to do was to sell my spare clothes. The notice was like a ray of light shining through desolating gloom.

I hurried back to my lodgings and packed up my best jacket, a pair of flannel trousers, two pullovers and a cricket-shirt. They were all fairly new, and I was confident of raising a large sum on them. My mind soared to beatific visions—a pound, thirty shillings, two pounds—why not? It was rotten luck that I should have to sell my clothes, but there it was. The money I would get for them would just about rescue me from my difficulties. Later on I would get a job and be able to buy better clothes.

In the meantime, food—not clothes—was the important thing. My mouth shed torrents of saliva at the thought of the food I would have when my clothes had passed over the counter of the tradesman whose aim in life it was to purchase gents' cast-off clothing.

With the parcel under my arm I hurried towards the shop. By now my attitude towards my poverty-stricken state was such that it seemed to me that everyone I passed knew I was penniless, and so regarded me with scorn and contempt. I hurried along furtively, carrying the parcel as inconspicuously as possible.

Like many people undertaking such a transaction for the first time, I had to pause outside the shop to screw up my courage, and to make certain that passers-by were not taking an intense interest in the proceedings.

At this moment it seemed at once degrading and abnormal to go into a shop and offer to sell one's spare clothes. A strange proceeding! Some moments passed, during which I read and re-read the announcement about cast-off clothes, before I could summon up the hardihood to enter the shop.

The man behind the counter was very business-like. When I mumbled a query as to whether he wanted to buy any clothes, he made no reply. Taking a pair of scissors, he cut the string round the parcel with great efficiency. Then he tumbled the clothes on to the counter.

"How much d'you want for them?" he asked briefly, and it was as though he said, "Wretched being, you come here selling your clothes in order to buy food. How much shall I, in the charity of my spirit, grant you for these worthless garments?"

I found it hard to state a price. It seemed to me quite possible that the man would give me two pounds for the clothes. On the other hand, the transaction was proving to be so wearing that I considered that if he threw down a pound-note on the counter, I would be glad to take it and go.

"How much can you give me?" I asked.

He looked at the clothes with sardonic indifference, and his indifference was wounding to me. My clothes, which I was selling because I was in such a state of desperation, were a matter of indifference to him. And by the same token, my desperate state was also a matter of indifference to him.

"I'll give you a shilling for them," he said.

If someone had suddenly, without any possible reason or justification, come up to me and slapped me on the face, I could not have been more astounded.

"A shilling!" I exclaimed, aghast.

I was tremendously indignant, and yet insulted and aggrieved, as one whose most intimate aspirations have been roughly, carelessly and indifferently thrown in the dust. How fantastic and naïve my visions of two pounds seemed now! I wondered how I could have been so utterly silly as to have imagined that I would get two pounds for these things on the counter. They had suddenly, by the magic of a few indifferent words, become transformed into worthless rags. Nevertheless, a shilling! I could not get over it.

"Are you sure?" I asked him. "A shilling?"

For answer the man picked up one of the pullovers. With true business instinct he had picked out the least valuable of the clothes I had brought.

"See that?" he inquired. "We're lucky if we can get rid of anything like that to anybody. We're swamped with them. We can hardly give 'em away."

I could not believe him; and anyway, what about the other clothes?

"What about the trousers, the jacket?" I demanded desperately. "They're practically new. Why, between them, they cost me thirty-five shillings!"

"Well, that's not much for a new pair of trousers and a jacket," he answered briefly. "And anyway, people are selling clothes, not buying them. They're a drug on the market, particularly now, just after Christmas. How do I know if I'll ever sell 'em? They may fall to pieces, for all I know, before anyone'll buy 'em. If I give you a shilling for 'em, it's practically giving it away, you might say."

I took the clothes and wrapped them up again. Nevertheless, even as I did so, I was tortured with doubt. A shilling—that was something. Think what I could do with a shilling just now.

Were not these clothes worth the alleviation, no matter how temporary, of this nagging, enervating emptiness of the stomach? The clothes—they were not very important, but a shilling was.

But, on the other hand, it seemed to me as though a principle were at stake. I felt that I would rather starve than be a party to such an absurd transaction as the sale of all my best clothes for a shilling. And anyway, looking at the matter from a logical standpoint, supposing I sold the clothes and got the shilling? The shilling would be gone, eaten up, before I knew where I was. And what would I do after that? I had nothing else to sell. . . . I would keep the clothes. I went out of the shop crushed and overwhelmed with disappointment.

The gateway to an avenue of hope had been rudely slammed in my face. Once again the thought beat a tattoo within my brain, as it had been beating for the past week: "What can I do?" Worse than the hunger and the deprivation was the sense of utter impotence, of being unable to lift a finger to alter my situation. I had always imagined in the past that when things got really serious one did something—somehow circumstances enabled one to do something. But what? "What could I do?" The phrase revolved in my mind, becoming meaningless, wearing a groove deeper and deeper, like a blunted gramophone needle travelling the same circle on a worn-out record.

CHAPTER IV

FROM PILLAR TO POST

OVER THE WEEK-END I stayed in my lodging in a state fluctuating from torpid indifference to intolerable craving for food and tobacco.

By the end of the long-drawn-out Sunday I seemed to have gone mildly insane on the question of food. I knew that the wooden top of a table is hardly to be recommended as an article of food, yet I could not help feeling that maybe if I were to take a bite at it—just a small bite—it might not prove to be so very unpalatable.

I now saw everything in terms of potential food. I wondered what it was like not to feel hungry, and marvelled that I had ever been in that privileged state. I wondered if I would ever again know what it was like to go about and not feel hungry; but I dismissed this idea as a Utopian dream. I wondered why people with enough to eat worried about anything else.

The intensity of my thoughts about food prevented me from

passing away the long, empty hours in reading. For one thing, my mind, no longer nourished by the body, was woollen, torpid and dead. When I took up a book my eyes roved uncomprehendingly over the pages, and saw nothing save occasional disjointed and disconnected phrases. These leapt out from the rest of the dim blur with a sudden sharp clarity, giving rise to painful associations and desires.

". . . He lit a cigarette. . . ." ". . . Let us dine at a restaurant tonight. . . ." ". . . She pushed her plate away. 'I cannot eat,' she laughed. . . ." ". . . He gave the commissionaire a handsome tip. . . ." ". . . He toyed with his breakfast. . . ." ". . . I am going out to lunch! . . ."

It was painful to read, for all literature seemed to be about food, about the delightful meals, eaten in the most casual way, by all kinds of inane and unappreciative people who didn't deserve what they got.

On Monday morning an idea came to me—an idea that seemed to be the solution of all my difficulties. I would go to the Relieving Officer! I would apply for relief! I was astonished that I had not thought of this before. Surely I would get something from him.

Because I had not eaten now for three days, it was with an effort that I arose to go to the Relieving Office.

When I got there I had to wait some time in a cold, cheerless room provided with a few hard benches, before I was called into the office.

"Have you applied for relief before?" the Relieving Officer inquired.

I told him that I had not.

Thereupon he took from a drawer several sheets of official paper, and with great care and deliberation put them in their respective order within a folder. Then he settled himself down to enter particulars about me on these various forms.

"Your name?" he asked.

I told him.

"Oh, so you're a Jew, then?" he asked.

"Yes," I replied.

"Well," he said, "we can't give you any relief here. You'll have to go to the Jewish Board of Guardians for that."

I was taken aback by this unexpected result to my application. With an effort I collected my wits. I had an elementary knowledge of the question of Relief, and I felt that the Relieving Officer had no right to refuse me relief on the grounds he had mentioned.

"The Jewish Board of Guardians is not in this area," I told

him, "and as I've lived in the neighbourhood for over six months, I'm entitled to apply for relief at the local Relieving Office. In any case," I went on, "the Jewish Board of Guardians isn't an official Relieving Office. It's entirely voluntary. They give you something if they can, but there's no law to compel them to."

My words appeared to impress the Relieving Officer. It was as though he reluctantly abandoned that which he had intended to make into an argument.

"Well, anyway," he went on, "what's your address?"

I told him my address, and then my age. Then he asked me if I were married. I told him I was single.

"We can't give relief to a single man," he said, suddenly very firm. "If I were you, I should go to the Jewish Board of Guardians."

"But I told you——" I began.

"In any case," he interrupted, "I won't give you any relief before you've applied to the Jewish Board of Guardians. That's final."

I felt too tired to argue with him any more. Moreover, the whole atmosphere of the Relieving Office filled me with distaste. This haggling for some begrudged relief made me feel as though I were a destitute pauper, and I desired passionately to cling to the belief that I was not—that I was merely asking for something that was my legal right. I was glad to get out of the place, even though I had not been given anything.

For a moment I pondered whether to undertake the wearying journey to the Jewish Board of Guardians. It was possible that I might meet people there who had known my mother and myself, for we had lived in the neighbourhood of the Guardians. It would become quite a local scandal (so I thought) if it became known that I had been reduced to the necessity of applying to "the Guardians" for relief. Possibly it might reach the ears of my mother, for she still kept up a fitful correspondence with one or two friends in the area.

However, I dared not risk the closing of yet another avenue of hope. It was a long and formidable distance to the Guardians' office. Nevertheless, I set off with slow determination.

Eventually I came to the offices of the Board. I was grateful for one thing—there was no deadly monotonous waiting to be done here. There was a waiting-room provided with benches, but this room was empty. There was a door on which was painted the words: "Jewish Board of Guardians. Office." I went up to this door and knocked.

"Come in," an austere voice said promptly.

Preparing myself for another ordeal, I went in, and found myself facing an official of the Board. I did not know whether he recognised me—I fervently hoped not—but I knew him. Part of the activity of the Board was loaning money free of interest to suitable applicants, the money being repaid in weekly instalments. My mother had taken a loan every year before Passover, in order to lay in an augmented stock of goods for the shop during this special period. I had made many visits to the office in order to repay money on this loan. My mother had also been a regular contributor of subscriptions to the Board.

As a general rule the clerk was in the office, and he had been the one to whom the money was paid.

On this occasion the official was in the office by himself. He was tall and thin, with a thin, aristocratic face. He was dressed perfectly, in the fashion of ten years previously. In general, he conformed to my ideas of a high official of the Civil Service, or even of a diplomat.

Perhaps in the circumstances I had hoped to find here a more kindly atmosphere than in the Relieving Office. Perhaps I had anticipated a tacit assumption that we were brothers under the skin. At any rate, my heart sank because he seemed impassive.

Seated behind his desk, he looked at me, and did not appear to derive any great pleasure from what he saw. And because he did not actually welcome me, I seemed to detect in his glance all that contempt and superior disapproval that are felt by some people towards those who apply for relief. I could not feel as impersonal to the situation here as I had felt in the Relieving Office, and therefore I smarted under a sense of humiliation. I felt that to him I was just another of those shiftless lads who "bummed it" from town to town, preying on charitable organisations and on sentimental old men in the synagogues. I was going to have a hard job getting anything out of him, I thought, looking at his unmoved official face.

"What do you want?" he asked.

"I've come to apply for relief."

"How is that? What are your circumstances?"

I explained.

"The Relieving Officer had no right to send you here," he said coldly. "We are not an official Relieving Office. We are a voluntary, charitable organisation."

It seemed to my wrought-up imagination that he emphasised the word "charitable".

"That's what I told him. But he said I must apply here first."

"He is quite wrong. It is an important matter of principle."

"Of course. I quite agree."

47

He seemed to resent my agreeing with him.

"What is your name?" he asked stiffly.

I told him.

"Where are you living?"

I told him.

"Are you married?"

"No."

"Oh! You are single, then?"

"As I'm not married, that's fairly obvious," I said sarcastically.

I was getting fed up with these eternal questions, that had not yet led anywhere, that stood as a barrier between me and food. I was tortured with impatience by the slow, imperturbable official routine, by these questions about my name, age, address, circumstances, and the peculiar significance attached to the matter of whether I was single or married.

"We cannot give relief to single men," he said frigidly. "We have not enough funds. We have to consider married men, with children, first."

This made me wild with disappointment and frustration and humiliation. It was for this that I had made a fruitless journey, answered interminable questions, faced humiliation, would have to walk back four miles, answer more questions, face more humiliation.

"What's the matter?" I snarled. "Doesn't a single man have to eat—pay rent? Has a man got to be married before he can get any relief?"

"We cannot give relief to single men," he repeated icily.

My impotence goaded me on. "What sort of a relief organisation d'you call this, anyway?" I stormed. "You scrounge pennies from the poor, and then you behave like Lord Muck when someone applies for relief!"

"Get out, or I'll call the police!" he said stonily.

"Call them! That's one way of getting board and lodgings, anyway!"

"Get out!"

I wanted to say or do something violent—something that would shake him once and for all from his official impregnability. But suddenly my reserves of energy collapsed, and I felt very tired. What was the use of bothering with these people, anyway? Who the hell wanted their niggardly doles?

But if only I could get some temporary form of relief, no matter how small; the price of a meal, something to fill up this nagging, debilitating hollow in my belly; something to turn the pale water in my veins to red blood again; something to transmit life to my brain and limbs. For a moment I thought of pleading with him to give me something, no matter how small. Then I knew I would never be able to plead for charity. I turned away, silent, trying not to feel like a beaten dog.

When I got into the street again I felt very tired. My knees were as jelly, my shoulders drooped. I had not the energy to hold myself upright. Those four miles; not one mile, but one mile followed by another mile, followed by another mile, followed by another mile—four miles, four long miles, endless miles.

Well, I have to get back somehow. Can't hang round here all day. Put the left foot forward. And now the right foot forward. And now the left foot forward. And now the right foot forward. And now the left foot. And now the right foot. Left foot, right foot. Left foot, right foot. . . .

When I got back to my lodgings I sat for a long time dazed and inert, whilst a black cloud threatened to descend before my eyes and blot out everything.

CHAPTER V

THE SKELETON IN THE MIRROR

By THE TIME I neared the Relieving Office, it was after twelve o'clock. It occurred to me that it would be useless for me to go here at this time. I would have to go after the dinner interval.

Nevertheless, once I had returned to my lodging the fatigue which overtook me seemed to make it impossible for me to do anything so energetic as to rise and go out and haggle with the Relieving Officer.

I was fed up with the whole business, anyway. I began to take the standpoint that I had got myself into a mess, and that I would have to get myself out of it without the aid of relief organisations. Like many people who have been badgered about by prying Relieving Officers, and have had no indications that any favour-able result will be forthcoming, I yielded to the emotion: "Let them go to hell; I'll get on without them."

So I lay on my bed, gazing unseeingly into space. Sometimes I would think of easy—delightfully easy—ways to get money, become rich, have as much food as I wanted.

Now, I would think, if I stood at the corner of a busy street in the centre of the town and begged each passer-by to give me a farthing. Only a farthing. What is a farthing to them? And supposing that two people each gave me a farthing. Already I would have a ha'penny! Not a very considerable sum, but already something better than nothing. But now, just supposing that four people each gave me a farthing. I would have a penny! You can do something with a penny! There are some places where you can get a cup of tea for a penny. But just a minute. Supposing eight people each gave me a farthing. I would have twopence. One can almost make a meal on that. But speculations such as these are mere trifles. Why bother about twopence? Supposing that no fewer than sixteen people each gave me a farthing. I would have fourpence! This is bliss. But if thirty-two people each gave me a farthing, I would have no less than eightpence. This is wealth, real wealth. But consider, wait a minute. Suppose that *sixty-four* people each gave me a farthing! O joy! I would then have—how much? How much is sixty-four farthings? I cannot reckon it. My brain struggles feebly with the problem. Sixty-four farthings . . . sixty-four farthings . . . it mumbles, but it can not translate the farthings into terms of pence, of shillings and pence.

And sometimes my mind turned to the problem of my circumstances—a problem which had become insoluble. I realised dimly that I should have done something, no matter at what cost to pride: should have begged, sung in the streets, done anything to get food. But now I was caught, trapped in the toils of hunger. I was too inert to make effort, to use initiative to secure food. I no longer cared. I felt vaguely that I ought to care; that indifference was death. But I could no longer care. I was no longer very much troubled by pangs of hunger. There was merely a dull, numb void where my stomach had been.

Then on the Tuesday night, when I rose momentarily from my bed, I caught sight of my face in the mirror. For the first time an arrow of fear pierced through the thick armour of my indifference. I saw in the mirror a skull covered tightly with thin parchment. Fear invaded me and concern flooded me. Indifference vanished. I turned hurriedly from the mirror. Once again the question recurred: "What shall I do?"

If only I could get some kind of odd job by which I could earn a few shillings. The idea recurred insistently. Some kind of job by which I could earn a few shillings.

Suddenly it seemed to me as if I had found a way out at last. I would go canvassing from house to house, asking people if they wanted their furniture repaired. This seemed to be an idea of positive brilliance. Even if I got only one or two jobs, and earned only a few shillings, it would make all the difference to me. I decided to carry out this project as soon as possible—the next morning.

On Wednesday morning I packed the most essential of my tools in a large attaché case, and set out to see whether I could get any orders for repairing furniture. Objective circumstances were none too bright. It was one of those grey, utterly gloomy mornings common in the middle of winter. There was a sharp touch of damp frost in the air. As I was feeling very empty and without strength, and was loaded with heavy tools, it was difficult for me to feel very optimistic about matters in general.

I stopped at my first street, which was fairly long and was entirely residential, without any shops or factories in it. It was with some effort that I nerved myself to knock at the first house, but when I did knock there was something of an anti-climax. No one was in.

I knocked at all the houses on that side of the street, but no more than four or five people answered the door. Most of these were indifferent and closed the door again as soon as they had opened it. One housewife was very annoyed by reason of having been interrupted in some domestic task.

I tried the other side of the street, telling myself that at any rate the responses could be no worse. But they were, both in quality and quantity. Only two people answered the door. One was an aged grandma, very nearly stone deaf, who invited me into the lobby and clearly had not the slightest idea of my business, even after I had howled my message down her ear for fully three minutes. The other was a burly, half-dressed ruffian who gave one contemptuous look at me, and with an angry "Not today!" shut the door with a bang.

What with the weight of the tools and my utter lack of strength, by the time I had reached the end of the street I could hardly walk. Nevertheless, the tantalising thought that I might miss just the one house where people might want me to carry out repairs lured me on like a will o' the wisp. I canvassed the next street and even the next.

The total result of that which seemed to me to have been a whole morning's work—though it probably did not take much more than an hour—was the awakening within me of the sleeping devil of hunger, an intolerable weakness and fatigue, and an ever-deepening sense of humiliation. I went back to my lodgings almost too worn out to feel the encroachment of utter despair.

I spent that afternoon, as I had spent the previous afternoon, lying on the bed, gazing unseeingly into space and conjuring up fantasies of a full stomach and pockets bulging with wealth.

The next morning I decided to go out canvassing once again. It was impossible that I could keep on with this sort of thing and get no jobs at all. And yet, circumstances proved otherwise. Still another morning of hawking my tools from house to house proved to me that people were not enamoured of the idea of having their

51

furniture repaired, or if they were, then they were above all reluctant to allow a complete stranger to repair it.

Moreover, I began to revise my ideas. After all, repairing furniture can be something of a complicated business. It may need all the resources of a well-equipped workshop to effect a relatively simple and quick repair. What would I do supposing someone actually wanted me to repair furniture, but that in order to repair it I needed a gluepot and brush, a bench, vice and cramps, not to mention handscrews, polish, screws and nails, timber, and so on? It was asking too much that I, a complete stranger, should expect people to entrust me with the money to buy even a few nails, let alone other materials, before they had seen me do a stroke of work.

These thoughts were sufficient to dissipate my visions of earning anything by repairing furniture. I went back to my lodgings determined that, come what might, I would waste no more energy or shoe-leather on a hopeless project.

I had not been in my room more than a few moments when I was aware of someone knocking at the door. I opened it, and found my landlady grinning at me politely.

"I knocked one or twice before," she said, "but you were out, seemingly. I was wondering if you could do a bit of a job for me, seein' that you're a carpenter, or whatever it is."

I was almost overcome by her words, the irony of which nearly caused me to burst into bitter laughter. Here I had been dragging my tools round from house to house, and all the time a job was waiting for me at my lodgings. It was enough to make a cat laugh.

"You know what it is," she went on. "Young people will damage things. On New Year's Eve we had a bit of a party in the sitting-room, and you'd never believe it, but what d'you think the young folk done?"

Like Brutus, she paused for a reply. I remembered New Year's Eve very well for a number of reasons, not the least of them being the inordinate noise that had gone on into the small hours in the sitting-room, which was the next room to mine. The noise had sounded as though people were alternately murdering each other and turning the furniture upside down.

As I could not guess specifically what they had done, my land-lady went on with an air of triumph:

"They went and broke in the settee! Now what d'you think of that?"

My thoughts on the matter were mainly technical. The one job she had for me might prove beyond my capabilities. A settee, after all, is an upholsterer's job, not a cabinet-maker's. I might end by turning the settee inside out and being unable to restore it to anything like its proper state. In ordinary circumstances I would have declined the job and told my landlady to get an upholsterer to do it for her. As matters stood, however, I would have been quite willing to try my hand at repairing a defective water-system or a leaking gas-pipe.

I therefore went with her into the sitting-room, and after examination of the damaged settee, set to work. My landlady left me to it.

I had a job at last.

CHAPTER VI

THE GODS LAUGH

I DISCOVERED THAT in spite of my acute desire for a job of some kind, in actual practice it was very difficult for me to work at all. Not merely my body, but my mind also could barely function. The simplest and most elementary step to be thought out and carried into operation seemed to offer insurmountable difficulties. It was as though I was trying to do the job at the bottom of the sea, encumbered with a deep-sea diver's outfit.

Nevertheless, ever before me, compelling, was the reward. In two or three hours I had finished the job. Then, agitated at the idea that, incredibly, I would be able to get something to eat, I hurried to tell my landlady that the job was done.

There was, however, a disappointment for me. It appeared that there were other jobs that wanted doing. Another man, in a far better position than I, would have been pleased. I, however, was cast-down. From my standpoint other jobs were superfluous and unnecessary. This one job had achieved my immediate purpose—to secure the means whereby I could eat and drink as soon as possible. Other jobs merely postponed the moment and prolonged the agony of waiting. However, as I was sedulously cultivating the pretence that I was working more from a desire to pass the time than from any immediate and urgent necessity, I found it impossible to ask my landlady to pay me already, when I had done only a mere two or three hours' work.

With weary reluctance I went on with the other jobs. The locks and bolts of various doors functioned badly, and, whilst I was no locksmith, I was able to effect an improvement by screwing up loose parts, oiling the locks, and so on. The top of my landlady's kitchen table was warped so that the different pieces resembled not so much a flat surface as the waves of a troubled sea. There were one or two other jobs. I went on working with dreary doggedness, with infinite toil.

At about half-past five I had completed the various repairs, and I calculated that I had worked about six and a half hours. Now that I had done the work I was glad. Visions of limitless wealth floated before me. I ought to get eight or nine bob for this.

Once again I went to tell my landlady that I had finished. She smiled amiably.

"That's good," she said. "Thank you very much."

She went on to discuss the weather, my chances of getting a job shortly, and other items of small talk. I burned with impatience, and nodded feverishly at everything she said. She rambled on and on, till I felt a mad desire to shout aloud with despair.

Gradually her flow of conversation exhausted itself. All the time she had made no mention of that which was to me the most important thing—payment for my work. And gradually the cold astounding truth dawned on me: she had no idea of paying me for the work! Either she was too mean and was resolved to get out of paying me if she could, or else she tacitly assumed that for various favours she had rendered me in the past—favours of which I had no knowledge or recollection—I had done the work for her in pure and simple gratitude.

I found it difficult to believe the second of these suppositions, though the first seemed to me to be quite within the bounds of possibility. My landlady, for all her amiable airs, was of a grasping meanness. Later events were to prove to me many times that people who knew that I was a woodworker were prepared to attempt to exploit my ability in order to get something done for nothing, or nearly nothing. With these people one was placed in the position of being a mean, tight-fisted wretch who demanded exorbitant payment for "trifling" work, which anyone with any decency at all would have been glad to do for nothing.

Nevertheless, this was my first experience of someone who, without the slightest claim on my gratitude or affection, presumed that I would do a day's work without pay. I was intimidated by having to ask for the money and being cast in the rôle of a mean, tight-fisted wretch. Precisely because I needed the money so desperately, so all the more I could not bear to ask for it. I ceased to think of payment as something to which I had a just right. I thought of it as a destitute person thinks of charity.

The conversation came to a stop. There was an awkward silence. I wanted to ask for the money, but all my energies were exhausted. I could not summon up the brazen effrontery necessary to ask to be paid for work I had done. I retired to my room, dumb and overwhelmed.

This did not last very long. By what right did this parsimonious landlady of mine, who had never done anything for me apart from collecting her rent every week, and who had actually threatened last week-end to evict me should I get more than one week behind with the rent—what right had she to expect me to spend nearly all day messing about with her precious furniture and doors?

I went to the kitchen and knocked again, not timidly now, but loudly and brusquely.

"Come in," my landlady's voice sang out in an over-sweet contralto. I opened the door, and went in.

"Hullo," she exclaimed, with arch surprise.

In spite of my indignation, I could not even now avoid feeling intimidated by the need to ask for the money.

"I thought maybe you'd pay me for the work I did today," I said, trying to appear very blunt and determined, but still feeling shame at the words I was uttering.

My landlady's face expressed surprise, even hurt.

"Pay?" she asked. She paused for a moment, and then, as one deciding to yield with good grace to an importunate demand, she asked with an air of naïve candour, "How much shall I give you? Will half-a-crown be enough?"

Two and sixpence for nearly a whole day's work! Even if I had charged her only a shilling an hour, the full cost would have been six and sixpence. In addition to that, it was always recognised in the trade that anyone who did private work charged at least the Union rate of pay. And she offered me half-a-crown!

Suddenly I remembered that, after all, I owed her a week's rent. I could always argue the question with her at the week-end, when I would have food inside me. And in the meantime—half-a-crown! My attitude changed suddenly. After having been penniless for days, and thinking sixpence the height of wealth, the thought that I could, without further trouble or argument, possess half-a-crown thrilled me and made me eager to agree.

"Very well," I muttered.

She opened her purse and handed me half-a-crown. I thanked her mechanically, and without further ado closed the door. My mind was a tumult of emotions—indignation, distress, shame, but, above all, exultation. I had half-a-crown!

Half-a-crown! Was I not rich, overflowing with wealth? Half-a-crown! Feverishly I hurried up the passage, rushed out into the street.

A merciless, punishing rain was pelting down. Ever and

again an aggressive wind howled with bellicose fervour and thrashed the raindrops on to the pavements and on to the shop windows. I was too impatient to go back for my overcoat. I ran through the seething street overcoatless and without a cap. All the time my mind was occupied with calculating what food I should buy.

I reached the dairy. This was the shop that sold that luscious Cheshire cheese—like rich, firm butter! I went inside and bought a pound of it. Tenpence gone; one and eightpence left. Half a pint of milk; another twopence gone (Northerners do not deal in that quaint coin, the farthing). A loaf of bread, twopence ha'penny; one and threepence ha'penny left. Quarter of butter, threepence; a shilling and a ha'penny left. What else? Three bananas, fourpence ha'penny; eightpence left.

Now, what else? The mind of your destitute individual is not concerned with the bare satisfaction of his momentary needs, and of saving for the future. He is obsessed with the idea of spending everything, of getting the maximum possible amount of goods or pleasure with the money he has now. Let tomorrow look after itself! One can always starve again. It is comfortable security that breeds caution.

I had the colossal sum of eightpence left, burning a hole in my pocket, what of its idleness. Then I remembered. A packet of cigarettes. But wait a minute! Tea, sugar! The eightpence suddenly shrank and became small.

Coppers went on a twopenny sample packet of tea, on sugar, and on a twopenny packet of cigarettes. I had to resign myself to having a wasted, utterly futile ha'penny left. Exultantly I hurried back, my arms and pockets filled with packages.

My room had a festive appearance, the table decorated with the food. Food! My spirit within me clamoured. I unwrapped the parcels and cut off hunks of bread and cheese to eat there and then.

But then I realised that this was an occasion not to be treated lightly. I realised that I was feeling wet and cold. Better to postpone the feast for a minute or two and make a fire. By a fortunate accident I had been sent twice the amount of coal I had ordered before Christmas, and there was still over a hundred-weight of it left. I would make a fire and do the thing in style.

I made a fire. It burned up brightly, and I was glad that I had made it. It added to the festive appearance of the room. Once again I was about to cut some lumps of bread and cheese and eat them there and then. Then, instead of cutting rude lumps of bread and cheese, I cut six slices of bread and buttered them liberally. Then I cut the cheese into small pieces. Then I sat down at the table. I was aware of a mysterious sense of uneasiness. . . . Wait a minute; get a book, and you can read while you're eating.

I rose and got a book. Uneasiness was deepening. Self-control, desire to get everything ready properly—all this was very well, very good. But why? . . . what? . . . 'what impelled me to behave like this? Sh! Sh! Sit down and have a good meal. You can have more, if this isn't enough.

Again I sat down at the table. I was aware of a sense of constraint, as though I were a stranger sitting at another man's table, about to eat a meal surreptitiously given to him by the woman of the household. Uneasiness grew. Then I remembered. Tea! Of course! What a fool I was! I would drink some tea before I ate anything. This would make me feel better. With relief I rose to prepare the tea.

The tea was ready. I poured out a cupful. For a moment I sat waiting—for what? Then impatience seized me. Enough of this! I put the teacup to my lips and drank. I was astonished. The taste of the tea was appalling! Like warm mud!

I paced to and fro, nervously pondering this mystery. Then a solution came to me. Of course! What a fool I was! After I had not eaten for so long it was natural that the tea should taste queer to me. It was necessary for me to rinse my mouth, drink some water. Relief surged through me. I rinsed, and drank cold water. The water had a peculiar taste. It was with an effort that I drank it. Then I sat down again.

I took a bite of bread. Then dismay seized me. The bread tasted like sand. Try the cheese . . . the cheese tasted like clay. . . .

It's quite clear, really. Nothing to make a fuss about. The cheese must be bad—the quality varies a good deal. The bread; well, the bread isn't much good either.

I sat down dejectedly. A numb misery had seized me in its grip. The fact was, in spite of everything, I did not feel hungry. It was incredible, amazing, frightening. I had not eaten for a week, and now I had some food I did not want to eat anything. I endured all the sensations of an impotent benedict.

I wrapped the food up again, and put it away very tidily. I remembered the cigarettes, for which I had craved so urgently during the last week. I lit one and smoked it obstinately to its end, despite the protest of palate and stomach. Then I undressed and went to bed. For long hours I stared blankly into the darkness.

Food . . . and I was not hungry.

CHAPTER VII

THE VALLEY OF THE SHADOW

THE NEXT MORNING I awoke and was hit on the head simultaneously with awakening. For a moment I was filled with alarm at this manifestation of unseen powers in my room, and strove to open my eyes to see who they were. My eyelids appeared to be stuck together, and it was with some difficulty that eventually I managed to part them. During my first attempts to see, I was struck several further blows on the head.

I was to a certain extent surprised to see the room exactly as it had been the night before. There was no sign of anyone apart from myself having been in it, nor were there any articles lying on or near the bed against which I could have struck myself.

Just then I was hit another blow on the head, and the truth dawned on me. My head was weak and empty, and when I moved my eyes in any direction other than in front, the blow struck me; inside the head, not outside. I ached in the stomach, in the legs, in the back—in fact it was quicker to realise where I was not aching.

I was ill, possibly quite seriously. I decided to stay in bed till I felt a little better. An uneasy sense of loneliness came over me. I had no one to help me. My landlady might be a thousand miles away for all the help she would be to me; she never came near the room from one fortnight to another. Besides, she was the last person I felt like turning to for assistance. To be ill in a strange place is not an enviable circumstance. I felt that I was on dangerous ground.

Suddenly I realised that this was the morning I had been awaiting impatiently for nearly a fortnight—the morning towards which I had reckoned and calculated days, hours, minutes, seconds; the morning I was to get paid at the Labour Exchange.

There could be no dallying on this morning. Nothing would keep me from getting my Unemployment Benefit. I clambered out of bed, and it came to me with a shock to discover how ill I really was, for I could hardly support myself. I suddenly felt very old, and the chill of death was in my bones.

I crawled about the room, dressing piecemeal, and making tea. The universal aching seemed to increase, making movement a painful and tardy process.

I allowed myself plenty of time in which to reach the Labour Exchange. Nevertheless, I arrived only barely in time to sign-on. The way had seemed interminable, the effort unendurable. A penetrating, devitalising chill turned my blood to icy water, making me shiver and writhe in numb agony. Yet the weather could not have been very cold; people walked about in the ordinary attire of a mild January morning, and did not seem to be feeling any great fall in the temperature.

I was afraid the clerk at the Exchange might see that I was ill. If he did, and felt he ought to report it, then I would be disqualified from benefit. Actually, by signing-on I was contravening the law, for one of the declarations a man makes implicitly every time he signs on is that he is "capable of, and available for, work"; which means, amongst other things, that he is not ill.

However, I was paid in a brisk and business-like fashion. Had the setting been in any way suited to the occasion as I saw it, there would have been a fanfare of trumpets, cheering crowds, emotional speeches, great rejoicings. However, I collected the money stolidly, in a manner fitting a very ordinary occasion, and left the Exchange.

I had decided long before what I would do when I was paid. I would go to the nearby café that advertised itself as being a "Home from Home". There one could buy dinners of good quality, the quantity being according to one's purse. Here I would feast myself to absolute satiety. With reckless prodigality I would order the largest meal on the menu, together with every possible accessory to it. If this proved to be not enough, I would order a second helping of everything (pretending somehow that it was for someone else). After this I would have at least two helpings of that supremely satisfying, if somewhat sickening pudding they made, and would then conclude the dinner with two large cups of tea.

This was the voluptuous, the rapturous vision that had floated before my mind's eye countless times in the past ten days. Many an unfulfilled stream of saliva had gushed in my mouth at that fair dream. I had garnished and ornamented it with many superstructural details: how, if my hunger were not satisfied by that first gastronomical debauch (as, indeed, how could it be satisfied—how would it ever be satisfied?), I would go somewhere else, have more tea and the richest, most nauseatingly sweet cake they sold. Yes, I would even buy myself that luscious bottle of cod-liver oil and malt for which I had yearned so desperately one night as I stood gazing into a chemist's window.

True, all this would mean that in one reckless hour I would be squandering money which I ought to be spreading carefully over a whole week. But what of that? I would at least have had one glorious and shining hour in the drab gloom of the week. Better one ecstatic repletion of the stomach than a succession

59

of grey, unfilling palliatives, merely teasing, not satisfying. I would have to go short anyway. I might just as well go short in the most enjoyable way.

That had been my anticipation of this hour. But how flat and dreary that vision seemed now! The very notion of eating a tithe of that gargantuan dinner of the imagination made me feel worse.

Nevertheless, I could not abandon this vision altogether. It was as though I would be repulsing that which had helped and cheered me in my time of darkest gloom.

So I went along to a café, where I reluctantly and with difficulty swallowed a cup of tea and a piece of cake. Then I went to a public library, where I spent the rest of the morning unseeingly turning over the pages of magazines.

At noon I crawled along to the "Home from Home", where I ordered a very curtailed and shrunken counterpart of "The Dinner". Halfway through eating it I gave up the task as one altogether impossible of fulfilment, despite the fact that I was leaving good, nourishing food which I had paid for.

Trembling, writhing with cold and weakness, I made my way back to my lodging. Despite fanatical notions I had on the subject of fresh air, I did my best to seal my room hermetically. Then, blessing the accident that had left me with a large store of coal, I made an enormous fire, drew my chair in front of it and lay there, relaxed and stupid.

Thus I spent that day and the succeeding days. I have vague memories of crawling about, a weak and enervated ghost, dividing my time between dull, restless hours in bed, and dull, apathetic hours in front of the fire. My body was one huge, nagging ache, and cold as a bleak winter's morning

It was a time of slow, enduring ennui. As near as is possible in a living organism I had no desires, no capacities, and, save for the aches and the cold, no feelings or perceptions.

The only matter I thought about to a successful conclusion was that of the fire. In spite of the fact that I sat so near to it that my trousers sometimes scorched, I still felt unendurably cold. But when the fire burned low, I felt even worse. Nevertheless, once relaxed in front of it, I could not summon up enough energy to get up to put more coal on. I would sit dully watching the flames sink lower and lower, the life-giving heat fading slowly away. "In five minutes by the clock I'll get up and put more coal on," I would tell myself. The five minutes passed, but still I could not get up to perform the task. Many evenings the fire went out, and there was nothing for me to do but go wretchedly to bed.

But more than the effort involved was the fact that when more coal was put on, the heat of the fire practically disappeared for a time. This I could not bear, and it was this question which occupied my mind a good deal, and which I eventually solved.

It occurred to me to make the fire first in one corner of the grate. When it was burning brightly, I added coal to the other part of the grate. When the first part of the fire had burned low, the second was burning up. Afterwards I added coal to that part of the fire which needed replenishing, and the result was that there was always some part of the fire giving out glowing heat. I imagine, however, that this solution came towards the end of the illness, for at first I had little energy for such efforts.

I suppose I attended regularly at the Labour Exchange, for I have no recollection of any difficulties, technical or financial, in which I would have involved myself if I had not. In addition to this, however, I forced myself to go out for walks. Each of these was an arduous struggle against overpowering torpor, apathy and weakness. Nevertheless, I was driven to engage in them in order to distract my mind, and also because I had a vague idea that exercise might do me good.

I forced myself to eat three or four oranges a day, although the idea of eating anything was repulsive to me and the juice of the oranges seemed to taste exactly like vinegar. Here again I was trying to aid myself to recovery. I also yielded sufficiently to circumstances to use a hot-water bottle in bed.

This hot-water bottle was literally an old wine bottle filled with hot water. Because of the care I took in pouring the boiling water very slowly into the bottle, it did not crack. I had hitherto always regarded hot-water bottles and their users with the stern contempt of youth for those who seek to pamper their weakly bodies. Now, however, I realised the advantages of a hot-water bottle, for at night my body was icy cold, though my head burned with febrile heat. The bottle filled with hot water suffused the bed with satisfying warmth, and when I woke in the small hours, as I invariably did, I was, towards the end of the illness, drenched with perspiration, which latter I regarded as a good sign.

With the strange carelessness of the young, I did not consider it worth while for me to visit a doctor. I felt quite capable of taking care of myself, or, putting it another way, that no doctor could really help me.

I diagnosed my illness as a kind of feverish chill, and put down as the basic cause of the illness and its severity the fact that my powers of resistance had been undermined through lack of food. Can you go to a doctor and ask him to cure you of the effects of starvation? This was how I reasoned with myself, though the real reason of my reluctance to see a doctor probably lay in a feeling of diffidence at the idea of telling him the cause of the illness.

The condition I have described lasted for about eight or nine days. Then slowly I achieved the ability to eat, the aches and pains gradually dissolved and disappeared, and I was able to walk about and perform my daily tasks without undue discomfort. After a few more days I was more or less recovered from the worst features of the illness, though I was still very weak and my face was a gaunt, pale mask.

Those who are believers in the philosophy of Candide's friend, Doctor Pangloss,—that "all is for the best in the best of all possible worlds"—may take comfort and inspiration from a perusal of the above experiences. The fact was, when all is said and done, that the illness had come at a very opportune time. One of the main characteristics of this illness, as I have shown, was my inability to eat anything. In view of my circumstances at the time, one may well ask, "What could be more opportune than that?" Thus one may perceive that under our present best of all possible systems of civilisation even illness may be a blessing, if it takes away the appetite. Amongst some people I might no doubt have been the object of commiseration and mournful sympathy, but amongst the unemployed and Labour Exchange circles generally my condition was one calling for congratulation, admiration, and even envy. Moreover, when it is remembered that I had planned to fling away my money, not in mere satisfaction of bodily needs, but to wallow in sensual gluttony, one may detect in the illness the hand of Providence ever outstretched to save the would-be sinner.

By the time my appetite returned to me I was enabled to square matters with my landlady and in addition have some shillings in hand. It is to my regret that I have to record that apparently I ignored the hand of Providence which had been outstretched to save me. In the first few days of my recovery those extra shillings, together with other shillings retained from that week's dole after the rent had been paid, vanished in sating my bodily appetites; and, sinful mortal that I was, it seemed to me that I had not had enough.

Thereafter, I settled down to exist on twelve and sixpence a week; that is, on six shillings a week after the rent was paid.

CHAPTER VIII

THE REVELATION

Amongst the inhabitants of the house in which I lived was one whom, because of the fact that I do not remember his name, and would invent another if I did, I will call Tim Stevens.

He was a burly, round-faced, garrulous ex-sailor turned bricklayer's labourer. He had been involved in some accident or another, and was now living on compensation, which I regret to say he spent mainly in drowning his lonely sorrows. I was not very keen on meeting with him, because when I did he engaged me in lengthy and tortuous conversation from which it was difficult for me to escape.

Generally we met in the bathroom, a dirty little hole with distemper crumbling from the walls and ceiling, and containing a minute bath which was eaten with rust and coated with slime. From the fact that the door was occasionally locked and the sound of splashing water could be heard, I deduced that sometimes it was actually used as a bathroom; but on the whole its function was that of a miniature laundry, or a place for washing crockery.

It was here that I spoke with Tim about a fortnight after I had begun to recover from my illness. He was looking rather pale and woebegone, and displayed little of his usual inclination to talk.

"I've not seen you for a week or two," I said politely, quaking lest this remark should involve me in a turgid monologue on his part from which I would have the greatest difficulty in tearing myself away.

"No," he agreed shortly. "A've been laid-up."

"I was ill myself a couple of weeks back, but——"

"Ah, I was cruel bad, I can tell ye. I was laid-up for a fortnight, d'ye see, and it left me as weak as anything." He coughed hollowly, and I, eager to tell someone of my own misfortunes, interjected with:

"That's just what happened to me."

"Ah," he went on, sombrely indifferent to the petty ailments of others. "I tell you, I was achin' all over——"

"That's just how I was!"

"Me back, me stomach, me legs, me 'ead——" he catalogued inexorably.

"That's just how I was!"

"I never touched a thing," he went on, with awful solemnity—"not a thing. Not a bite. I couldn't bear the *sight* o' food!" He frowned portentously, to illustrate this appalling circumstance.

"That's just how it was with me!" I exclaimed in wonder and delight.

This man was a fellow-sufferer—more, a brother, a comrade in distress! I wanted to shake him by the hand, go away with him to some quiet, secluded corner, where we could mutually dissect, probe and exhaustively discuss our identical symptoms; analyse them, see what precise differences, if any, there were, and generally have a heart-to-heart talk about our melancholy experiences.

Apparently he did not share my enthusiasm. Rather did he appear to resent the assumption that I could have been as seriously ill as he, or that any illness could in any way be compared with his.

"I was burnin' like a fire," he challenged darkly, "but most of the time I was as cold—as cold as a bloomin' iceberg."

Sensing his hostility to my idea that we had been victims of exactly the same symptoms, I refrained from any further comparisons.

"You must have been pretty bad," I conceded reluctantly.

"Bad!" he exclaimed with hoarse fervour. "Bad! You've said just the right word, mate. I was bad. Cruel bad. I was achin' in the back——"

"And in the legs?"

"*And* in the legs. *And* in the stomach——"

"You had no appetite, eh?"

"Appetite?" he asked. His tone was one of amazement and scorn, as one who would ask, "What sort of frivolous question is this? Don't you realise I was *ill*?" "Appetite? I couldn't touch a thing. An' I was achin'——"

"You felt weak, eh?"

"Weak? If you'd ha' given me five pounds—no! a hundred pounds—to walk a mile,"—he paused impressively and fixed me with his gaze to make sure that I really appreciated the grave import of his words—"I couldn't have done it," he ended slowly and heavily.

"Really! And what——"

"Say, the doctor said it was one o' the worst cases of 'flu he'd come across this winter."

"The 'flu! Is that what you had—the 'flu?"

"Yes, that's what was wrong wi' me—the 'flu. I reckon that's what you must have had, an' all. Didn't you go to a doctor?"

"No," I said lamely, and went away.

So that was what had been the matter. The 'flu. A common, everyday illness. An illness that overtook all kinds of people; people living in normal everyday circumstances as well as those who existed in conditions of acute starvation.

I had spoken with a man who had described to me how he had been suffering from certain symptoms identical with mine. It appeared that he had been ill with the 'flu; therefore it followed that I also had probably had the same illness. This revelation had an effect on me altogether disproportionate to its apparent unimportance.

Because of the fact that I had had pneumonia a number of times as a child, I had always regarded the 'flu as a petty, trifling illness—merely a rather severe form of the common cold. I had not known that its effects could be as severe as they had been in the case of Tim and myself. These symptoms had numbed my spirit, for I had regarded them as a portent—a portent of slow but sure descent to extinction. Gradually my strength would dwindle away, and I would die. That was how I pictured it, and I had been at once too passive, too proud and too ashamed to seek assistance.

But now all this must end—this passivity, this morbidity, this hiding in one's lodgings, like an animal preparing to die in some jungle retreat. I was alive and recovering. I would recover and live. I still had a hold on life, and a right to life, like anyone else.

I was as one whose sleep is intermittent and vaguely terrible with nightmare. Each time he wakes to find it is still night, and it seems that the healthy light of day will never come. Then he wakes to discover that at last it is day, and everything is normal again. So it was with me. I had not, after all, been suffering from some wasting disease, the outcome of unendurable privations, the prelude, perhaps, to lingering, isolated death. I had been victim of an ordinary illness, the 'flu.

I sat down at the table in my room in a vaguely exalted mood. I was about to prepare my plans for a new assault on life.

Firstly, I must change the relaxed, sloppy, passive methods of life, so easy to get into, so hard to get out of. A regular routine, that was the need of the moment.

Then there were a number of friends I'd had, with whom I had gradually lost contact when I moved away from the neighbourhood in which my family lived. I would visit these friends again, renew the friendships, keep my outlook broadened to external things, instead of narrowed down to myself, like an Indian fakir with his eye perpetually glued to his navel.

There was an uncle and aunt whom I had visited a good deal when I was a child, though I had dropped out of the habit as I grew older. I had met my cousin some months ago, and she had asked me why I didn't come to see them more often, particularly as I was now living by myself. I would visit them fairly regularly from now onwards.

So much for that. I would also make a definite, planned search for work. I would not go job-hunting indiscriminately. To do so now, towards the end of January, in the slackest period of the slackest trade year that had been known for a long time—this would be a mere waste of time and shoe-leather.

It seemed to me that the bigger firms would be suffering from the twofold effects of the slump and the slack season. I would go to the small handshops. The same things had to be taken into consideration here also, but circumstances would differ in individual cases. A small order, which a large firm would disdain, would keep a handshop fairly busy for a few weeks. A chance order, and a small employer is prepared to take a man on. Therefore, I would inquire at the handshops. One never knew what would turn up.

So it was that I set out to look for work. I felt a certain grim satisfaction in being out and about again, in being one of those who, potentially, still have a part to play. I was no longer a pale, mournful invalid, languishing in his lodging and resigning himself to his fate. I was one who was walking about the town looking for a job.

Before long I reached the neighbourhood in which I had decided to look for work. Eventually I reached the first cabinet-making shop. It was small and dingy, and badly in need of repair, as are most small cabinet-workshops, and many large ones. I opened the door and entered.

A small, stocky man was working in the dark, cramped room. He turned round when I came in, but said nothing. I noticed that he had green eyes, like the eyes of a tiger.

"Want any cabinet-maker's improvers?" I asked.

He gazed fixedly at my chest.

"How much d'you want an hour?" he asked my chest.

"A shilling."

"What can you do? Are you used to handwork?" he inquired of my chest.

"I've always been used to handwork," I replied, feeling uncomfortable because he persisted in speaking to a part of my anatomy instead of to me.

"Have you got a full set of tools?" he asked, still restricting his gaze to the upper part of my torso.

"Yes, I've got a set of tools," I assured him.

"Well, I'll give you a trial," he said casually. "You can start tomorrow morning at eight o'clock." He lifted his eyes to my face for an instant, and dropped them again immediately.

I went out stunned. I had not merely got a job, but got one at the very first place at which I had inquired.

CHAPTER IX

A NEW START IN LIFE

WHEN I HAD recovered from my first excitement, my thoughts turned to the question of how I would manage till I received my first wages. My circumstances were none too favourable for starting work. I had no money, and very little food. I needed money for fares (for the workshop was two or three miles away from where I lived), and particularly I needed money for food.

I had intended to pay my aunt and uncle a visit that night, and after a time it occurred to me that when I was there I would explain my position to them. I would ask them to lend me some money till I got my wages and the Unemployment Benefit for the days I had been out of work.

Accordingly I went along that night to visit my relatives. They were concerned about my appearance, and told me that I looked very ill. I told them part of the truth, saying that I was just recovering from a severe attack of the 'flu.

Conversation ranged now here, now there. The health and activities of the different members of our scattered family, the state of trade, the weather, were discussed and disposed of. All the time I strove to take my part in the conversation I was aware, with guilt, that I had come here not merely to pay a family visit, as they supposed, but to borrow money. Their friendliness to me, their tacit assumption that I had come to pay a visit after the manner of nephews, made me feel uneasy and guilty.

Time drifted on, and still I had not broached the all-important question. Finally, my uncle, who himself had been a cabinet-maker before age and ill-health forced him to retire, asked me about my prospects of getting a job.

"As a matter of fact," I said, "I'm starting tomorrow——"

"Tomorrow?"

". . . Yes—but . . . you see, I don't happen to have any money."

"No money?"

"No. You see, I should be getting the dole the day after to-morrow, and with it being towards the end of the week, as you might say, I really haven't got enough money to last me till I get paid on Friday, or go and get the dole."

This was the most I could bring myself to say. I had not the hardihood to utter openly and shamelessly the fact that I had no money at all, now, at this moment. I could not bring myself to tell them that the very possibility of my keeping the job depended on whether they lent me anything.

My aunt and uncle looked at each other anxiously and held a whispered consultation. And suddenly the truth dawned on me— not merely was I' hard up, but so were they. Hitherto I had shrunk from approaching them, or others, for money—tacitly assuming that they had money. But it appeared that others as well as I could be poverty-stricken. After all, I was not some peculiar isolated being that the slump had selected for its one individual victim. The slump had come down with a heavy hand on hundreds of thousands, on millions of people. And amongst them were, not merely myself, but these relatives of mine.

There was my uncle, after fifty years or so in the cabinet-making trade. At an age when people in the more wealthy section of society were considered little more than middle-aged he had been forced to give up his work, a mere wreck of a man, glad to be able to hobble along to the synagogue on a fine day. My cousin and her husband lived with my aunt and uncle, and both were out of work, and so, in a family of four, of which my aunt and uncle were both semi-invalids, none was now a wage-earner.

Small wonder, then, that when I came along in the middle of the week to try to borrow some money, looks of perplexity and anxious consultations were exchanged.

Finally my aunt spoke in a tone of exaggerated cheerfulness.

"Well, we'll go to the shop, and we'll get you plenty of food."

They asked me what kind of food I would like, whether I wanted this or that, and finally my aunt returned from the nearby grocery shop with various goods that had been obtained on credit. Money was not mentioned.

After further conversation, which avoided economic matters, I took my leave. I had plenty of food now, but still no money. It would be necessary for me to walk to work the next morning with my tools. I would have to walk to and fro from work until that distant time, forty-eight hours away, when I received my wages.

The next morning I arose early, and allowing myself ample time, set off to walk the three miles to work. The tool-box was a burden that sapped my low reservoir of strength. Nevertheless, if I was feeling weak physically, my morale was high. I was filled with a pugnacious determination to seize this opportunity to rehabilitate myself, and to free myself from worry and hunger.

I whiled away the tedious and enervating journey to the workshop with optimistic thoughts of the future, ever and again changing my tool-box from one shoulder to the other. At last I drew near the workshop, and in a few moments I was able to set the tool-box down. My hand was numb with fatigue, so that when I lifted it to wipe my damp forehead, the hand dropped down again of its own volition.

I knocked at the door, thankful to be able to wait and rest for a few moments. After I had knocked again, the door opened, revealing my employer. He had evidently just got out of bed, and with a sleepy grunt he beckoned me to come into the workshop. Once I was inside he withdrew to inner regions, first vouchsafing me the information that he would be back soon, and telling me to unpack my tools.

There before me was the emblem and sign of Starting Work Again—a bench bereft of tools and shavings, the bench I was to work at, my bench. Once again the feeling surged in me of renewed hope for the future. I deployed my tools in strategically necessary places, and proceeded to make a fire for the glue-pot.

My employer (I still did not know his name) returned and gave me my first job, which was a gramophone cabinet. Most of the pieces were already cut and planed to size. I had to complete what was done of this, then "mark out", "bore", "dowel", "knock up", "cramp" and "clean" the job, after which I would turn to making and fitting the doors and the lid.

With wit and will held in a tight, unrelaxing grasp, I set to work with sustained and concentrated energy. Already I was fit only to spend the rest of the day in bed. But I still had the capacity to stand on my feet and work with some show of energy, and it behoved me to make the best use of what strength I had. Later on, in the afternoon, I could make an excuse—say I felt unwell: purely temporary, of course—and then go home for the rest of the day. Tomorrow is Friday. I will not have to carry my tools to work, and anyway, a day ahead is another day travelled on the highroad to returning health. Saturday, only half a day's work. Then the week-end before me, with two days' money and a week's dole in my pocket!

So I rushed at the work, eager to get my first job over. The boss came in and silently began on his own work. I was relieved in that he in no way interfered with me. He assumed that I knew my job, and he left me to go ahead with it. That was how I liked it.

Dormant reserves of energy came to my aid, and I planed, bored, cramped and cleaned as one inspired. Ever and again fatigue made attempts to numb my joints, relax my limbs. A cloudy blanket threatened to descend on my brain and confuse me so that I would not know what to do. But I kept the gates of my being tightly closed, so that fatigue could not insinuate itself anywhere.

The morning passed in an agony of slowness. When I hoped it

was nearly dinner-time, the boss first broke silence by saying, "It's nearly half-past ten. If you like, you can have a bite while you're working; I don't mind." He then left the workshop, no doubt to have a bite himself.

His magnanimity in no way cheered me, and the announcement of the time caused a pang within me. I did not feel that I could hold out much longer. Nevertheless, there was one bright side to the picture. The fact that it was only half-past ten meant that I was making good progress. But I did not relax my efforts. I felt that I had only to open the gates of my being ever so slightly to the forces of fatigue to be overwhelmed by them. Once again an eternity of hellish effort.

Dinner-time came at last, and none too soon. In spite of myself, efficiency and dexterity had slumped alarmingly within the last twenty minutes or so. But now it was dinner-time, and I had an hour in which to eat and recuperate. The prospect was sufficiently cheerless. No money, no warm or stimulating drink, no cigarettes. Nevertheless, the period of rest alone was something for which I was abundantly relieved and thankful. I had an icy draught of cold water as a prelude to my sandwiches, and sat on the bench to eat and cogitate over the future.

Soon all this would be over. I had a job. A job meant money with which to buy the necessities and the minor luxuries of life. In a week's time I would be able to buy a cup of tea and a packet of fags without thinking twice about it. Soon I would repay, and more than repay, my aunt and uncle. Soon I would be able to send money to my mother again. Soon I would get lodgings away from the memories of the last months. Soon I would be an everyday member of society again, not an outcast pauper. Soon, soon, soon.

Work was resumed. But I was no longer the tautly strung individual of the morning. My brain hesitated, my hands lagged. Soon I was ready to give in. To go on would only damage whatever hard-won prestige my morning's work had yielded. In an hour, I decided. At three o'clock I will tell him I suddenly do not feel well. This would be a good excuse both to get away and counteract any fault-finding. And maybe I would ask him for a sub! Two, three shillings. . . .

I found it difficult to make up my mind when to finish work. It always appeared that if only I could finish one particular operation, then the job would be fairly complete, and therefore my boss would have less reluctance in agreeing to let me stay away for the rest of the day.

When I finally decided that I would finish work, my employer came to me and said he wanted moulding put round the lid. I thought I had better do this before I approached him about finishing work. When I had fixed the moulding on the lid, however, he wanted more mouldings fixed on other parts of the cabinet—lots of mouldings, fixed in every conceivable place. An hour passed, and it was, as near as I could judge, about four o'clock. Suddenly my employer came to me and said:

"You ought to be a bit quicker on the job."

For a moment I hesitated between telling him that I did not feel well and would like to go, or informing him of the obvious fact that if he had rested content with a gramophone cabinet, and not a collection of ugly and superfluous mouldings, the cabinet would already have been finished. However, before I could say anything, he went on:

"But after all, you know, it's your own business. You're on piece-work. If you take longer on the job, you earn less, that's all."

I was astounded. I thought he must have made a mistake.

"Piece-work!" I exclaimed. "I'm on hour work!"

He smiled with affected astonishment.

"Hour work? Who told you hour work? What hour work?"

"Why, didn't you——?" I began.

"Hour work!" he said derisively. "I never take anyone on hour work. It's only piece-work here. Nobody pays me hour work."

With this he walked back to his bench and made a show of working, as though nothing had happened.

For a moment I was overwhelmed. How could it be piece-work when I didn't even know the price of the job, did not know how much work he would yet expect me to do on the job, before he declared himself satisfied? So this fellow thought he could fool me, did he? Of all the bloody cheek! I went up to him.

"Look here——" I began, unable to prevent my voice from quivering with anger.

"What d'you mean, 'Look here'? Who're talking to?" he demanded sternly. His green eyes glared at me. They reminded me of the eyes of a tiger.

It was difficult for me to shake off the attitude of disciplined obedience to an employer. For a moment I was intimidated. Nevertheless, I thrust the inhibition aside roughly.

"I came here at a shilling an hour," I told him. "And I'm going to get a shilling an hour."

"Don't talk nonsense," he said briefly, almost with indifference. "You get four shillings and sixpence for that gramophone cabinet, not a penny more."

"I'm not going to argue with you," I said. "Either you give

me seven shillings for seven hours' work, or I'll smash all those sideboards you're working on."

The idea came to me only as I uttered it; nevertheless, having uttered it, I meant what I said. There was, after all, no signed agreement between us. I possessed not the slightest legal proof that my employer owed me a farthing, or, for that matter, had ever seen me before. And, like quite a number of shady employers, he was trying to take advantage of that fact.

I felt therefore that I had nothing now to lose. I might as well at least get a certain amount of satisfaction out of teaching this insolent exploiter a lesson. My previous experiences with two of them had taught me that there was only one way to deal with these individuals. Heated words, calling the police even, meant nothing to them. You had to do something they thought you would never dare to do—give them a damned good hiding, destroy something of equal or more value than the money out of which they were trying to swindle you. This taught them something, gave them something to remember.

"You pack your tools and go!" he said brusquely. "I don't want any of your bloomin' cheek!"

"Give me the seven shillings and I'll go!" I said heatedly. "But unless I get that seven shillings, and get it straight away, you'll have to make yourself some new sideboards. Don't think I'm just fooling you, either."

I went up to my bench and got my mallet. I walked with it towards the sideboards.

"What are you going to do?" he asked, in sudden alarm.

"I've told you what I'm going to do!"

"You're mad!" he gasped, "a real lunatic! I'll call the police, that's what I'll do!"

"Go on, call them."

He hesitated a moment, his green eyes shifting uncertainly. Then he put his hands in his trousers pocket.

"Here," he said agitatedly, "here's your seven shillings. Take it. I'll be only too glad to see the back of you."

With my mallet still in my hand, I took the money. I went up to my bench and packed my tools. Then, not another word passing between us, I left the workshop.

Out in the street the incidents of that day recurred to me like the incidents of a nightmare. Was it really that morning that I had arisen in the austere, chilly gloom, had a cup of tea and a slice of bread and butter, shouldered my toolbox, and with many calculations of the future, set out to work? Were these the happenings of this same morning, or were they a dream I had dreamed a long time ago? The long, exhausting hours in the workshop, which to me were to have been the prelude to renewed hope; their outcome in that primitive and beastlike scene in which we had bared our fangs and snarled over a few coins—he with baleful greed and I with a panic fear of frustrated need; these things recurred to me and filled me with humiliation and the facile despair of the sick.

Of the flames of hope that had burned so vigorously that morning there was left now only dead ashes. I was without hope now. Something that had been taut and straight within me had given way.

CHAPTER X

LAST STRAWS

THERE ARE TIMES in a man's existence when it seems of necessity that the fates are working against him. Rational though his beliefs may be, events take place which force on him the illusion that somewhere above him baleful spirits, inscrutable and pitiless, plot out his destruction.

So it was with me at that time. After the *débâcle* of my attempt to find a job, it seemed to me that nothing much worse could happen. But the baleful spirits had still one or two more tricks in store. It was as though they had decided that I was not yet sufficiently cast down, had not yet grovelled sufficiently in the dust.

When I returned to my lodgings and entered my room, it seemed to me that I was either dreaming or else had somehow got into the wrong room. The room I had left that morning now looked like something between a laundry and a cheap lodging-house for down-and-outs. Hung diagonally across it was a length of rope, on which was suspended an unsavoury collection of shirts, socks and other garments that looked as though they had been washed but not cleaned. Sprawled before the fireplace was no other than Tim Stevens, the ex-influenza patient.

"What——" I began.

"It's alright," he said cheerfully. "You an' me's goin' to share this room from now on."

I felt a bit sick.

"How's that?"

"Well, you see, the landlady's gone an' let two rooms upstairs to a young married couple. My room was one o' the two. Now, ye see, this room is really to let to two people, for sharin', see? And the landlady says for me to share this room with you."

"I see," I said.

I felt suddenly homeless. The sailor's bed was crammed against one of the walls. His none-too-clean utensils took up most of the space on the table and the shelves, his clothes hung on the line. My books had been displaced from the shelves and piled hugger-mugger in dirty corners to make room for his belongings. Papers, books and clothes that had been in the chest of drawers had been dumped unceremoniously on my bed.

Not merely were my privacy and convenience gone, however. The very air and light had been taken away. The windows were shut tight, and the thick velvety curtains, which I had never used, were drawn together. The air was thick with the stench of some incredibly foul tobacco that he was smoking. I felt shut up in a stinking little den, peopled normally by boozers, degenerates and gamblers. The place had now that atmosphere.

"Well," Tim said cheerfully, "sit down and make yourself at home. I reckon we'll be alright together, don't you?"

"Yes," I said reluctantly.

"You know," he went on, with affable companionship, grasping his knee with his huge palm and belching a cloud of filth from his pipe, "I've often thought to myself—funny, isn't it?—'Now, 'ere's me, living up 'ere by myself. Now there's that young lad down there, living by 'imself as well. Now, why shouldn't the two of us share a room?' And now 'ere we are, sharin' this room! Funny, isn't it?"

Tim's artless joy in that he now had someone to share his boozy sorrows was disarming. I could but make the best of things, although the idea of sharing a room with him was distasteful to me. Our interests were poles apart. I knew that he got drunk, and often reeled home in the small hours of the morning. With this garrulous, pipe-smoking drunkard sharing my room, I could see small possibility of being able to utilise my spare time in study, reading or writing.

I would have to move elsewhere. But where? Of the different lodgings at which I had previously inquired, this had been the cheapest, the only one I could afford on the dole; for I had been out of work when I first came here, and had stayed even when I was working. Even if I found some other suitable place, I would have to pay a deposit before I moved in—a large item to an out-of-work receiving twelve shillings and sixpence a week. Moreover, not many landladies accepted young men who were out of work; you were forced in the end to stay at places like this, or even worse.

There was nothing I could do but make the best of things till I could find some way out of this position. Something within me was becoming deadened and indifferent. I did not care much
74

now what happened. I did not expostulate with Tim about the manner in which he had disposed of my possessions, about the window, the pipe or the washing. I put my things together in a more convenient form and then ate a slight meal that seemed to consist mainly of solidified tobacco smoke of a particularly virulent type. Although I wanted to rest, I also wanted keenly to escape from Tim Stevens, the pipe and the room. So I went off to repay my aunt and uncle for the food they had given me.

I found myself unable to confess to them that my job had proved to be a failure, so I merely intimated that I had borrowed some money and was thus able to repay them.

My aunt demurred a good deal about accepting money for the food. I began to hope that in spite of all the efforts I might make to persuade her to accept it, she would refuse. Moreover, the mere fact that I wanted her to refuse forced me to insist that she accept it. We had just reached the stage where it seemed to me that I might decently end my efforts to persuade her to take it, when she yielded reluctantly to my protestations, and accepted the money.

After a time I took leave and set off to walk back to my lodgings. When I was about half-way back, and was gazing into a shop window, something suddenly seemed to go wrong with the ordered working of the universe. For a moment everything spun madly around. Then the pavements sloped up towards the sky; the sky leaned drunkenly down to the pavement. I wanted to run somewhere for help, but fear and uncertainty kept me chained to the spot.

I closed my eyes and clenched my teeth in sick agony. Then everything became still again, but a curious unreality masked the true face of everything. The long, busy street, the lights, the people—these things were not from real life, but from something seen on a stage. The street had the flat, two-dimensional appearance of stage scenery; the people were puppets in a crowd scene.

The illusion filled me with a breathless horror. I began to hurry back to my lodgings. The road seemed tortuous, endless.

Slowly, with reluctance, things became normal again. But I had been badly shaken. I trembled with weakness and fear.

I reached my room too fatigued and shattered to worry very much about the altered circumstances that now ruled there. Tim Stevens was lying in bed, still puffing at his pipe. He was a none-too-savoury object as he lay there, half his gross and fatty body exposed above the bed-clothes. He greeted me amiably, and appeared to wish to enter into a lengthy conversation. I was, however, in no mood for conversation, lengthy or otherwise. With a curt word or two, I undressed and got into bed.

75

It was difficult for me to compose myself to sleep. The air in the room was, if anything, thicker and more stinking than ever, with the vile tobacco. The windows were still shut tight, with the heavy black curtains drawn across them. I felt shut up in a fetid-smelling box.

After a time I fell asleep. It seemed hardly a moment had passed when I awoke again. The light was on and someone was moving, none too quietly or deftly, about the room. Tim Stevens, still smoking his pipe, was making himself some tea.

When he saw that I was awake he offered me some, and though I had in any case intended to refuse, I could not but reflect that I would have had to be badly in need of a cup of tea before I would have accepted it, for the tea was the colour, and appeared of the consistency, of dark brown paint. I asked him irritably why the hell he didn't go to sleep, instead of fooling about in the early hours of the morning.

"That's all right," he said cheerfully. "We sailors are used to this. You know what it is—four hours on an' four hours off—the watches, yer know."

I silently condemned him and his notions of existence into the nethermost hell. It was with some difficulty that I managed eventually to persuade him to turn off the light. After a time I heard him crawl, with many hoggish noises, back to bed.

This, however, was not his last interruption. Two or three hours later he was up again, making himself another incredible cup of tea. By now I had decided that the situation was impossible. At all costs I would have to move to another place. The thought of having to endure more nights like this, even till I moved out, was intolerable. I would complain to the landlady. Much good that would do!

He turned out the light again, and then, with some astonishment, I heard him move towards my bed. I thought he had mistaken his direction, until a few moments later I heard him whisper a suggestion to me. At first I found him merely incomprehensible, but afterwards light dawned on me. Loathing and revulsion filled me, as I indicated tersely what I thought of him and his suggestion.

"Now, you do' wanna get mad," he said ingratiatingly. Nevertheless, I noticed with relief that there was fear in his voice. "There's nothin' to it really——"

He shuffled back to bed making sheepish noises. After this interruption I found that sleep had vanished. I waited for the morning as for the Millennium. It seemed as though Eternity passed before the morning, bringing with it light and sanity, came again.

CHAPTER XI

SURRENDER

THE NEXT MORNING, when I was returning to my lodging after a fruitless search for work, I made my decision. I would write to my mother, and tell her I would like to come to London.

It had always been my intention to join my mother and sisters in London, but circumstances had never seemed to favour the project. When I was working it seemed foolish to throw up a job to go to London on the off-chance of finding another. On the other hand, when I was not working youthful pride made it seem to me as though I were running to my mother and sisters to escape those troubles and responsibilities which, by electing to live on my own, I had undertaken to shoulder should they arise. My mother and sisters had promised that if they heard of a job for me they would let me know, and so I could come to London. However, the matter had hitherto remained a vague idea which might never come to fruition.

But now there were two factors that made me decide to write that I would go to London if I could. The first was that the events of the past few weeks, and particularly those of the past few days, had reduced me to the end of my tether. It seemed as though something within me had been strained and strained, and at any further tension it might snap. I was afraid of the consequences to me should any further untoward events arise. I felt the need of being near to those who could help me.

The second factor was that I had evolved the naïve illusion that there would be more work in my trade in London than there was in Forgeton. Even during the slackest periods I had seen vanloads of furniture from London being unloaded in the wholesale furniture districts of Forgeton. It seemed to me that two things followed from this. The trade in Forgeton staggered weakly from one miserable season to another, because of the influx of furniture from London; and, *ipso facto*, there were more chances of a job for me in London than there were in Forgeton.

I made up my mind. I would write at once.

When it came to writing the letter, however, I found the task more difficult than I had anticipated. I could not bring myself to write openly that my difficulties were the reason I wanted to come to London. I, who had declared proudly my ability to look after myself, was now, at the onslaught of difficulties, admitting defeat.

In the end I compromised by writing a rather diplomatic letter in which I hinted that I was getting a little fed up with

77

being constantly in and out of work. I mentioned my reasons for supposing that I would get work more quickly and regularly in London, and ended by saying that if my mother knew of any-one who had some sort of job for me in London, I would come as soon as she let me know of this.

It was with mixed feelings that I posted the letter. What would happen? How would my mother respond to the veiled phrases of the letter? Would she read any urgency in it and act promptly, or would she take my mealy-mouthed phrases at their face value, treat the matter casually and at her ease? It might be a month before anything definite was settled. A month. . . .

I need not have worried about the response to my letter. Less than twenty-four hours after I had sent it I received a reply. The fact that an answer came so quickly—in almost the minimum time it was possible for a reply to be sent—was in itself an answer to my letter.

I opened the letter, and the first thing I saw was a postal order for ten shillings. I was filled with emotion. This, then, was the reply. I sent out a timid, uncertain call for help, and immediately, unequivocally, help was given. The matter was to me wonderful and stirring beyond measure. I did not see it merely as one in which I wrote a letter hinting that my circum-stances were a little difficult, and received in reply, somewhat prosaically, a postal order for ten shillings. I saw the incident in a far wider, more universal aspect. I saw in it the fact that when human beings are in need of aid, other human beings will come to their assistance. And this realisation was marvellous and overwhelming in the extreme.

After a time it occurred to me that although I had read the letter, not a word of it had penetrated to my brain. I read it through again carefully, finding, to my surprise, that it was not from my mother, but from my elder sister, Sadie.

From Sadie's letter I saw that possibly my own letter had not been quite so vague and diplomatic as I had imagined. At any rate, my mother had acted with promptness, urgency and efficiency. Neither she nor my younger sister was in a position to help me financially, as things were going very hard for them that winter. Nevertheless, my mother 'phoned up Sadie at the office where she worked, and asked her to come to see her that evening (the evening of the same day on which I had sent my letter). When Sadie arrived, my mother told her of my circum-stances as she interpreted them from my letter. She adjudged that I must be in fairly desperate circumstances to write such a letter.

Sadie had discussed the matter with her husband, Ted, and

they invited me to come to stay with them till I found a job. They sent me the ten shillings as part of the cost of a coach ticket to London, saying that I should find the rest out of my unemployment benefit. They were sorry they could not send me more, but Ted had been off work for ten days with a severe attack of the 'flu, and they had not much money at the moment.

This, then, was the letter. Gratitude and relief surged through me. Safety, security, aid were within my reach. In eight days' time I should be in London, away from all this. There I would get a job, rehabilitate myself, be a normal, self-respecting member of society who earned his bread by the sweat of his brow, and not something very near a pariah outcast, one living on the edge of destitution and degradation.

My only regret was that I could not go to London at once. Already, in the one day prior to getting Sadie's letter, I had depleted my week's dole of twelve and sixpence sufficiently to have only barely enough money left to pay the rent, let alone use any of it for buying the ticket to London. Also there were one or two matters that needed my attention before I could leave for London. And then I was supposed to give a week's notice to my landlady, or pay a week's rent in default.

So it was that I endured another week of hunger and of life in Tim's company. But ever before me, shining like some incredible vision, was the knowledge that in six days, five days, four days, three days, two days, one day, tomorrow, I would leave all this behind.

My last night with Tim was even more disturbed than usual. In addition to interrupting my sleep by making tea in the early hours of the morning, he persisted in getting out of bed every half-hour or so and gazing anxiously through the window. It transpired that he was under the urgent illusion that there was a fire raging in the neighbourhood. Nothing I said to the contrary had any effect. I thought that maybe he was going crazy, but I didn't care.

After a night such as this I awoke hollow-eyed and weary. Nevertheless, it needed but one glance at the clock to galvanise me into activity. It was nearly eight o'clock. I still had one or two things to pack, and I ought to have something to eat before I caught the coach to London at nine o'clock. I tumbled quickly out of bed and hastily made my preparations to leave.

Tim watched me with sheepish curiosity from his bed. Every now and again he made some conciliatory remark, such as:

"Ye're not nowty wi' me, are ye?"

"Let bygones be bygones, eh?"

"Let's part like good pals."

"I wish ye luck, an' a safe journey; ye know that."

To all of which I answered hurriedly and briefly.

Finally, at twenty to nine, I loaded myself with my luggage, a heavy portmanteau and two full attaché cases. I was desperately afraid that I would miss the coach to London, but my vitality was now so easily exhausted that at the prospect of having to rush with this burden to the coach station, I felt inclined to give up the whole project.

I felt at once desperate and careless of everything. On the one hand I was desperate because I had spent all my money on the coach ticket, and had barely sufficient coppers left to last out the day. On the other hand, the mere accident of waking up late, with its consequence that I must now rush to the station at top speed—this filled me with a counsel of despair that made me wish to fling everything aside, not bother yet about going to London, not bother about rushing to the coach terminus, not to bother about anything at all, but just flop down somewhere and let everything go to utter wrack.

It was only by a strong effort that I managed to prevail upon myself to make the attempt to get to the coach station in time. It was a quick quarter of an hour's walk, even if I were un-encumbered, and I had only twenty minutes in which to do it carrying the portmanteau and attaché cases.

With a curt word of good-bye to Tim, I made my way out into the damp, misty street. I decided that the only tactic that would get me to the coach station in time was to make one hurried rush, not resting, not pausing, not even shifting the portmanteau from one hand to the other. I set off with long, hurried strides, pre-tending to myself that I was not carrying anything. Very soon I was bathed in perspiration. My overcoat seemed to clog my movements, as though I were swathed in thick blankets on a hot summer's day. I continued to rush towards the terminus, my heart pounding, the sweat dripping from my forehead.

Half-way there I gave up and rested for a few moments, not really caring whether this meant that I would miss the coach. Then, changing the portmanteau and attaché cases from one hand to the other, I set off again.

Soon I was on the main road, and there were many clocks to tell me that I had only a few minutes in which to catch the coach. I continued onwards in torture, seeming never to get any nearer to my destination.

Bathed in sweat I entered the coach station at three minutes past nine. I was convinced that the coach had already left. To my surprise and relief, I found that not only had it not yet started, but it did not even seem ready to do so for at least a few minutes.

After showing my ticket, I staggered towards the coach, settled my luggage in the rack and occupied my seat.

The way was now clear for me to get to London. The part I now played was a purely passive one. I had merely to sit in my seat, allow the perspiration to drain off me, the fatigue to wear away, and meanwhile the coach would be taking me to London.

END OF BOOK TWO

BOOK THREE

OUT OF THE FRYING-PAN

CHAPTER I

IN LONDON

THERE WAS A humming and grunting of engines. The coach moved out of the station and drove portentously through the main streets of the town. It was queer for me to realise that thus, on a sudden, I was leaving the town in which I had lived all my life. I was leaving all this behind. I was leaving, perhaps for ever, these streets and everything connected with them. It was as though I were leaving, without farewell and without explanations, the friends of a lifetime.

But it was too late now to sentimentalise and feel sad. Inexorably, undisturbed from their stony tranquillity, the streets wheeled round and vanished. The suburbs, indifferent and impassive, watched us speed on our way.

The macadam road sped swiftly beneath the tyres of the coach. The countryside, curtained with mist, grey and melancholy, hovered by and was gone. The naked skeletons of trees at the roadside wept mournful tears at the passing coach. Inwardly I bade farewell to all the passing landscape. It was bare and wintry now, but I had known it in the fair flower of summer. Then the fields were undulating patches of ploughed land, the hills swept nobly to the horizon, the grass was vivid green. Then the sky was all blue and gold, the trees were rich and prosperous with many leaves, the hedgerows were riotous with flowers.

The engine purred with comfortable satisfaction as it raced along the flat road, and then it moaned and whined with plaintive effort as it toiled up the hill. Now it sang with triumph, and now it groaned dolorously. But with every fleeting moment more and more distance separated me from the town in which I had hitherto spent all my days. It seemed as though, in rushing past this landscape, I was hastily and unceremoniously rushing past all that I associated with my youth.

The short grey winter's day drew to its haggard end, and still the coach raced on its way. Through the evening we travelled still. We had stopped twice—for dinner and for tea. Each place where the coach pulled up was rather intimidatingly high-class for me, and at each of them I confined myself to ordering a cup of tea and a piece of cake. Even after this drastic economy I found myself with exactly a penny left. It occurred to me that I was entering London in the best style of the heroes of conventional literature, for all of them seemed to arrive in the Metropolis with nothing but the proverbial penny in their pocket. I was imitating the best models.

We passed through busy towns and suburbs, brightly lit and filled with Saturday night shoppers. Soon the coach began to travel through the West End of London. We drove through streets decorated with neon signs that urged one to buy So-and-so's Beer, and perpetually advertised cigarettes that would not harm the throat. Hotels, theatres and restaurants swam by in a glittering stream. The roads were crowded with hectic traffic, and pavements overflowed with passers-by. There was an air about the streets of busy, efficient enjoyment—on the one hand the resources of a mighty town harnessed for the purpose of giving amusement, pleasure, diversion and relaxation to the million; and, on the other, a purposeful, almost grim determination to be so diverted and amused. It all seemed very far away from unemployed demonstrations, the Means Test, "No Hands Wanted", and slack seasons.

Finally we drove up to the terminus at King's Cross. I was in a state of suspense, for, like most physically and mentally sick people, I was constantly inventing causes for anxiety. I had been anxious during most of the journey in case no one should meet me. What would I do then? I had no money for travelling, and it was beyond my strength to carry my belongings very far.

These anxious speculations came to a sudden end, for awaiting me in the coach station I saw Ted, my brother-in-law. A vast relief filled me. Now my worries were over. Now I was with friends; food and security were mine. I hurried up to Ted, who had not yet caught sight of me.

In a sense my condition was similar to that of one recovering from a long and exhausting illness. Such people are generally filled with a morbid desire to recount to others in great detail all the chronicle of their suffering, perhaps even gilding the lily by exaggerating their very sufferings to make them more poignant, more capable of arousing sympathy in the listener.

"Thank goodness I'm here at last!" I said fervently to Ted. "The last few weeks——"

Ted, however, did not seem inclined to pay very much attention. He interrupted me with a certain firmness that could not but strike me at once. I felt wounded and embarrassed and ashamed of myself. I did not like whining, in myself or in others, and to have it indicated to me that I was engaging in this unhealthy pursuit rather damped my first ardour.

We travelled by roaring, rushing tube trains, ascended and descended lifts a good deal, and hurried along many subterranean passages. London seemed to be honeycombed with underground passages, through which hurried endless, eternally moving streams of people. The underground passages reminded me of the scene in "Alice in Wonderland" in which the White Rabbit is hurrying along the tunnel, glancing anxiously at his watch.

"Dear me," he is saying, "I shall be late to meet the Duchess."

Here everyone seemed to be afraid that they, too, would be late to meet the Duchess.

Eventually we reached the suburb in North London where Ted and my sister lived. We ascended the steps of the house, Ted rang the bell, and there was Sadie with a welcoming smile on her face.

"Hallo!" she said brightly. (Was her smile too bright?)

"Hallo," I answered, and somehow I was disturbed by vague forebodings. Suddenly I felt that maybe I was imposing on them. "I didn't expect to be back here so soon," I added, trying to drive these thoughts away.

We ascended the stairs and went into the living-room.

"Well," Ted said heartily (was his voice too hearty?), "take off your coat and sit down."

Sadie had gone out of the room, but now she returned, bringing a large plate of food that had an exceedingly appetising smell.

Immediately I felt very hungry. Sadie took the top plate off, revealing sausages, mashed potatoes and onions. How appetising it looked! How hungry I felt!

"Well, sit down and have a good meal," said Ted, with his casual kindness.

Suddenly I was filled with embarrassment. I felt no longer a guest, but a dependent, one who depended on the charity and kindness of others for his food and shelter. I had a sudden desire to renounce the food that was before me, leave Sadie and Ted, endure homelessness, suffering and privation, rather than be under obligation to others. But such a course was obviously madness. What could I do now? I remained, mute and hesitant, at the table.

"These are funny sausages," I stammered.

"Haven't you seen that kind before?" said Ted. "They're

Parisian sausages, you know—very high class. We don't accept any responsibility for them, though."

I laughed awkwardly, toying with my knife.

"Well, eat up," said Ted heartily, with a certain impatience. "There's plenty more where they came from. Have a good tuck in. I suppose you can do with it, after—er—after your long journey on the coach."

Suddenly, with impatience, I pushed aside all embarrassment and began to eat. When I had finished, Sadie, with the calm assumption that I had not had enough, brought in some more. And, with eating, my uneasy feelings melted away. Joy and relief took their place. I was amongst friends now.

CHAPTER II

GENUINELY SEEKING WORK

MY MOTHER, WHOM I visited the next day, was anxious about the past, but relieved now that I was in London. I did not go into details about what had happened, merely vouchsafing the information that I had been ill with the 'flu. I arranged that I would visit her fairly often, though I lived some distance away.

On the Monday I arose with the determination to find a job as soon as possible and settle down in the city which was now the venue of my existence.

First of all I signed on at the Transfer Counter at the nearest Labour Exchange, and made a Transfer Claim for benefit. I had heard that these Transfer Claims could take a very long time in coming through from the other Exchange, and did not anticipate my own claim coming through for several weeks. I was therefore agreeably surprised when it came through in a few days, and I was paid on the Friday in the usual way.

After I had been to the Labour Exchange I went to look for a job. During the rest of the morning and in the afternoon I walked about, religiously and thoroughly seeking to familiarise myself with the districts through which I passed, and with any neighbourhoods where there might be agglomerations of cabinet-making workshops. Unfortunately the first day ended without success, for I came across hardly any cabinet-making places worthy of notice.

The remainder of the week, and many succeeding weeks, passed in a repetition of that first day. I set myself to an intensive course of job-seeking. Day after day I walked the streets to the point of exhaustion, pursuing the baffling phantom of work. On

85

one or two occasions it seemed as though I would be able to catch hold of a job, grasp it firmly and make it mine. But the job slipped elusively from my grasp, and I was still unemployed.

Gradually it began to dawn on me that my economics had been at fault when I had assumed that because London exported furniture there would be more favourable opportunities there for a job. I began to perceive now that if the industry in London was bigger than in the provinces, it was because, amongst other things, the man-power at its disposal was greater. And if crisis hit the industry in London there were just as little prospects of getting work there as when crisis hit the industry in the provinces.

Sometimes I thought that maybe it would be better for me to return to Forgeton, where, if any jobs were going, I would have a better chance of finding work than I had in London. However, from one or two letters I received from friends in Forgeton, it appeared that trade was, if anything, worse than before. For this reason alone it was futile to think of returning there, apart from many practical difficulties. Like a black and stifling cloud that grows ever larger, unemployment hung low over the whole country.

However, I felt it incumbent upon me now, more than ever, to get a job. Firstly, I must be able to repay Sadie and Ted, and cease to burden them with my presence. Secondly, I must justify my reason for coming to London. I had said that I would assuredly get a job more quickly there. I must justify this statement, otherwise they would think that I came to London for other reasons.

So I walked eagerly about the streets, seeking in vain the magic words "Cabinet-Makers Wanted". And never was there any sign that cabinet-makers were wanted. But always the weary, the resentful, the irritated reply, "No, we have no vacancies". Always the blunt phrases, "No hands wanted", "No vacancies".

I was a quick and energetic walker, and in my search for work I covered long distances—too long sometimes. I started out about nine o'clock in the morning and returned about five. During the day I rested but little, partly because of a compelling desire to find work, and partly because of an innate impatience which made it impossible for me to dawdle along the streets or rest long in a coffee-shop. Even the dinner hour pause, when I ate my sandwiches in some public space or in the shelter of a coffee-shop, was one which I could only observe with reluctance and impatience. I had a peculiar dislike of public libraries as places in which to rest or read, and so I avoided them.

I found that in London one could spend an enormous amount of time and shoe-leather looking for work. In my own town the matter had been fairly simple. The cabinet-making firms were on the whole concentrated into two relatively small areas. It was therefore possible to find out fairly quickly whether any jobs were going. London, however, was so vast that one did not know where to start or where to finish.

I got rather weary of giving my name and address to different firms and never receiving the letter they promised. Never once did any employer ever carry out his promise to "let me know in a day or two".

In addition to walking about looking for work, I answered a certain number of box-number advertisements in the papers. However, I never once received any reply or acknowledgement to the letters I sent (all of which contained a stamped addressed envelope).

Of the very rare number of advertisements for cabinet-makers in the press at the time, only a small proportion gave the name and address of the firm which was advertising. The others, no doubt, took advantage of the hard times to be able to secure, under the anonymity of a Box Number advertisement, the best workers at cut-price wages.

Some employers who did give their names and addresses, however, were often very vague about their requirements. Like many unemployed, I occasionally wasted whole mornings going after jobs which I should not have bothered about had I known one or two more facts about them. Unemployed men, expecting a certain minimum rate of pay, walk, cycle, or waste fares for long distances to go after a job, only to discover that the rate of pay is far below what they are prepared to take. Or else men who from principle or bitter experience are opposed to working piece-work in their particular trade, discover that they have travelled a long distance about a job that is on a piece-work basis.

Similarly, many employers advertise for one type of worker when they mean another; or they advertise for men, and when the men apply for the job, they discover that only superhuman, polytechnic geniuses are wanted.

On one occasion a firm advertised for woodworkers, and asked all applicants to phone. The term "woodworker" of itself is rather vague, as there are many kinds of woodwork and many types of men who can be described as "woodworkers". Woodwork, however, can range from semi-skilled botching to highly skilled accuracy, and widely differing rates of pay can be asked by the workers concerned.

This advertisement gave no indication of the kind of woodwork concerned, or of rates of pay. I phoned up the number given and announced to the man at the other end that I was a woodworker and was inquiring after the job that was advertised.

The voice asked:

"Can you read blue-prints?"

This requirement had not been mentioned in the advertisement. However, I felt that at a pinch I could read blue-prints, and so I answered yes to this question.

The voice went on:

"Can you use machinery?"

This question rather annoyed me because it seemed to me that if the firm wanted woodworking machinists who could read blueprints, they should have said so, and not advertised vaguely for "woodworkers". The trade of a woodworking machinist is definitely different from that of a woodworker, and is recognised as such. I had never used machinery.

However, I had worked fairly close to a circular saw and overhand planer on several occasions, and, as these are fairly simple machines, I felt that I could work them without difficulty. Also, I was keen to get a job, so I answered that I could work machinery.

"What machines?" the voice asked.

"Circular saw and overhand planer," I answered.

"Nothing more?" the voice asked.

By now I was curious to know what sort of a job this was, anyway. They advertised for woodworkers, and it appeared they want woodworking machinists who could read blue-prints. I indicated that I had only mentioned the circular saw and overhand planer because I had thought that this was all they would require of a woodworker; actually, I said, I was familiar with all woodworking machines.

The voice became a little more cordial at this, and proceeded to go into detail. Apparently I would be expected to supervise matters in general, and act as woodworker, woodworking machinist, setter-out, foreman over a gang of ex-schoolboys, packer, van-loader, etc. I listened incredulously. I did not see how anyone could be all these things simultaneously and efficiently.

"D'you think you can do it?" the voice asked.

No one is more facilely optimistic than an unemployed at the prospect of a job. It was a tall order, but I would have a try. In any case, I was curious to know about the job.

"Of course I can," I said, trying to sound at once very efficient and rather contemptuous of the puny nature of the work involved. I went into an explanation of an imaginary job I had had two years ago, which was just like this one.

The voice at the other end was keen now. "How much will you be wanting an hour?"

I thought for a moment. Such a job obviously carried with it a high wage. However, I would compromise.

"One and ten an hour," I answered.

"One and ten!" exclaimed the voice, with horror.

I was astonished. "Why, how much are you prepared to pay?"

"Well," the voice announced, "we've had men simply *begging* for the job at one and four an hour."

I was filled with indignation and contempt.

"If you like," I said suavely, "I'll come over to your place and crawl on my hands and knees for the job at a shilling an hour."

There was no reply save the sound of the receiver being slammed.

I was fortunate on this occasion, however, for I had only wasted tuppence replying to an advertisement which I would not have bothered about had I known one or two more details. There were many times when I, like many other unemployed, wasted a whole morning walking to and from a job because the advertisement gave a totally wrong impression.

A furniture shop in Edgeware Road announced a job for a cabinet-maker, able to do repairs and to "touch-up" furniture. As I was fairly skilled in repairs and was an experienced amateur French polisher, I decided to go after the job.

Applicants were asked to attend at the shop from two till four that afternoon. I walked to the place, and arrived just after two o'clock. Already there were over a dozen men waiting for the job. They stood around at the back of the shop, all sunk in funereal gloom, eyeing each other furtively.

Finally the interviewing began. The manager walked up with that somewhat royal air affected by managers of small and unimportant concerns. He began to interview the first applicant in a tiny plywood-constructed office. The interview lasted for a quarter of an hour, and then the applicant emerged looking somewhat shattered. He went away without a word to us.

One applicant after another was seen, each interview taking from ten to fifteen minutes. In the meantime more and more job-seekers were arriving.

Finally the interviews were brisked up until they took a mere four to five minutes each. I felt that I had at least as good qualifications for the job as any there. I was ignorant at the time of the almost superlative capabilities that a mere advertisement in the Vacancy Columns of the Press can bring to the surface.

Suddenly, after a dull eternity of waiting, it was my turn for the interview. I entered the plywood office.

"Are you a cabinet-maker?" asked the manager, with dignity. I told him I was.

"Can you do repairs?"

"Yes."

"Can you touch-up furniture—fit, and so on?"

"Yes, I can do all that kind of work."

"H'm. Have you ever done any lino-laying?"

I was astonished at this question, so astounded that I told the truth.

"No, I've never done any lino-laying."

"Never done any packing, or anything like that?"

"No." (Furniture packing is quite an art on its own.)

"Well, you won't suit us," he said very firmly. "We want a man who can pack furniture and lay lino, as well as doing repairs."

I went out somewhat dashed, particularly at the prospect of the joyless walk back. It was only when I was half-way home that it suddenly occurred to me that I ought to have asked him why the hell he advertised for a cabinet-maker able to do repairs, when all the time he wanted someone who could repair furniture, pack furniture, lay lino, and, possibly, was adept at piano-tuning, paper-hanging, plumbing, and other complementary aspects of the furnishing trade.

No less annoying than such experiences is the futile, if benevolent sympathy of some people for an out of work. Their hearts bleed for the unemployed in general, and for you in particular. They cannot bear to part from you without giving you some hope for the future.

"I know Mr. So-and-So," they say. "I'll speak to him about you. I'm sure he'll give you a job."

If they wanted to give you hope, they have succeeded. Life becomes promising. As one who is likely to get a job in a day or two, you spend a few coppers of your dole on luxuries you have not permitted yourself hitherto. You are filled with hope. And you wait. You wait for the job that never comes.

When this sort of thing happens a few times, and the days pass without any job having materialised, it becomes merely disheartening. It increases rather than diminishes hopelessness. It makes the prospect of a job seem more than ever far away, a taunting, unattainable mirage on the horizon.

Search here, search there, scan advertisement columns, tramp the streets from morning till night, the plain fact was that there were no jobs. During the whole of this period of unemployment I was never once sent after a job by the Labour Exchange.

CHAPTER III

A RIFT IN THE LUTE

THE CONTINUAL SEARCH for work began to have its physical effects on me. I became more weary and worn out from day to day. The quest for a job became a grimly monotonous torture, a long-drawn-out struggle against fatigue and weariness and intolerable boredom. I drifted towards a general condition of debility and exhaustion.

These physical effects were accompanied by a sickness of the mind no less disagreeable. When the first glamour of security and regular meals began to wear off, I became increasingly uneasy and dissatisfied with my situation. As the days passed I felt a growing sense of humiliation at my position of dependence. I longed to be free and independent, to be in the position of one who was able to give, rather than of one who received.

I began to become aware of a growing sense of isolation. Each night I returned from long, fruitless trudging through the streets, had some food, and then settled down to read. There seemed to be nothing else to do.

I did not know anyone else of my own age or interests, nor was I likely to find anyone whilst I was out of work. I had no money with which to go out and amuse myself.

Soon I exhausted Ted's small library and I began to feel bored. I had not joined the local library because I was constantly expecting to move, possibly from the neighbourhood, if I got a job.

Ted tried on one or two occasions to persuade me to join a club or organisation. I promised that I would, but always finally evaded the matter. In my unhealthy state of mind I felt very reluctant to join any organisation. It seemed to me to be too great an ordeal to have to come in touch with new people, to have to talk to them and make a favourable impression on them.

On Saturday nights I went to the pictures. Occasionally I went with Sadie and Ted to visit a friend. But these were isolated diversions in the arid waste of evenings.

Moreover, I was uneasy even on these occasions. On Saturday nights I was spending money which was not my own. In the state of mind I was in at the time this weighed on me. And when we visited a friend it seemed to me that I was merely in the way. The friend, after all, did not know me. I was Sadie's brother, and so the friend was polite to me, even though ordinarily he would not care a damn about me.

It did not occur to me that there might be anything morbid or exaggeratedly sensitive about these and other unspoken ideas that held sway in my mind. I readily accepted all such ideas at their face value, and assumed that any honourable individual would think in the same way, were he in my position.

So I became ever more gloomy and morose. I spoke to Sadie and Ted only when they spoke to me, or when it was necessary for me to say something. When any of their friends visited them, or when I went with them on a visit, I endured the ceremony of introduction as one endures an ordeal, and then effaced myself as much as possible. Conversation, in the light and friendly sense of the word, became a lost art to me. I was able only to confine myself to essentials, and spoke as though it were a crime to say an unnecessary word, or to mention subjects that were not absolutely relevant.

One Saturday night Ted seemed to have forgotten that I normally went to the pictures on this night. On all other Saturday evenings, when tea was over and the various household duties performed, he would give me some money with which to go to the pictures. So off I went, returning in time for supper.

On this Saturday evening I sat reading in the kitchen, waiting for Ted to make the usual suggestion. Ordinarily, I had never been very keen on going to the pictures, but now that the prospect of going seemed in doubt, I realised that I would miss this weekly adventure if I did not go.

I puzzled over what I should do. If Ted found I had missed going to the pictures, he would no doubt think I had been silly not to have reminded him. On the other hand, I was chary of reminding him; it would be to assume as a right that which, after all, was a friendly gesture. Eventually I decided to go for a walk. I could always say I had preferred it to the pictures.

I usually hung my coat on the door of the front room, so I went to the front room for it. In front of the fire Ted was reclining on one of the easy chairs, and Sadie sat on his lap. They were conversing in low, intimate tones.

They turned suddenly, as I entered, and half disengaged themselves.

"It's alright," I blurted. "I only want to get my coat."

I was about to go out as quickly as possible, when suddenly Sadie sidled from Ted's knee. She smoothed her skirt, and straightened herself angrily.

"I'm sick of this!" she burst out. "There doesn't seem to be such a thing as privacy in this place! Why don't you go out somewhere for once? He goes moping round the place with a face as long as a fiddle! Won't say a word to anybody! I don't believe you want a job! And anyway—oh—what's the use of talking!" She flung out of the room.

The attack was overwhelming in surprise and in volume. In a daze I left the room, and stood hesitatingly in the lobby. The world was suddenly menacing and savage. That this should have happened . . . here . . . in Sadie's place. . . .

Ted stood before me, his face twisted with embarrassment. He said something lamely, but it meant nothing to me. I was sorry for him that he should feel under the necessity of apologising. And whilst I wanted to pretend that the incident had had no effect on me, I was acutely ashamed of the fact that there were tears in my eyes. I tried to brush past him.

"Just a minute," he said, detaining me with his hand. "You know, Sadie's going to have a baby."

The announcement momentarily surprised me. But at the moment I was primarily and above all concerned with myself. Surprise faded. I wanted to go away, get out of this place.

"You see," Ted's voice came, "at such times women have a tendency to get rather excited about things. Ordinarily they wouldn't bother about them for a minute. You mustn't get upset about what Sadie said. She'll be sorry about it afterwards. Particularly if she finds you taking too much notice of it. Just go on as though nothing's happened. Don't let it change your plans about staying here."

I felt sorry for him, but I wanted to go away. I brushed past him.

He called after me, "Aren't you going to the pictures? Here!"

The pictures? A mere trivial mockery. A quarter of an hour ago, everything that was ordinary and commonplace. Now something too stupid to bother about. I made some reply, and stumbled down the stairs.

Out in the street I assiduously rubbed salt into my wounds. Sadie's words repeated themselves. Each phrase was as the lash of a whip. "Goes about with a face as long as a fiddle. . . . Why don't you get a job? . . . You don't want a job. . . . Why don't you go somewhere? . . . Moping about the house. . . ."

I would never go back there again—never! I would rather starve than accept another crust from them. Or from anyone else, if it came to that. I would get some lodgings somewhere. Better starve in independence than feast in humiliation.

For about an hour I strode furiously along the streets, fuming over Sadie's words, breathing undying determination never to go back to her house.

Gradually I calmed down. What was the good of making a fuss, anyway? I ought to have known that something like this would happen. A young couple like Sadie and Ted wanted privacy. I was bound to get on their nerves. A three-roomed flat was small enough for the two of them, but with me hanging around they had nowhere to turn.

Sadie was quite right. That was the bitterness of it all. Yes, they had no privacy. Yes, I walked about with a face as long as a fiddle. Yes, there was never a smile on my face. Yes, I never went out anywhere. Yes, I never said a word to anyone. Yes, I couldn't get a job.

But not wanting to get a job? No! This was absolutely unjust! Was it for that that I had tramped the streets all day long, been humble and subservient and striven to get work at anything and everything, in order that I might return in triumph and say that I had a job and would repay them? No, this was absolutely unjust! She had no right, *no right*, to fling out that contemptuous taunt, that taunt so wounding to the self-respect of the dependent unemployed, that taunt that came so glibly and easily to the lips of those who have a job.

But what was the good of getting mad about that, either? The real cause of the quarrel was, simply, that I was unemployed, and that circumstances had compelled me to seek assistance from others. This sort of thing inevitably led to quarrels, enmity, arguments and counter-arguments between those who gave and those who received. Sadie and Ted had done very well by me, and maybe the present incident was merely an accident of the moment; but nevertheless, inevitably, relations would tend to be strained in the circumstances. It was up to me to take the step that would dissipate any causes of ill-feeling. I would leave. Not immediately and in a manner rendering future friendship impossible. I would leave in a week or two, purely as something desirable for all concerned.

I felt calmer now, and no longer in the mood for reckless thoughts or deeds. I did not want to return to Sadie's place any more than before. But it was obvious that to do anything else was mere stupidity. And, having returned once, I might as well stay until a favourable, unmelodramatic opportunity presented itself for me to leave them.

Nevertheless, as I walked back I was doubtful about my reception. Maybe Sadie's attitude towards me had worsened in my absence. Maybe both Sadie and Ted had decided that it would be better if I left them.

I pictured the scene. Sadie keeping to her room, refusing to be drawn into any dealings with me; Ted enacting the part of a man who in spite of everything is his wife's husband; Ted taking me aside and saying quietly, "Look here, I'm sorry . . . but I think that on the whole it would be best if you left us now and found some digs for yourself. You see how things are . . ." and so on,

94

and so on. I chilled with humiliation at the thought. To become one who wasn't wanted, was cast aside, had not been wanted all along, had been an intruder all the time, if only he had the eyes to see it.

In my mind's eye Sadie and Ted became transformed. They became comfortable, secure, complacent, and inappreciative of the hardships of others because of their own security and comfort. They had everything that I had not—jobs, wages, married life and comradeship, a home, friends—everything. From the narrowed outlook that life in these circumstances so often produces, they gazed, uncomfortably perhaps, at me, a shabby, thick-booted intruder. And together they decided, with many self-comforting reasons and subtle, psychological interpretations, that on the whole it would be best (for my own good, of course) that I should go.

Ted might say to me:

"Of course, we don't want to see you hard up, or anything. We'll let you have some money every week."

And I would mutter proudly:

"That's alright. I don't want any money. I'll manage alright by myself."

For a moment I felt again conflicting emotions as to whether I should return. But it was clear that there was no alternative. I decided that I would behave as though nothing had happened, as though I had merely been out for a walk.

Ted opened the door.

"Hullo," he greeted me. "You're just in time. Supper's ready."

I was taken off my guard by his attitude, and felt at once relieved and suspicious. I followed him upstairs uneasily. For a moment I waited doubtfully in the lobby, and then, as one who nerves himself for a desperate act, I walked into the front room.

Everything was just as it usually was at supper-time. The table was neatly laid. Sadie was pouring hot water into the teapot. Ted was spreading marmalade on slices of bread.

"D'you want bread and cheese, or bread and marmalade?" he asked. "There's nothing very elaborate tonight, I'm afraid."

"Have you had a long walk?" asked Sadie.

Her voice was not quite so casual as Ted's, or maybe it was too casual.

I replied briefly and nervously. I suddenly felt somewhat of a fool, one who made much of small incidents. Nevertheless, it was difficult for me to realise that I was not a stranger at their table. Ted and Sadie behaved just a little too much as though nothing

D 2

had happened. It was ostentatiously obvious that nothing had happened.

"Say," said Ted suddenly, "we want you to do a job for us."

"Oh, yes!" Sadie exclaimed. Her voice was eager and relieved.

A sudden hope flamed up in me, a certain pride. They wanted me to do a job—one of the things which I could do but they could not.

"What is it?"

"We want you to make us a bit of a wardrobe. Nothing very elaborate, you know. In fact, not a wardrobe in the ordinary sense, at all. We—er—we're not too flush with money just now, and we'd like you to keep the cost as low as you can. Can you do that?"

"Yes, I daresay I could," I replied.

A sudden desire to be of use, to justify my presence in their house, had swept up within me. But I carefully suppressed all outward signs of it.

"And how much do you think you could make it for?" asked Sadie.

"Oh, for a few bob—three or four bob," I answered casually.

"Three or four bob!" they exclaimed.

"Yes," I replied. I had known that I would astonish them, and could hardly keep the pride from my voice.

"But how could you make a wardrobe for three bob?" asked Ted suspiciously.

I had already noticed their lack of accommodation for clothes. I had thought the matter over, and had meant to approach them about it. Now I explained to them how it could be done for a few shillings. Briefly, the idea was one of shelves in a recess in the wall, and a curtain.

"Why, that's a jolly good idea!" exclaimed Sadie.

"It's a good job we've got you in the place," Ted said heartily. "Otherwise we'd have had to spend about five quid on a wardrobe."

"Yes, it *is* a good job we've got you in the place," Sadie agreed fervently.

Suddenly suspicion reared its head again. They were trying to get round me, that's what it was.

"You can't fool me," I thought.

I felt very cunning and knowing.

CHAPTER IV

THE MEANS TEST

Aₗₜₕₒᵤ𝗀ₕ I ʜᴀᴅ decided, with great altruism and magnanimity, that I would eventually leave Sadie and Ted, circumstances made it imperatively necessary that I should leave them in any case—altruism and magnanimity notwithstanding.

For one thing, the baby was due soon. There would be no room for me in their flat during such a time.

Apart from this, there was the economic aspect of things. Sadie would be leaving her job shortly, which meant that Ted would have to bear their joint financial burdens on his none-too-considerable wage.

Then there was the Means Test. That was the most final argument of all. If I remained out of work a month or two longer, I would come under the operation of the Means Test.

The laws in connection with the Means Test were, as has been amply testified on many occasions, somewhat paradoxical. Anyone in my position—that is, one who was living with relatives who were adjudged to have sufficient income to support him— would be cut off benefit altogether. On the other hand, by the simple process of leaving home, the out-of-work could make fairly certain of securing most of his benefit. The result was that he was debarred from living with those whom it was most economical and natural to live with, and whom it was possible to repay with all or most of his dole. The Government, in some recondite way, regarded it as more eminently within the divine order of things if homes were broken up and dole-drawers starved in strange lodgings. True, the matter was not placed so crudely before the people. This illogical farrago of half-baked idiocy was termed "economy".

Be that as it may, these various reasons meant that I had to find lodgings. I settled eventually in a cheap room a mile or two away from Sadie and Ted, and once again I was "living on my own". Once again I was living on twelve and sixpence a week—that is, on six shillings, after the rent had been paid.

Of course, now that I was in London and near my relations, my position was better than it had been when I had had to live on twelve and sixpence a week in Forgeton. Nevertheless, in essence my circumstances remained the same in London as in Forgeton. I still had an income of only twelve and sixpence, with all that this implied. Any assistance I received was negligible, both for the reason that I discouraged attempts to help me and gave others the impression that I was "managing" alright, and

97

because those who normally would have helped me were in no position to do so now.

In the meantime the weeks passed, and still no job came. During my first weeks in London I had told myself that within two months at the most I would certainly manage to get a job. Nevertheless, the two months passed and I did not get a job. Three months passed, and, all efforts notwithstanding, I was still no nearer to getting work. Four months passed, and still I had no job.

A peculiar fear descended on me—the fear that the strange incredible thing would happen to me that had happened to a vague anonymous mass of people: the fear that I might be out of work for a really long time.

Nevertheless, man has to adjust himself to his environment if he is to survive. My attitude towards being out of work changed— in my surface consciousness, at any rate. Slowly but surely the first keen edge of the urge to get work became blunted. I began to become accustomed to being without a job, and unemployment became the normal, not the abnormal way of life. After I had been denied work for months, a job became something remote and unattainable, a vanishing possibility dim and distant on the edge of the horizon.

Time passed, and I changed still further. I looked for work, but I was afraid of getting a job. Getting a job had become such an enormity, it was something so striven for and held in such high value, that of necessity a job became something formidable, something that no ordinary man could cope with.

Unemployment, with all its personal and social implications, breeds a sense of inferiority and a lack of confidence in the one unemployed. This, together with the exaggerated proportions which the job has now assumed, makes the acceptance of a job a feat of heroism in one who has been unemployed for a lengthy period. Let those who prate about "workshy's" please note this fact.

Thus it was that I began to know at first hand those recondite forces that mould the inner life of an out-of-work—forces as subtle and powerful as the elements, for, like the elements, their work is scarcely noticed except after the passing of time. Unemployment began to wreak within me those changes that have been wrought in so many unemployed. Lack of confidence, a sense of inferiority, the gradual but certain conviction of being a useless and unemployable member of society—these began to become part of my second nature.

With the passing of time, the shadow of the Means Test grew ever larger. That which was formerly a far-off danger that possibly will never be encountered, drew very near now, and overwhelmed the future. I had no illusions about the Means Test authorities, and considered them quite capable of reducing my twelve and sixpence to a mere nothing. In my more worried moments I even anticipated that by one of their freak, illogical actions they might cut me off altogether.

Certainly, I had known a distant relative of mine in Forgeton, who had been in receipt of the full amount of unemployment benefit for a single adult. His circumstances were exactly similar to those I was in at the present time, for he had been living on his own. Nevertheless, when the Means Test made its savage debut his benefit was cut down to ten shillings a week. How he managed to exist, I don't know to this day. Consequently I anticipated the Means Test with much misgiving and uneasiness.

When a policeman knocks at the door of a house and offers the unprepared occupier a summons, the latter as a rule experiences feelings of alarm and dismay. That is how an out-of-work feels when the clerk at the Labour Exchange gives him a form. That is how I felt when the clerk gave me a form.

At first, when an out-of-work has only begun to sign-on, he may be given a number of different forms. As a general rule, these deal merely with routine questions that need clarifying, or with details that still remain in doubt. But when one has been signing-on for a few months, and each succeeding pay-check records, as unemotionally but dreadfully as fate, the ever-mounting total of Cum. Tot. Dys. Pd.* (the number of days for which benefit has been received), then the out-of-work begins to dread the day on which he will be given a form—The Form.

As the total of Cum. Tot. Dys. Pd. reaches towards the 156 mark, the man or woman knows that the Means Test is near.

So it was that when my box-clerk flipped the pages of my claim, and took out from them a buff form, I was filled with concern and dismay. I had anticipated this moment many times. Yet, as is often the case when people urgently hope that something will not come to pass, I had almost convinced myself that it would not happen. Well, it had happened. Here it was.

Out in the street I read the form. It stated that my normal benefit would expire, and therefore I was to make a claim for Transitional Benefit. Transitional Benefit? Quite a polite name for the Means Test, but I didn't like it, anyway. Transitional to what? One was passing from one stage to a lower stage, and this lower stage was termed Transitional. It did not open up a very bright perspective.

I had to give answers to the many questions that were printed

* No doubt the official "cypher" for "Cumulative Total of Days Paid".

99

on the form: what my income was, and its source; whether I was in receipt of a pension, and if so, what type, and how much; whether I had any savings, and if so, how much. The instructions for filling up the form stated that if answers to the questions were in the negative one had to write None or No—to leave a blank space was not sufficient. Consequently, when I had filled it up, my form was a mass of None's and No's.

Amidst the None's and No's I had one lone item on the Income side:

Income.	Source of Income.
12s. 6d.	Unemployment Benefit.

On the Expenditure side was the following:

Rent .	.	.	.	.	.	. 6s. 6d.
Gas, Coal, etc.	.	.	.	.	.	6d.
Miscellaneous (Food, etc.)	.	.	.	5s. 6d.		

Income and Expenditure totalled up very neatly—twelve and sixpence each.

The next time I went to sign-on I returned the form. After that I waited to be summoned before a Committee. I understood that this was the next step in the procedure of the Means Test. Nevertheless, time passed and I was not summoned before a Committee.

One day a man knocked at the door of the house where I was living. He announced himself as a representative of the Public Assistance Committee, and asked to see my rent-book. I was not in at the time of his call, and so after he had seen my rent-book, the P.A.C. representative merely asked my landlady one or two formal questions, and then went away.

This incident was something far less intimidating than anything I had anticipated. I had thought of some callous bully of a man hectoring me about my means of subsistence, and, in the manner of many of these officials, insisting that I could sell this or that, and telling me of all kinds of improbable ways by which it was "possible" for me to manage without Unemployment Benefit.

However, even this little incident would have proved rather unpleasant were it not that I was on very friendly terms with my landlady and her husband. In the course of friendly conversation with them I had explained my position, and did not mind them knowing about my private affairs. The matter would have been very different if the Means Test man had made inquiries about me from a landlady who was a stranger to me.

Finally came the day when the clerk at the Labour Exchange handed me another form. This buff form contained my fate.

I walked some distance from the Exchange before I could prevail upon myself to read the form. There was a good deal of small print which I did not bother to read. I came across the words "Determination for Current Period", followed by the written entry "At the rate of 12s. 6d. a week, from 19/5/32".

I read the form over again slowly from the beginning, until the incredible fact dawned on me that the P.A.C. were allowing me the same amount as I had been receiving under normal Unemployment Benefit.

Possibly I was crazy, or society is crazy. At any rate, because certain people had graciously decided to grant me twelve and sixpence a week on which to live, I was filled with exultation, with joy. I walked back to my lodgings on air.

I continued signing-on at the Labour Exchange twice a week in the usual way, but once a month a clerk of the P.A.C. called at my lodging and left a form for me to fill in. The form was never posted, but was brought by hand, and had to be returned by the applicant in person the next morning.

I became expert at making up my budget on these forms. It was very easy for me to fill in my various items of income and their sources. The answer to this was: Unemployment Benefit, 12s. 6d. Any other income, None. Expenditure: Rent 6s. 6d., coal, gas, etc., 6d.; Miscellaneous, 5s. 6d. Total Income 12s. 6d. Total Expenditure 12s. 6d. "None" to this question and "No" to that, and there you were—my existence in a few scribbled words. Nothing could be easier.

Sometimes, in a desire to be a little more original and not answer the questions in the same rather toneless way, I would write under the item "Miscellaneous": "Food, clothing, amusements, fares, postage, etc., 5s. 6d." On one occasion at least I particularised even more minutely, and wrote: "Food, clothing, amusements, bootlaces, haircut and razor-blade, 5s. 6d."

Having duly completed the form, my next job was to take it up to the offices of the P.A.C. the next morning. Here various beneficiaries of the Means Test leaned against the damp stone walls, waiting until they were called by the clerk who was in charge of their case. Each clerk was in charge of a district, and we were each under the charge of the clerk responsible for the area in which we lived. In my Means Test experience I was rather fortunate, and not the least way in which I was fortunate was the clerk in charge of my district. He was a quiet, somewhat careworn, middle-aged man, of gentle manner. He would open the door of his office and call our names half wearily, half apologetically.

When I entered the office he would glance over my "budget",

refer to the dossier that contained details of my "case", and then ask:

"Any change in your circumstances?"

"No."

"Well, sign here, please."

I signed, and it was all over for another month.

LIFE ON TWELVE AND SIXPENCE

IF YOU, THE reader, will assume that you are in the position of living on twelve and sixpence, the assumption might prove to be instructive.

You leave the Labour Exchange on Friday and you have in your pocket a ten-shilling note and half a crown. You may comfort yourself with the reflection that not until another 168 hours have passed will you receive any more money. On this ten-shilling note and half a crown you must make do until one more week has passed and once again you are going through this same routine of going into the Labour Exchange and coming out again with a ten-shilling note and half a crown. So your life passes from one Friday to another, from one twelve and sixpence to another.

If you were the perfect unemployed man or woman, something resembling a cross between a calculating machine and a lump of wood, you would leave the Exchange devoutly determined that you would spend your money only on that small portion of extreme necessities that you could afford. But Nature, in creating man, failed, unfortunately, to foresee the phenomenon of unemployment; and so no separate species of mankind, no dull, brute-like creature, was evolved for the satisfaction of Ministries of Labour.

You, being something still resembling a human being, will leave the Exchange with your mind occupied with the vast amount of your needs and the small possibilities of gratifying them.

Little things, that a person who is earning wages scarcely bothers about, have now assumed great moment and significance in your thoughts. Maybe your shoe-laces have broken and been tied together and broken again, and it is now imperative that you buy another pair. Maybe your razor-blade will no longer shave you, and it is necessary for you to buy another one. Possibly you need a haircut; but how can you afford it? Your trousers are falling to pieces, they have been patched too many times; but you don't know how you are going to get another pair. It is raining, your feet are wet, you squelch water at every step. Your shoes are cracked beyond repair, the soles are dropping off in pieces, the heels have worn down to nothing. How to get new shoes, how to get these old wrecks patched up? Your socks are full of holes, darned beyond repair—wait till you can afford to buy new ones. Your overcoat and jacket are shabby, worn, ragged? These are mere trifles.

The question, the main question, is what food you should buy, and how much—or little—of it. Tomorrow you will be paying six and sixpence rent, and you will have only six shillings to spend.

Unfortunately, however, you once squandered your money on tobacco, and now, unemployed wretch that you are, tobacco is more than ever necessary to your peace of mind, calm of nerve. For a time you struggle against spending twopence * of the six shillings on a packet of cigarettes. As a general rule, you end by going into a shop, and, not without pangs of guilt, buying a two-penny packet of cigarettes.

Thus it is that you learn one of the first lessons of unemployment—that is, that whereas an unemployed man may deprive himself of necessities in order to obtain a fraction of the minor pleasures of existence, he can never enjoy it as his more prosperous neighbour might. He is tortured by the fact that he spent money on this when he ought to have spent money on that.

Maybe you have been going hungry for the last few days, and have not known what it is to have a decent meal. Now that you have this ten-shilling note and two shillings and four pennies in your pocket, you are seized with a desire to have a good, warm, filling dinner somewhere. Strange temptations and desires assail you (unfortunately, Nature failed to create you fitted for the rigours of life on the dole), and what of your weeks and months of penury, of joylessness, of going short, of boredom, of tightening your belt, of constantly having had to deny yourself everything you wanted—because of all this you have a strong imperious urge to have at least one wild luxurious fling with your money. You become possessed of the idea not merely to have a good meal, but to have a splendid meal, a meal better beyond comparison than any you have ever had.

There is more even than this: You want to go somewhere bright and gay, lively and happy. You are fed-up with spending empty days of grey joylessness in harsh want. Compelling desires surge up within you to know what it is to be free from these chains of hunger and need. You would like—whisper it—you would like to go to the pictures this afternoon.

* The price of a similar packet of cigarettes would today be fourpence.

But there is a stern reality, and you must face it. You have five and tenpence on which to live until next Friday. You must abandon these wild dreams and cut your coat according to your cloth. Better go home. At the grocery shop choose with care and calculation those most essential—no, not the most essential, they are too expensive—the cheapest foods on which you can make some pretence of living.

Not only on the Friday do you think, feel and agonise thus. You will know the same yearnings, the same deprivations and the same unfulfilment on the morrow, and on the day after, and the day after that. You will know it this week and the next, and untold weeks hence. Existence has become one long enforced abstemiousness, life one eternal doing without.

That is life on twelve and sixpence—if it can be called life. It is doubtful whether anyone could survive such an existence for very long. In actual fact I myself lived on twelve and sixpence a week for only a fairly short time. On my twenty-first birthday (in August of that year) I received an altogether unexpected birthday present. The P.A.C., with a startling lack of logic, decided that now that I was twenty-one I could not live on the amount they had thought sufficient for me when I was not yet twenty-one. They therefore increased my weekly transitional payment to the amount of benefit for a single male adult. This was then fifteen and threepence.

In addition to this, my position improved, as far as help from my mother and sister in the East End was concerned.

I had always done my best to give them the idea that I was "managing". My sister's husband was trying to assist his own mother and his two unemployed brothers, and I had no desire to be an additional burden on him. Nevertheless, on twelve and sixpence a week it is difficult to keep up for very long the pretence of "managing".

Round about the time my dole was increased I went to visit my mother. It had been raining for nearly a week, and my shoes were in a very bad condition. When I entered the kitchen my mother exclaimed in astonishment at the way my shoes squelched water over the floor.

"Why don't you get your shoes repaired?" she asked.

"Well, I happen to be out of work," I answered uncomfortably.

My sister, who was also in the kitchen, said with some surprise, "But you get the dole, don't you?"

This was so startling that I laughed bitterly. I had hitherto kept silent on the amount of "dole" I was getting, but now I explained that the amount did not allow for such trifles as shoes that needed repairing. They were horrified. My mother did not know
104

anything about the dole. While she knew that the amount of unemployment benefit I had brought home when we were living in Forgeton had been rather small, my unemployment periods had been brief, and she had not bothered very much. I now discovered that she had credited the authorities with a sweetly reasonable attitude that was rather touching to contemplate. She had thought that they would "understand" that now that I was living on my own I could not exist on such small benefit as I had brought home in the past. She had imagined that my benefit was at least sufficient to prevent me from going hungry, and to provide for such necessities as the upkeep of shoes and clothes.

Similarly with my sister. Immersed in the routine of home and shop, she had never thought very deeply about such questions as unemployment, despite the fact that unemployment reached her both through the shop and through the family. She saw unemployment purely as an absence of work, and therefore as an inability to spend money on the pictures, on holidays, and such-like luxuries.

To make matters further complicated, I had not been aware of their lack of knowledge on the matter. I had assumed that because they could not afford to help me they did not like to refer to the question.

Now, however, these misunderstandings were cleared up. My mother decided that my shoes were hopeless, and not worth repairing; from which it will be observed that an out-of-work's very lack of money causes him to lose more than those who can afford to have such matters attended to in time. Although she could ill afford it, my mother bought me a new pair of shoes, and also insisted that from now on I must visit her for meals at least three or four times a week. I had still not enlightened her altogether on the matter of how much benefit I was receiving, and no doubt my mother and sister had the idea that these three or four meals were not so much a necessity as an opportunity to allow me to put a shilling or two by for my other needs.

After this incident I visited my mother and sister in the East End a few times a week, and was given something to eat. This to a certain degree helped to take the first sharp edge off my constant lack of food.

Maybe I will give some people the impression that I was insatiable, and therefore it is with some hesitation that I state that even with an income of fifteen and threepence and a few meals per week, I did not lead a very satisfactory existence. In fact, looking back, I have never been able to distinguish any sharp difference between the time when I was living on twelve and sixpence a week and the time when I was getting fifteen and threepence and three or four meals. There is no sharp line of **distinction**; it is all one long, uninterrupted period of grey gloom.

It happened that very occasionally I managed to supplement my dole. Once every few weeks I earned a few shillings here, got an odd job there. Nevertheless, even these badly needed aids were too rare in occurrence and too short in duration to affect the general grey gloom of the days. The few shillings I earned on these sparse occasions prevented my situation from becoming too unbearable and desperate, and enabled me to survive that which otherwise I could not have borne.

There are a number of people who spend their time making ingenious calculations on the minimum amount on which an out-of-work can live. These people like to give the impression that if they themselves were unemployed, they would be so scientific and organised that they would make a profit out of it.

For myself, however, I cannot pretend that I was unemployed in any very distinguished way. I invented no ingenious menus, I engaged in no mathematical calculations. I lived merely from hand to mouth, budgetless, without calculations. Had my income approached some reasonable standard (no matter how remotely), I would undoubtedly have made some attempt to budget my income, as a matter of course.

I often thought that it would not be so bad if I could have no other outlay than food and shelter. But there were always other items—razor blades, shoe-laces, fares, baths, haircut and clothes.

Clothes have an altogether unexpected way of falling to pieces when one is unemployed. There are times when even an out-of-work has to buy new clothes. During the first year of my period of unemployment I bought myself the following clothes:

1. A pair of trousers.
2. A pair of tennis shoes.

The trousers were a tragedy, and so, if it comes to that, were the shoes. There came one Friday when I realised that I would have to buy myself a pair of trousers. I went to one of the cheap stores, and after having been measured paid four and elevenpence for a pair of trousers. Thus, practically the whole of the money which I had for food was spent on a pair of trousers; I could see no alternative. When I got home I found that the trousers were about six inches too big for me. I took them back, and after I had engaged in a desperate argument with, apparently, every member of the staff, from the errand boy to the branch manager, was given another pair. These fitted me fairly well, but they mysteriously fell to pieces in the course of about three weeks. After I had walked about for a week or two in the trousers I had been wearing before, I was sufficiently fortunate to be given a pair by someone.

I bought the tennis shoes at that time of the year when most people are beginning to think of thick woollen underwear. I happened to be rather sensitive about my appearance, and did not like going about in the autumn in a pair of white tennis shoes. Therefore, in addition to paying two and elevenpence for the shoes, I spent another sixpence on a bottle of shoe dye. This stuff made the calico part of the shoes seem a good imitation (from a distance) of ordinary black leather, but the rubber joining the soles and the uppers remained obstinately white—which gave the shoes a peculiar appearance. In addition the rain soaked very easily through the uppers of the shoes, whilst I had to become accustomed to a peculiar, cautious way of walking in wet weather; for it was very easy to slip, particularly when running hastily across a wet road.

Life is full of shabby hardships and disappointments such as these for the unemployed. Wherever the out-of-work turns to try to satisfy his burning needs, he finds himself powerless because of his lack of money, he is suddenly pulled up short by the chains of economic circumstances.

With rare exceptions, day in and day out, week in and week out, month in and month out, life went on in the manner I have described.

END OF BOOK THREE

BOOK FOUR

SOME ENCOUNTERS

CHAPTER I

THE CORUSCATING CARPENTER

ONE MORNING, AS I scanned the Vacancy columns of my land-lord's newspaper, I saw an advertisement for joiners, carpenters or cabinet-makers. The firm which was advertising gave an address in the Empire Exhibition Grounds at Wembley—some Pavilion or other.

This was the first job for woodworkers that I had seen advertised for some time. I was eager to go after it. Nevertheless, I did not possess the money for the fare to Wembley. On a sudden impulse I approached my landlord, explained the position, and asked him if he would lend me the money to travel up to Wembley. It was the first time I had ever attempted to borrow money from him, and normally I would never have thought of doing so. However, the glamorous vision of a job and wages was not to be denied.

My landlord earned a precarious living as a house-to-house pedlar; his wife earned a little, when she could, as a char-woman. They scraped along from day to day, from penny to penny. Moreover—and I had not thought of this—if I got a job in Wembley I might move away from them. Consequently it says much that my landlord, with an appearance of hearty cheerfulness, unhesitatingly lent me two shillings.

I hurried out and boarded a bus to Baker Street Station, from where I took the train to Wembley. Because of my impatience, the journey seemed endless, every pause at a station a crime against me. Every minute was precious, and with every passing minute some other joiner, carpenter or cabinet-maker might have taken the job which I felt ought, for numerous diverse reasons, to belong to me alone.

At last we reached Wembley. Here I inquired my way to the Exhibition Grounds and, after I had been given the directions, very nearly ran there.

I soon discovered, however, that it was one thing to get to the grounds of the Exhibition, but quite another to find my way to the factory I sought. There were few people about, and those who were could either give me no directions at all, or, what was worse, gave vague directions that led me nowhere.

For what seemed a very long time I hurried impatiently amongst the skeletons of the Exhibition, which, under a grey and mournful sky, had the dejected air of those who once knew a grandeur and magnificence that are now but a memory.

There seemed to be no way of getting directions to the place I was seeking. Ever and again I came across job-seekers who, like myself, were searching forlornly for some Pavilion or another, that now housed a factory. Occasionally I found that I had strayed into a barbed-wire entanglement from which there appeared to be no escape. How I had got into these ingenious traps, and how I could get out of them, were problems that exercised my mind a good deal.

Finally, when I was giving up all hope of discovering the whereabouts of the place I was seeking, I saw an energetic young man striding towards me. His confident and alert bearing stamped him, to my mind, as one of those rare, superhuman personages who really knew where they were going in this God-forsaken place. Hurrying towards him, I asked my way.

"You're going the wrong way, buddy," he said cheerfully. "Better come with me. I'm going there myself. I'll show you where it is."

I was filled with relief, now that I had found someone who really knew the way. At the same time it was rather awkward that we should both be going after the same job. Who would go in first? And supposing the one who went in first got the last job available? I occupied myself for some time with such questions. Finally my companion asked:

"Are you after the job that's going?"

"Yes," I replied. "I've been looking for the darn place for about two hours."

"I'm going after that job as well," he returned briskly. "What are you?—joiner? carpenter?"

"I'm a cabinet-maker."

"Oh, I'm a joiner and carpenter or carpenter and joiner, whatever you like to call it. Been out long?"

"Oh, a few weeks," I answered cautiously.

"A few weeks, eh? Tough, that is! I've only been out since last Sat'day. Jus' been working at the Bamboozle Film Studios. Making two bob an hour night work, I was."

"Two bob an hour! Crikey! But I bet that job didn't last long."

"Eighteen months," he replied carelessly.

"You won't get two bob an hour at this place, I don't suppose."

"Maybe not. But if I don't get the rate I don't take the job."

"Neither will I," I answered uncertainly, afraid of my own words.

I envied him his ability to speak these strong, confident words. And why shouldn't he? Whilst I had been pining in unemployment for nearly a year, he had been earning two bob an hour. Moreover, he had probably known very little unemployment, and had been able to obtain a thorough mastery of his trade. He could afford to talk that way. But could I?

Eventually we came to the place we were seeking. My companion strode through the gate and into the first workshop as though he had been primarily responsible for turning the firm away from the edge of bankruptcy to prosperity and affluence. With assured self-confidence he demanded to be shown where the foreman "hung out in this joint". A young man in dirty overalls directed us (or maybe I should say him), and in answer to our (or maybe I should say his) query as to what they were paying in this lay-out, intimated with a discreet air that the foreman would tell us.

After we had walked through one or two workshops that resounded with the noise of hammers and saws, the joiner's foreman was pointed out to us. He was a ·young man of about twenty-five, small and thin, with red hair and a vacant expression. He was himself working at the bench, and looked up in surprise when we drew near. The joiner approached him first, whilst I stood a short distance away.

After there had been some conversation, I saw the foreman say something to my companion. The joiner exclaimed in loud, astonished tones:

"What! One and four an hour! Christ, I've just been workin' at the Bamboozle Film Studios, and getting two bob an hour night work! One and four an hour! Blimey!"

The foreman shrugged his shoulders, and the joiner left him. As he came towards me he said ironically:

"Go on, you'd better try *your* luck, mate."

One and fourpence an hour seemed to me to be a very desirable wage; until I could get a hold on employment again, at any rate. The highest I had earned before this period of unemployment was one and a penny, which, in view of my age and local circumstances, could have been considered quite a high wage. Furthermore, there certainly seemed no prospects of my being able to get a rate higher than one and fourpence an hour, or, having got such a job, to be able to keep it. I went up to the foreman.

He seemed to be a very sleepy and absent-minded individual,

but about his sleepiness and absent-mindedness was an air of disapproval of me in that I was the companion of the coruscating joiner. He gazed dreamily about a foot above my head. After a couple of minutes he enunciated with apparent difficulty the question:

"You . . . a . . . joi . . . ner?"

"No, a cabinet-maker."

At these words the foreman fell into a trance. He gazed with dumb rapture at some beatific vision on the ceiling in the far corner of the room. Then reluctantly, with difficulty, he struggled back to mundane, material things.

"I took on . . . enough men . . . this morning . . . " he mumbled with great weariness. "Call . . . in a day or two . . . if you . . . like."

I had a sudden impulse to kick him hard, do something that would waken him summarily from his dreamy reverie. I had a heart-rending vision of the thousand and one ways I could have spent the money I had wasted on the fare coming here.

However, there was nothing I could do. He was merely exercising the rights of a foreman to hire and fire.

The joiner was hanging about with an air of deep disgust.

"What a —— wage!" he exclaimed when I drew near. "One and four an hour!" And then suddenly he shouted to the workers at the bench, "Foreman? Foreman? I thought he was the —— glueboy!"

Following his cue I shouted:

"If that guy's foreman, they ought to make me general manager!"

Then, feeling that we had redeemed somewhat the futility of our search for work, we swaggered out of the place very defiantly.

CHAPTER II

A COMMERCIAL INTERLUDE

I WAS WALKING along one of the main streets of North London, when suddenly my way was barred by a burly individual whom at first sight I imagined to be an impecunious bookmaker with a strong taste for drink. I found his first remark somewhat startling.

"D'you want to buy a suit, Guv'nor?" he asked me avidly.

No thought was farther from my mind at that moment than buying a suit. Furthermore, how this tout imagined, in view of my appearance, that I could afford to buy a suit is something I have never been able to comprehend. It is true that I happened to be wearing a new pair of bootlaces, but I doubt whether these gave me a more than usually opulent appearance.

"No, thank you," I muttered, and prepared to continue on my way.

However, it appeared that the matter was not to be ended as simply as all that.

"'Ave a look at some of our suits," he said with hoarse fervour. "They're goin' cheap!"

No matter how cheap the suits may have been going, they would still have been far too expensive for me.

"No, it's alright," I said. "I'm sorry, but I don't want a suit."

Once again I prepared to go on my way.

"Jest 'ave a look!" he implored desperately. "Jest 'ave a look—it won't do yer no 'arm!"

Once again I repeated my euphemistic phrase that I didn't want a suit, though what I really meant was that I could not afford one. But it was of no avail. The tout had apparently decided that if no one else in London would buy one of his suits, I would. However, even if I could have afforded to buy a suit, I would never have bought one at a shop that employed a tout.

His insistence that I should view the incomparable suits, and my refusals, were repeated a number of times. The tout's capacity for insistence seemed inexhaustible, and my only means of escape appeared to lie in knocking him down and walking over his recumbent body. On the other hand, whilst it would have given me great pleasure to perform the latter, I did not feel capable of achieving the first and more indispensable part of this enterprise.

Before I was quite driven to such desperate measures, however, a solution to the problem occurred to me—a solution, moreover, in keeping with my sentiments about shops which employed touts: I would take the tout at his word. He had urged me to view his suits without risk, loss or obligation on my part. Apparently nothing would gratify him more than that I should just glance at the incomparable suits. Very well, I would glance at them.

I signified to the tout that I had yielded to his entreaties. I graciously consented to view the suits.

My decision caused a magical change in the tout. He adopted an attitude of dog-like devotion. A mother's croon to her newborn babe could have been no more tender than the obsequious voice with which he thanked me. With eager servility he directed my attention to the suits that were the marvel of the sartorial world, and the ideal towards which our civilisation had been struggling for so long. With poetic rapture he pointed out first this suit and then that. It appeared that through some mysterious agency—possibly telepathy—the tailors had made these suits with only one person in mind—me.

The tout, however, was not to know that in Forgeton I had been friends with a tailor. In an otherwise reasonably amicable friendship there had been only one flaw. That was my friend's passion for pausing in front of every tailor's shop window we passed on our walks through the streets. Conversation was halted, discussion was abandoned, wit became stale whilst, in the most technical language, my pal dissected every garment he saw displayed. He would point out to me how this suit was badly cut, how that suit was badly pressed, how this suit hung badly, and that suit didn't even fit the wax model in the window.

I saw now a golden opportunity to profit by my pal's technical harangues. Useless for the tout, with beatific rapture shining in his eyes, to expound to me the beauties and perfection of suits at the low price of £5 5s. I pooh-poohed his words with scorn. For every suit I had a phrase as lethal as a rifle-bullet.

"No. Don't like it. Doesn't even fit the model."

"Don't like that one. Look how it's pressed."

"No, can't say I like that. Very badly cut, I think."

Slowly but surely an almost tearful desperation began to master the tout as I mercilessly punctured his idyllic raptures. What of my ignorance of the subject, I used these phrases of condemnation rather erratically and wildly. It was thus fairly easy for the tout to disprove them. Nevertheless, I had one last implacable retort to all his pleadings.

"I don't like the pattern," I said adamantly.

After a time, he turned to me. "You don't like the patterns? Come inside the shop. I'll show you plenty of patterns—lovely patterns."

For a moment I hesitated, and then I had yielded to a fool-hardy impulse to carry this thing to its logical conclusion. I entered the shop. Here the tout triumphantly handed me over to the true denizen of the place, whilst he went outside to try to lure other passers-by to follow my example.

The denizen, a tall man with a bald head, treated me with scarcely concealed contempt. His phrases might be polite and suave, but his attitude appeared to be that anyone who was sufficiently foolish to yield to a tout was fool enough to yield to anyone.

"So you want to see some patterns, do you, sir? Very good, sir. We've some nice patterns here, sir. I'm sure you'll like them, sir."

By now I was sorry that I had ever entered the place. However, I could not but go on with the farce. The denizen took a roll of cloth and demonstrated it to me lovingly, caressing it with his fingers.

"See what a nice pattern," he wheedled.

I examined it searchingly, as though I expected to find a hole in it, or something.

"No, I'm afraid I don't like this one."

The denizen was not unduly disturbed. After all, it was only the first one he had shown.

"Very well, sir; I'll show you another one. You're sure to like it."

He brought another pattern. But my heart was not to be moved. He brought another. I dismissed it. He brought another. Perforce, I had to dismiss that. I began to hope that by now he would give up in despair. But no, the man was indefatigable. He brought out a ladder.

"Wait," he said, and his tone was that of one who at last is about to reveal to the persistent inquirer the mystery of mysteries. He climbed up the ladder, and from the top shelf brought down a roll of cloth. My nerve was beginning to be a bit shaken by now, but there was nothing else for it. I had to declare that I did not like the pattern. Unlike the others, this really was a nice pattern, and good cloth. I would very much have liked to have had a suit made of it.

The denizen may have been disappointed, there was certainly a wild gleam in his eye, but apparently he had no intentions of giving me up as hopeless. Once again he climbed the ladder. Once again I sternly disliked the pattern. The denizen climbed the ladder again and again, and each time I declared my unequivocal dislike of the pattern.

I began to feel more desperate than the desperate salesman. The patterns danced before my eyes. My head was beginning to whirl.

"Is there no end to this?" I thought.

It seemed as though there were no end to it. Apparently the denizen was prepared to go on showing me patterns till doomsday. Finally it seemed that there was only one thing for me to do. When the denizen brought me the next pattern, a repellant pattern of loud checks in a very poor cloth, I declared myself, somewhat critically, to be satisfied at last.

And now what? My original intention had been that at this stage I would say politely, "Well, good morning," and walk out. But now, in the cold light of reason, this seemed to me to be a somewhat hazardous undertaking. I was intimidated by the fat tout and the thin denizen.

"I'm glad you like this pattern, sir," said the denizen. "Very tasteful, I think. And one of our best cloths. Not many people would choose such a pattern. They would go in for something cheap and showy."

I intimated by my attitude to this speech that I was modestly aware of the fact that as far as pattern and cloth were concerned, I was indeed a connoisseur.

"You would like a suit of this material, would you, sir?" he went on.

"Oh—er—yes," I stammered. I could not think of anything else to say.

"If you will pay a deposit, I'll measure you for the suit immediately, and you can have it in twenty-four hours."

A five-guinea suit ready in twenty-four hours! He must think me a greenhorn altogether. My indignation emboldened me.

"I'm afraid I haven't the time just now. I'll be passing in a couple of hours, and I'll have more time then."

"But it won't take me long to take your measurements! Only a few minutes!"

"I haven't got any time just now. I told your t—— your salesman that before I came in here."

"But it will only take a few minutes—I assure you!"

"I'm sorry. I'm already late for an appointment."

I would have walked out of the shop now, but the denizen, no doubt an experienced strategist, blocked my narrow exit from the far end of the counter to the floor of the shop, the door and freedom.

"Just leave a deposit, a small deposit—anything!" he implored feverishly. His mask of suave politeness had dropped away, revealing the unscrupulous trader, greedy for an easy customer, for any customer.

"I'm sorry. Not now. When I come back later. I haven't got any money with me just now."

That which I meant literally he chose to take figuratively.

"But you needn't pay the whole five guineas now! Not at all! Thirty shillings will do! A pound!"

It had been incredible to me all along that either he or the tout should imagine I could afford to buy a suit. Its corollary—that I had money—seemed to me even more incredible. I had not even seen a pound-note for months. Pound-notes of a new design had recently been issued, but I didn't even know what they looked like.

"I'm sorry. I haven't brought any money with me. I didn't expect to have a suit made."

"That's nothing! Just leave a small deposit! I'll measure you straight away!"

There was a vindictive gleam in his eyes now. I responded to it.

"I've told you," I said firmly, "I can't leave a deposit now. I've no time."

"Well, just leave a little. Say ten shillings. I'll give you a receipt."

"I can't leave ten shillings."

"Five shillings, then. I'll measure you straight away."

"I'm sorry. Not just now."

"Leave only half-a-crown, then! It'll be just as good. It'll be a deposit. Then you can come back later."

That which I had originally thought of as a joke was becoming a sordid farce. I did not bother to make further excuses. I felt that the denizen knew now why I had come into the shop. That was alright with me. Let him learn his lesson. I edged towards the centre of the shop. The denizen continued to entreat, to importune.

"Deposit! . . . receipt! . . . half-a-crown! . . . measure! . . ."

I edged my way, practically pushing the frantic denizen before me, to about two yards from the door. Then the tout, sensing that something was amiss, entered the shop. He gazed at the imploring denizen and me with heavy gloom.

"What's the matter?" he asked threateningly. "Ain'cher suited, guv'nor?"

I'd had about enough of this. Ignoring both of them I marched to the doorway, and glaring at them, snorted:

"No! I'm not suited! And I don't want to be suited, either! If you want to know something, I've been out of work six months, and I haven't got a single ha'penny on me. So next time someone tells you he doesn't want a suit, maybe you'll believe him!" And with that I began to flee from the shop as fast as I could, though to the eyes of passers-by I was merely walking rather hurriedly.

When I was a safe distance away—about fifteen yards—I glanced back. Both the tout and the denizen stood in the shop doorway and gazed after me. In their gaze I saw many conflicting emotions. There was rage, and the compelling desire to murder me as brutally as possible. There was astonishment in that this person who spoke quietly with a strong Northern accent, and was thus by all Cockney standards a hopeless simpleton, should thus have fooled them. But above all there was anguish— anguish that The Perfect Fool of a Customer should have slipped through their fingers just when he seemed most securely caught and trapped.

CHAPTER III

THE HOPELESS SPECIMEN

For the first time for a number of weeks I saw a job advertised. I hurried along to the firm which was advertising, fuming impatiently because I had no money for fares. Also, the firm was situated in an obscure back street of which few people had heard. No one seemed to be able to give me positive directions as to the way there.

When eventually I reached the place and asked if there were any vacancies, I was told that a number of men had already been taken on, but I could go upstairs and see the foreman if I so desired.

I climbed up three flights of stairs, and finally came upon a narrow landing at the end of which was a small cubby-hole. A man was leaning against the wall, his hands in his pockets, a look of dreamy and hopeless abstraction in his eyes. When I came on the landing, he started out of his reverie.

"You come fer a job?" he asked anxiously.

"Yes. Where's the foreman?"

"'E's in that office. 'E's seein' a feller now."

"Oh. Are you going in next?"

"Yes, I'm next."

He leaned back against the wall and lost himself in reverie again. Ordinarily I would have been anxious and impatient because one job-seeker was in the office and there was this man to go in before me. But this man aroused no anxiety in me. Shabby and long unemployed as I was, I yet felt superior to him. I felt that if the foreman came to his office door and saw the two of us, he would inevitably choose me before this man. We were both shabby and both eager to get a job, but there was an obvious difference between us. I was young, and this meant much in the silent war for a job. In this new era in the trade, when energy and speed were beginning to oust skill, the employers preferred the younger cattle to the older. Moreover, they could generally hope to pay much less for a young worker than for an older one.

However, the difference in our ages was not the main point. That which made me so confident in competition with this other man was his whole attitude and appearance. It was the attitude and appearance of one who has been defeated by life, of one who carries on the struggle for existence mechanically and hopelessly, out of mere habit. Looking at him, one reflected that no employer would give him a job. The man had been

117

so defeated he would lose a job if it were given to him on a plate.

My thoughts were interrupted. The "office" door opened and the other job-seeker came out. The foreman poked his head through the doorway and said brusquely "Next, please!" The other man went into the office.

"Any luck?" I asked the departing job-seeker.

"He's taken dahn abaht a thahsen pertiklers, an' he ses he'll write ter me if he wants me," he replied with disgust.

I was somewhat cast-down. I knew all about these places where the foreman took down a thousand particulars and said he would let you know. It meant he'd already got all the men he wanted, but took your name and address on the offchance that he might need you; maybe you were prepared to work for a good deal less than most. I had come to regard this giving of "particulars" as a futile waste of time, for nothing had ever come of it.

However, here I was. I might as well stay and see what happened. The cubby-hole door opened and my predecessor slouched out. I went in to speak to the foreman. The interview consisted of him asking me my name, address, age, length of period in the trade, where I had last worked, how long I had worked there, why I left, whether I was used to this class of work (two postcard photographs of remote, Lilliputian bedroom suites shown), how long I had been unemployed, what rate of pay per hour I would work for, my replies to these questions, and his information that if he wanted me he would "drop me a card". Then I went home.

A few days later I was surprised to see an advertisement in the paper for twenty-five cabinet-makers. I felt that here at last I had a chance to get a job. The trouble with job-seeking in the cabinet-making trade was that most places, when they did advertise vacancies, wanted only one or two or three cabinet-makers. You had no chance. Inevitably someone who lived round the corner of the place had snapped up the job before you found your way there. When a firm advertised for twenty-five cabinet-makers—well, you had a bit of a chance. I went after the job with some optimism.

The place was not as large as I had imagined it would be. It was set in the middle of a lost piece of waste ground and was small, square and built of brick. As I approached it I could hear the familiar whining and bellowing of woodworking machinery. The concrete space in front of the factory was covered with tumbled and chaotic refuse. Bicycles, unprotected from the rain, leaned drunkenly against each other and against those which were

118

supported by the wall. As one who judged a factory as much by its outside as by its inside, I was not very favourably impressed.

When I pushed open the door of the factory the roar and scream of machinery leapt out suddenly, as caged animals might make a mad leap for liberty when they see that their cage has been inadvertently opened.

The factory was about 50 feet square, and seemed to be almost entirely filled with machines, and with piles of wood in various stages of being worked up. Scattered here and there in the midst of the confusion were benches at which cabinet-makers worked. Sawdust filled the air like a fog. The clamour of the machines beat frenziedly against the walls.

I stood hesitant for a moment, wondering who I was to interview and where. I was even less enamoured of the place than before. I was concerned by the fact that if I worked here I would be surrounded by unprotected dangerous machinery and swift-moving belts and pulleys. But more than this I was concerned with the thick, sawdust-filled atmosphere. An atmosphere like this clogged up the nostrils with sawdust and forced one to breathe through the mouth. I was susceptible to bronchial catarrh, and my trade was an unhealthy one for me under the best conditions.

"'Maker?" a young machinist near me bawled.

"Yes."

He motioned me towards the other end of the workshop.

"See that guy over there?—the one in the shirt-sleeves. He's the guv'nor."

Threading my way through the machines and piles of wood towards the man in shirt-sleeves, I recognised another man who was waiting before me to see him. It was the hopeless and defeated individual I had met when I last applied for a job. I felt unreasonably irritated at seeing him here, in front of me again. It seemed to me to be a sign of a degradation that was overtaking me—that I ran after the same jobs as this broken-down out-of-work, achieving the same lack of success.

The man in shirt-sleeves was engrossed in energetic conversation with a smartly dressed young man. I reluctantly took up my station behind the defeated one, hoping, for some reason, that he would not recognise me and attempt to draw me into conversation. Because of the noise of machinery, however, he did not notice me at first, but stood staring vacantly into space. I was able to observe him closely, and saw that he was indeed far more degenerate than I had first noticed.

His face appeared to be a pale yellow colour, and all the muscles were slack and loose in a foolish, undisciplined fashion. Here and there odd hairs sprouted over his face, as though he had

shaved himself, but very unsuccessfully. He had long since forgotten how to stand straight, for his shoulders drooped over his
body, in the manner of a cabinet-maker bending over his work;
he leaned to the right, as one who had spent years working at the
bench. The tips of his fingers were stuck nervously into his
trousers pockets, as though there were something inside the
pockets which might bite them. His clothes were worn and
greasy, and, together with his cap and shoes, had long since
lost the shape they had when they were new, and now served
merely to emphasize in grotesque detail every line and pro-
tuberance of his body.

Suddenly he realised that someone was observing him, and he
started guiltily. Then he smiled in a foolish, wavering, then
joyful fashion.

"What, you 'ere?" he asked, and I found myself annoyed in
that his tone seemed to express the tacit belief that we were of the
same stamp, that he and I were comrades. I was annoyed with
myself for being annoyed.

"Yeh."

"Come after a job?"

"Yeh."

"You didn't get that job las' week, eh?"

"No."

"Neither did I. They advertise for 'makers, an' when you get
there—'We'll write to you', they say. The bastards!"

"What about this place? They advertised for twenty-five cabinet-
makers, didn't they?"

"Yes, that's right. Twenty-five," he agreed anxiously, and
stared open-mouthed at me, as though expecting me to say
something very important.

"I don't see how they can get five in here, never mind twenty-
five."

"You're right!" he agreed vehemently. "They couldn't get
five in here, never mind twenty-five. The bastards!" He leaned
confidentially towards me. "It's a lahsy 'ole," he whispered
hoarsely, "a lahsy 'ole."

"You're right. I'm not too keen about taking a job here,
anyway."

He looked at me cunningly. "No piece-work, eh?" he
whispered.

"Not for me. I never work piece-work."

"That's right. Piece-work ain't worth a light to yer, an' that's
a fact. I've tried it. No more piece-work for me."

"Good for you. Piece-work in our trade is just a bloody
swindle."

He was about to say something vehemently, but beneath the roar of machinery a shout floated to our ears. The smartly dressed young man was going away, and the shirt-sleeved guv'nor was beckoning to us. My companion took his finger-tips out of his pockets and tried to straighten himself smartly, though his shoulders still drooped. He shambled over to the boss.

I watched the various machinery processes going on around me, as well as the efforts of the isolated cabinet-makers to work in a space within which they could barely turn round. Suddenly I saw that the broken-down individual was making his way back towards me.

"It's piece-work!" he shouted, "piece-work!"

The boss was looking in my direction. "Piece-work?" I asked.

"Yes."

"Oh, very well." I turned away disappointed, in disgust.

My companion was behaving like a crazed man. As he walked towards the door he turned to the workers on either side of him and yelled out:

"Piece-work, eh? Piece-work!—the bastards!" Varying this with: "It's a lahsy 'ole, I tell yer—a lahsy 'ole!"

I felt ashamed and sorry for him. Workers who, whatever the reason, do not get or take a job, generally walk out of the place without further ado. This man's open and unashamed disappointment, hatred and derision embarrassed me. I tried to make it clear from my bearing that I was in no way connected with him.

Outside the man kept up a running fire of furious commentary on the hardships of the cabinet-making trade in general, and the piece-work system in particular. I felt a sense of distaste in being with him. However, he seemed to be going the same way as myself, so I walked sullenly by his side.

"See what they've brought the trade to!" he exclaimed passionately. "It ain't worth a light now—not a light! You go fer a job and—'Give 'em piece-work,' they say. Piece-work! An' the bastards take it!"

I remained silent. Mere expostulation, as such, had never seemed to me of much use. Either act, or talk with a view to action. But mere complaints, and complaints to one who could do nothing about it, this was futile.

However, the defeated one did not seem to care particularly whether I listened or not. He seemed glad enough of the opportunity of someone to talk at, someone at whom he could ventilate all his accumulated frustration and disappointment. He shuffled rapidly by my side, his face a mask of bitterness and despair, his hands and the whole of his distorted frame twitching and jumping to give emphasis to his words.

And suddenly it was as though I saw a vision. The man at my side was not another being, a stranger. He was myself after the lapse of years. Here was my Future, set before me in flesh and blood and skin and bone. This was what I would become after years of tramping for jobs and not getting them. This was what I would be like when I had so lost confidence that even when I got a job I would be unable to hold it. This was what I would be reduced to: defeat, frustration, bitterness, endless self-justifying tirades.

No wonder I had been uneasy when he reappeared before me. No wonder I had regarded him with distaste. No wonder I wanted to be rid of him.

CHAPTER IV

IN HOXTON MARKET

I GOT FED up with the usual routes I followed when I was looking for a job. I knew the streets too well; they were loathsome. Mean, narrow and dirty, they were running sores on the body of London. Houses that were squalid and tumbledown alternated with squalid and tumbledown workshops. The only difference between the houses and the workshops was that people lived in the one, whilst people worked in the other. In the one was enacted the process of procreating, bringing forth, tending and rearing the raw material for the other.

No, I had no liking for the task of tramping the district round Hackney Road and Shoreditch and Hoxton—even less liking than I had for taking lengthy walks or expensive tram rides to Edmonton and such-like areas and asking stony-faced, calculating men—denizens of the new robot-run factories—for a job.

However, I was not in the position to do only those things I would like to do. Each day in the first few months I made my rounds, hoping stubbornly, not daring not to hope. And if the morning yielded nothing, the afternoon still held a bleak, inscrutable promise, like that of the fabled oracles who foretold the future in mystic, incomprehensible phrases.

One day, tiring of the usual routes, and thinking that perhaps streets unexplored and away from the main centres of the trade might yield that which I had hitherto sought in vain, I walked through many unfamiliar back streets, making my way towards Hoxton and Shoreditch.

After a time I came into a main street of the neighbourhood. A shabby and down-at-heel neighbourhood, its main street was a shabby and down-at-heel imitation of more prosperous main streets. But maybe I am wrong there. This street was no more an imitation of more prosperous streets than the district was an imitation of more prosperous districts. This main street had a character of its own.

At first so narrow that two vehicles abreast could scarcely have driven along it, the street curved round, and on a sudden gave way to a width like that of a market square. Shops that sold variously very second-hand gramophones and wireless sets, home-made peppermints and cast-off clothing, gave way to all the hubbub and commercial furore of a market. It was a market —Hoxton Market, to be exact.

Progress in Hoxton Market becomes difficult for the would-be job-seeker, anxious to reach the job-seeker's hunting-grounds. The pavements become more and more choked with slow-moving passers-by and dawdling shoppers. Clamorous shop-keepers, stall-holders and assistants—all filled with a fine frenzy of salesmanship—shout, joke, chaff, bawl, wheedle, orate and declaim the excellence of their goods.

As I passed a shop that sold, amongst other things, bacon, an assistant whose nose was red with the cold and whose hands were blue from the same cause, dashed out of the shop as though he had suddenly noticed that it was on fire.

"'Ere y'are now!" he bawled. "'Alf a pahn of the best fer eightpence!—'alf a pahn fer eightpence!"

I was about to refuse, and then I saw that this was unnecessary; the assistant was shouting to the world in general, and had probably not even noticed me.

Opposite the shop a stall-holder was advising mankind as a whole to buy his eels. These latter, unaware of their impending fate, were sluggishly engaged in somehow futile manœuvres of slow and tortuous movement in zinc tanks.

From all sides resounded the chopping of butchers' cleavers, and voracious advice from the shop assistants to buy "'alf a pahn o' the best" at a price foolishly, idiotically, almost insanely below the level of that price which would have been charged by these establishments had they been business enterprises instead of, as they obviously were, philanthropic societies governed by men whose sole concern was the welfare of their fellow-citizens.

At the corner of a pavement a broad, well-built man wearing a large trilby hat was repeating in tones of grave admonition:

123

"Don't fergit now, ladies an' gentlemen. I've something very special for the two fifteen. Don't fergit my special for the two fifteen." Despite his air of dark profundity and of really knowing something very special indeed about the two-fifteen, nobody seemed to be taking any notice of him.

Nearby was standing a somewhat decayed old man with a nose like a beetroot. He was dressed in shabby old clothes, and had a rather sheepish air of late and overdue repentance for a life of hectic dissipation. Wordless and immobile, reflecting on goodness knows what joyous moments of the past, he silently proffered a lemon to the passers-by. His stock-in-trade struck me as being rather meagre, but it was scarcely more so than those of similar decayed penitents whom I passed at regular intervals afterwards. The combined stock of the whole sorrowing crew could probably have been bought up for a shilling retail. These atoning merchants all seemed to be members of a society of repentance. Their penitence, however, was at least equalled by an ambition and optimism that would have appalled even Samuel Smiles. They looked for profit and sustenance to such articles as a yard of elastic, a box of matches, a pair of bootlaces, all of which were held mutely, and apparently without further interest, to the gaze of the passer-by.

There were men who suavely explained the incomparable excellence of their carpet-soaps, and there were women who sold fifth-hand silk stockings and dresses and books and magazines. The place was a hectic centre of commerce where tiny streams of coins merged together to become a river of trade.

As I made my way towards Pitfield Street, I saw that a group of youths were the cause of jubilant excitement amongst a crowd of youngsters. It was not difficult to see why: the youths were obviously a band of roving street musicians and comedians. One dragged a heavy portmanteau which no doubt held the "props" of the troupe, whilst the others carried severally a banjo, a drum and a flute.

The groups paused at the entrance to a street opposite the middle of the market. Great excitement, speculation and ecstasy from the children! The portmanteau was opened and a large red, faded carpet flung on the ground. Passers-by began to congregate on the pavements and on the roadway in front of the performers. These latter began to don grotesque wigs and beards and generally to prepare themselves for their performance. They behaved as nonchalantly as though for all the world they were in the privacy of some dressing-room. In the meantime the excitement of the children became so intense that it appeared as though some of them might give way under the strain. They crowded in front and at the side of the troupe, their eyes large and round with wonder and delight. From them came an incessant chorus of "Ee!" and "Coo!" and various other anticipations of the amazing delights which were shortly to emanate from the troupe.

"Get back!" ordered one of the players. "Go on! Over to that wall there!"

The children, impudent enough on occasion, allowed themselves to be cowed and intimidated by this tyrant who possessed the power to prevent them from seeing the absorbing wonders if they did not behave themselves. Abashed, but still giving vent to anticipatory delight, they squeezed over to one of the walls, where from now on they played the role of an appreciative gallery.

In the meantime the performers had pulled their trousers up to their knees, and, to the shrill amusement of some of the women onlookers, stood with their socks, garters and hairy calves displayed before the audience. Now they put Turkish or Egyptian fezzes on their heads, and cloaked themselves with what appeared to be queerly decorated curtains. Now they began blacking their faces.

At first I had been inclined to dismiss the whole proceedings and continue on my way. But now I was caught up in the anticipation and excitement of the rest of the crowd. One did not see an affair like this every day! I waited eagerly for the performance to begin.

Soon there was a pang-a-pang-a-pang from the banjo, a portentous thud on the drum, a preliminary blare from the flute, and a scarcely suppressed cheer from the kids. The next moment the banjo, the drum and the flute were rattling away at some popular effusion of the moment. It was a queer sight to see these lads, in their outlandish wigs and make-up, strumming, puffing and banging away with mechanical efficiency at some sophisticated American trifle. What they lacked in style they compensated for in vigour, and it was heartening and invigorating to watch them.

This effort concluded with a brave flourish, and then the players, handing their instruments over to the fourth of their number, began their performance in real earnest. Chanting some weird, gibbering song, they pranced up and down the carpet in their stockinged feet, made salaams, turned somersaults and generally acted the fool with great zest and crudity. As this act was obviously a farcical imitation of the supposed customs, behaviour and dress of Oriental races, it brought superior laughter from the bystanders. The children screamed and crowed with delight, and went into transports of merriment.

A little sobered now by the acrobatics of this turn, the performers turned down their trouser legs, removed their beards and fezzes and resumed their instruments once more. Banjo, drum and flute made their preliminary noise, and then the fourth of the company lifted up his voice and informed the world that he was heading for the last round-up. The instrumentalists certainly had a strong sense of rhythm, and they plonked and boomed and brayed in perfect time and accord. The singer managed to give a fairly convincing impression that he was dying of a broken heart, and the far-away expression in his eyes whenever he uttered the poignant phrase "B-b-b-boo, b-boo, b-boo," was in itself extremely touching. When the song died away into silence there was rapturous applause, particularly from the children.

The instrumentalists now turned themselves into a Nigger Minstrel Troupe. They began to indulge with great rapidity in a somewhat repetitive triologue which went something after the following style:

"Ah say, Sambo."

"Yeh, Snowball."

"Ken you te-ell me why does a chicken cross de road?"

"What's dat, Sambo? Why does a chicken cross de road?"

"Yeh, dat's what Ah said, Snowball. Why does a chicken cross de road?"

"Well, Ah guess Ah dunno why does a chicken cross de road. Maybe you ken tell us. Say, Darkie, why does a chicken cross de road?"

"What's dat you say, Snowball? Why does a chicken cross de road?"

"Yeh, that's what Ah said. Why does a chicken cross de road?"

Eventually, after much verbal ascertainment of the exact nature of the question, it transpired that the answer was because the chicken wanted to get to the other side—as most of us had suspected for some time. The children greeted the solution with ecstasies of delight, all except one girl with a dirty face, who had known the answer all along, and didn't think this fact was sufficiently appreciated by her colleagues.

Having disposed of this recondite problem, the minstrels began to intone a mournful song about a darkie far away. It occurred to me that maybe I had better go now. It was after twelve, and my long walk would be wasted if I didn't get a move on. At that moment someone touched me on the shoulder. It was the fourth of the company moving quietly amongst the crowd.

"Spare a copper for the entertainers," he murmured. "Out of work lads tryin' to earn an honest penny."

I was utterly confused. I had no money.

"I'm sorry. I haven't any money," I mumbled, and lurched out of the crowd.

The collector's face seemed to me to express hatred and contempt for those who enjoy a performance and give nothing to the performers.

I hurried away, confused and ashamed. It seemed to me almost as if I had stolen something from these lads. And they were out of work, like me.

THE DOWN AND OUT

ONE DAY MY wanderings took me near Liverpool Street and into the City. This was an interesting change from my usual round, so I continued through the narrow, roaring canyons of streets that were filled with all the agitated sound and movement of the centre of the City, and crowded with motor buses, clerks, typists, bank messengers and messenger boys.

Eventually I reached the Strand, and wandered up towards Charing Cross. I felt a bit tired by now, and, stimulated by the unusual, almost holiday nature of the walk, and possibly because it had been pay day at the Labour Exchange, I decided to have a cup of tea. Eventually I went into one of those eating-places so numerous off the Strand round about Charing Cross—the kind of place that is regretfully conscious that it is only a café, but aspires to be a restaurant.

I had just been given my cup of tea and had sat down when the door opened slowly, hesitantly. Then in came one of the most ragged, down-at-heel men I had ever seen. Furtively, with caution, he crept through the door. Then with a sudden accession of haste he scuttled to the first table in his path—my table. I eyed him with astonishment. He was so extraordinarily, unbelievably down-and-out.

His clothes; they were ragged, patched, in holes. The jacket was too large for him; the trousers, contrarily, too short. On his head a shapeless rag sat insecurely on a tumbled heap of hair. His shoes were bound with string; paper and rags were stuffed into gaping mouths at the toes.

For a time he sat there, hunched up and cowering. Ever and again he writhed convulsively, as though seeking to achieve surcease from the activities of an unseen army of vermin. A semi-congealed stream ran from his nose, and with a swift movement he wiped it on his slimy sleeve. His face was damp, and this impressed you, not as perspiration, but as though he had washed and not dried himself. He had a rank growth of four or five days' beard, and somehow one could not imagine what he would look like without it; it was impossible to think of him clean-shaven.

After some moments it must have occurred to him that a down-and-out such as he could never expect to be waited on by a self-respecting café-proprietor. Wearily he dragged himself to his feet. For a moment he gazed fearfully around, as though expecting that someone would come up to him and throw him out.

From some receptacle in the lining of his jacket he produced, miraculously, some money. One, two, three, four, fivepence ha'penny, I saw him count slowly and uncertainly from one hand to the other.

He shuffled up to the counter, where the café-proprietor's fat wife prepared herself for the difficult ordeal of pretending that he wasn't there, and that, anyway, she wouldn't lower herself to serve him; whilst all the time he was, and she would.

"Tea," he said hoarsely. "One o' them," pointing to some rock-cakes.

He was served and his money taken.

Once more he sat down facing me. Fear, anxiety and weariness disappeared from him. The whole of his energies were bent on the task of absorbing the tea and the cake as quickly as possible. Savagely, intensely, he threw hot tea into his mouth, gulping, swallowing, coughing. Then he grabbed the cake, tore vicious bites, champed his jaws, followed with more tea.

In a few moments his orgasm was over. He sat there immobile, gazing hollowly in front of him. Then gradually fear and exhaustion returned. He writhed, glanced furtively over his shoulder, drooped himself wearily, then started, his eyes gliding in terror once again.

On a sudden impulse it occurred to me to offer him a cigarette. When one offers another a cigarette, it is customary for the recipient to say "Thanks", or something to that effect. But when I offered him one, he grabbed it in the most ungentlemanly way, without uttering a word. He waited for a light, and when it was given, inhaled deeply. Then he leaned his head dejectedly on his arms. Smoking, after one has been deprived of that luxury for some time, commencing again on a nearly empty stomach, can be rather an unpleasant experience. . . .

Then he lifted his head up and cautiously put the cigarette to his lips again. Suddenly he began to speak, and at first it was as though he spoke, not to a casual stranger, but to people who sternly demanded that he give an account of himself.

"I tramped the country, lookin' for work," he said hoarsely. "But yer can't get any work—nowhere! I tried—honest. I been out six years."

Then he blinked hard, and looked at me strangely, as though he saw me for the first time.

"Boy," he said, "never go on the road." The hoarseness of his voice gave him an air of intense seriousness. "You'll be driven from one town to 'nother. A vagrant, that's what they calls yer, a vagrant. Y'ave to go in the spike, else you get locked up. The police is after yer all the time. An' they'll nab yer as soon as they can lay 'ands on yer. Fer nothink at all. Nothink. . . ." His voice drifted away, the intelligence faded from his eyes.

"I slep' out," he mumbled, "las' four—five nights. Cold . . . bloody awful, the cold. Underneath the arches."

"Underneath the arches." The words had a familiar ring. They were from a popular song, declaimed with much enthusiastic romanticism in music-halls all over the country. "Underneath the arches, I dream my dreams away." That was how it went.

I happened to look up. I saw that we were the objects of amused observation by the proprietor and his wife. The proprietor smiled hurriedly at me in an anxious fashion, as though to say, "I assure you, this is most unusual. Not our regular type of patron, at all, I assure you." His wife adopted a look of superior indifference and went behind the counter.

The tramp looked up. He saw the café proprietors gazing at him, coldly inimical. He shrank from them. Hurriedly he got up, made for the door. He gave one look round, and I saw that fear had leaped into his eyes again. Fear of what? Fear of the café proprietors, of the police, of me, of all society. . . .

CHAPTER VI

A PROMISING JOB

WHEN I SCANNED the Vacancy Columns of the newspapers in my search for a job, I followed, if subconsciously, a definite method.

All the advertisements were in rigid alphabetical order, and so, after a time, I ceased to plough my way through the whole list, but first turned my attention to those beginning with the letter C. Jobs for cabinet-makers generally headed this section, and it was easy to tell at one glance whether there were any jobs going.

If, as was generally the case, cabinet-makers were a drug on the market, and employers failed to evince even the most luke-warm desire to employ any, I turned to the W column. Here I searched for jobs for woodworkers.

If, as was generally the case, the need for woodworkers was at a low ebb, I scanned the rest of the W column to see if, under the category of wanted, someone might be sending out an urgent call for men to fill any kind of vacancy which by the most elastic stretch of imagination I could conceive myself as capable of filling.

If, as was generally the case, the employers that morning were desperately, imperatively in need of every type of worker except the type to which I belonged, I searched the column F for any-thing remotely connected with Furniture. By this time I would be resigned to the fact that civilisation was managing to totter along with only the minimum of assistance from cabinet-makers and woodworkers, so I was not very surprised if nothing turned up under F. I now went painstakingly through the whole list of Vacancies, and ended, as a rule, by resigning myself to the fact that yet another day was lost, devoid of any definite jobs for me to go after.

One cold morning in February I opened my landlord's news-paper at the page for advertisements of Vacancies, and scarce had I begun to study the small print than it was as though some-thing leaped from the page and hit me in the eyes. No need to study section C! No need to travel patiently through the dis-appointing columns! There, right at the top of the page, a double-column display advertisement for—for—hold me, someone—for cabinet-makers! At last, in a world that scorned cabinet-makers, a world that failed to evince even the palest of interest in cabinet-makers, that worthy and unappreciated body of men had been elevated to their true rank in the society of workers. No lowly small-print advertisement tucked ignominiously away amongst capstan operators, coremakers, charge hands and chief engineers, mark you, but a banner decorating the top of the page, a banner in large print. See what the advertisement says:

Wanted Immediately, Cabinet-Makers and Improvers. Also Fitters, Polishers, and Improvers. 1/10 per hour for good men, also overtime, with extra rates of pay. Bonus for quick workers. Annual Holiday with Pay. Work all the Year Round. Apply Immediately, Bash, Crash & Trash, Furniture Manu-facturers, Sweatingham.

What dizzying prospect was this? I stayed to read no more. I put on my overcoat and hurried out into the street.

I was galvanized into an energy I had not known for a long time. I strode swiftly along. My mind was occupied with glowing visions of a new and brighter future. Good Wages! Bonus! Overtime! I was not very keen on the idea of overtime, I decided, but nevertheless, if that was a condition of accepting the job, then I was in no way inclined to spurn it. Besides, it would mean an extra few shillings a week, and a few extra shillings a week would come in very handy, particularly during the first few weeks after starting work.

I felt confident as I had never felt before. The space devoted to the advertisement was so large, and the terms offered were so favourable, that an acute need for workmen must be denoted. Moreover, they did not advertise for a mere one or two men, but for an unspecified number of workers of all grades. The fact that they were working overtime, and offering such unheard-of concessions as bonuses and holidays with pay—all this added to the impression of an urgent need for workers. I had started out early in the morning, and ought to get to the factory fairly early. I seemed almost certain to get a job.

So I hurried through the keen, gnawing cold of the February morning. I wished that I had money for fares, for after a short time my strength began to lag, and yet I must keep on hurrying. Delay might mean losing the job. If only I had money for fares! By now I could have been at the factory gates.

It seemed an endless journey, but finally, when I had begun to think that I could not keep up the pace much longer, I saw in the distance the name of the factory I was seeking painted large on the factory building. I made a spurt, eager to get finished with the ordeal of hurrying.

When I approached the factory I saw a group of men standing about on the corner of the pavement outside. My heart sank when I saw them. They did not look as though they were waiting to go in and ask for jobs. I could tell that because they seemed in no way tense or eager. Rather they appeared to be standing idly and without any particular task. I felt that they had already been in to ask for jobs, but that all vacancies had now been taken and they were just standing about talking before they went their several ways.

Nevertheless, I could not give up my hopes, and regard my long walk as futile, merely because of the aspect of some men outside the factory. I would at least have a try, whatever these men said. They were, after all, fully grown men of an average age in the middle thirties. Perhaps the factory had room for me, a younger fellow, even if it had already disposed of all jobs for fully grown craftsmen in the trade.

I walked towards the men, in the meantime seeking for some indication of the offices or inquiry department. As I reached the group, one of them came up to me.

"Hey, son," he said casually. "You goin' in there for a job?"

"Yes," I answered. "Are there any jobs going yet?"

"There's a strike on," he said briefly.

It was as though he had struck me. The real meaning of the alluring advertisement suddenly became plain. After my romantic visions, everything suddenly became grey and prosaic. It was a biting cold February morning. There was an ugly, rather repellant factory before my eyes. And there was a strike on.

"Oh," I said feebly.

The men gathered round me in an earnest, questioning group.

"You wouldn't want to blackleg, would you?" asked one of them.

"I——" I began.

"If you go in there," said another, "you're letting us down. You're letting *all* cabinet-makers down."

"I——" I began.

"Our fight's your fight, mate; remember that," another interposed.

"We've all got to stand together—all cabinet-makers, no matter where we work, whether we're out o' work, or what. Standing together, that's the thing. If we stick together we can win anything," said the first one who had approached me.

I managed to get a word in.

"It's alright!" I said hastily. "I'm not going to blackleg on you. I'm a Union man myself, anyway."

Their faces lightened immediately.

"Oh, you're a Union man, eh?"

"That's different, then."

"A Union man! That's the stuff!"

"What branch, mate?"

The last question rather stumped me. I had meant that I was a Union man in the spirit, even if I had never come into contact with my Union in any shop at which I had worked, had scarcely ever heard it mentioned, and had never been asked to join.

"Well—er—I'm not exactly in the Union now," I answered awkwardly. "But I'm one of you, anyway."

The man who had first approached me slapped me on the back.

"That's the stuff, mate. Believe me, things would be a lot better in the trade if we had more young fellows like you."

I was inclined to think that maybe he was merely trying to

flatter me in order to disarm me of any notion of blacklegging. Nevertheless, they all seemed sincere and honest men.

Now that I knew that there was no job for me in the factory, I felt no longer interested in the whole affair. I could not be interested in the strike or in anything. The combined effects of the raw cold of the morning and the long walk on an empty stomach were having the result of making me feel slightly sick. I wanted to go away. Nevertheless, for reasons of politeness I felt it necessary to evince some interest in the position.

"What's it all about?" I asked.

"Oh, you know what the guv'nors are like. You let 'em get away with one thing, and, sure enough, they want something else. Then they want something more."

"That's right," I assented mechanically.

"First the guv'nor puts a time limit on all the jobs. Everything had to be made in a certain time. Then he brings a feller along with a stop-watch. He watches every move you make, an' times yer. I shouldn't be surprised if 'e timed us when we went in the bog. And now the guv'nor wants us to go on piece-work, work overtime without anything extra, work Sat'day afternoons an' Sundays—I don't know what he doesn't want."

"He seems to want a lot," I said feebly.

"He doesn't know himself."

"Nothing's enough for them."

"The more they get, the more they want."

"He won't get away with it this time, though. We won't stand for it."

Another worker was approaching, and apparently most of them recognised him.

"Ah, look who it is," they exclaimed in friendly derision.

"What's the matter?" asked the newcomer.

"What d'you think's the matter? There's a strike on!"

"A strike? What for? What d'you want to strike for?"

They told him.

"You're not going to blackleg, are you?" they asked jokingly, as though the very idea was somewhat humorous.

"Anyway, it's no good you going in there for a job. He only wants blacklegs, and you're not a blackleg. You don't look like one, anyway."

"A blackleg," said one of them, "is a man with a dirty face and a dirty neck—doesn't wash behind his ears. But you washed yourself this morning. You look quite clean."

The newcomer disregarded these remarks.

"Wasted a —— tanner," he said in tones of chagrin. "Why the hell can't we get to know about these strikes beforehand?"

"Well," said the first one, "you know now. You spread the news rahnd amongst the boys. And you as well," he added to me; "tell all the boys there's a strike on here."

"O.K.," I agreed, though I could not think of any of "the boys" to whom I could impart this information. I decided that the time was favourable for me to move off now.

"Well, so long," I said. "And I wish you luck."

"Good for you, son," the other answered. "And if you come round here for a job when the strike's over, the boys'll remember you. We'll remember you didn't blackleg on us."

As I walked away, his words recurred to me. And my disappointment became transmuted into a sort of sombre pride. I was proud not merely because he had spoken those words to me. I was proud because here were plain men, the very stuff of the rank and file, men who worked at the bench, my mates, cabinet-makers, who in this time of unexampled distress could stand together and cry halt! to the attack of greedy employers, could organise a strike, and when a potential blackleg came along, they could put the issue to him plainly, simply, without any highfalutin words.

CHAPTER VII

THE SCARLET WOMAN

I GENERALLY FOUND the evenings to be the most empty and boring part of my days of unemployment. I got through them somehow—by reading, talking with my landlord and landlady, visiting my mother and sister in the East End, and so on. Nevertheless, in the flat and stale existence which is unemployment, a longing for something diverting, exciting and stimulating constantly torments the one unemployed. It would be with feelings at once of disappointment and relief that I realised that the long evening had come to an end, and it was time for me to go to bed.

Some evenings, irritated by a sense of frustration, I would stroll aimlessly through the streets, attempting to experience a vicarious enjoyment in thronging crowds, glaring cinema signs, and busy shopping centres. One Saturday evening when I was feeling more than ever in need to be in the midst of a diverting environment, I walked to the West End and gazed incredulously and hungrily at the theatres, cinemas, shops and restaurants which by the very fact of their existence tacitly assumed a world of carefree prosperity.

This sybaritic world of neon signs, wide clean streets, taxis, giant shops, well-dressed, carefree people, attracted me strongly.

On occasions, if I was not too tired, I used the West End as a kind of escape-valve for my frustrated desires for an evening of startling, miraculously gladdening enjoyment.

One night I walked through the West End, and eventually found myself in that region which contains Green Park, Hyde Park Corner, and St. George's Hospital. I turned back and began to walk quickly, for it was already after eleven o'clock, and I had a long walk to my lodgings before me. As I hurried along a young woman paused in front of me. It seemed to me that she asked me something.

"Beg your pardon?" I said, pausing.

"Would you like to come home with me, dear?" she asked, smiling.

I was surprised. Women of this kind did not show any desire to make my acquaintance, for my clothes made it clear that they could not hope for any gain from me. I was further surprised because I had thought that street-walkers (which was what I assumed this girl to be) were blousy, painted drabs; whereas this young woman seemed pretty and unspoiled. Her manner was gay and fresh. Her eyes, particularly, seemed to express an amused, almost contemptuous happiness.

"No, thanks," I answered.

It seemed as though she were about to lay a detaining hand on my arm and expostulate with me. From references to prostitutes which I had occasionally come across in literature, I had gathered that they might become abusive if spurned.

"In any case," I added, "I haven't got any money."

"Haven't you? Oh, I'm sorry, mate. But that doesn't matter. Come home with me for the evening. I want someone to talk to."

She uttered the words with a sort of ardent impulsiveness. Her eyes smiled happily as she spoke. I could not decide whether she was Irish, Scotch or Welsh; her accent seemed to have the brogues of all three.

Maybe I had made a mistake? She certainly didn't bear out my idea of a prostitute. For a moment I stood undecided before this altogether unexpected invitation. In the long, arid waste of evenings here at last was something piquant and unusual. Should I pass it by? It did not take me long to decide. The girl was very attractive to me.

"Alright," I agreed.

I was reassured against some vague doubt by reason of the fact that she smiled up at me again happily, and there was gratitude in her smile. Rather daringly I permitted myself to feel friendly towards her. Again I thought she was very pretty. She had red-

135

gold hair which was attractively, but not extravagantly arranged. Her small nose was saucy and slightly upturned, whilst her eyes were large and bright, and seemed alight with inward happiness.

By her direction we turned and walked in the direction of Victoria Station. I did not know the neighbourhood, and for a moment uneasiness took hold of me again. Supposing she was just playing some sort of a prank with me? She certainly had that expression. Or maybe I would get mixed up in something?—something ugly or frightening. After all, in a place like London one never knew what ugly, frightening things might be hidden beneath the surface. My thoughts were interrupted.

"You know," she said happily, "I was just going to go home when I saw you."

"Oh."

"Isn't this rain awful? Not very much of it, y'know, but it is a nuisance, isn't it?"

"Yes, it is." We were about to cross a street, and I kept my eyes open for traffic.

"Yes, I do hate the rain," she said mournfully. "Oh—be careful!" she exclaimed.

I gazed at her in surprise. She had laid one detaining hand on my arm, and the other on her breast.

"Oh, I'm scared to death of the traffic! I always think I'm goin' to get knocked down. I'm sure that one o' these days I'll be killed by a motor-car."

"People who think that kind of thing——" I began sombrely. She interrupted me.

"Are you Scotch?" she asked.

"No."

I thought the question abruptly irrelevant.

"I'm Irish," she replied, and giggled as one bashfully confessing something rather derogatory.

"Oh. Been in London long?"

She laid a hand on my arm again, as one who is about to retail information of great importance and wishes the utmost attention. All gaiety of manner had dropped from her. She was very much in earnest.

"I was in Liverpool," she began dramatically, hurriedly. "And I was out o' work. Couldn't get a job—anywhere. Then I came to London."

"How?" I interspersed.

She ignored my question. The sentences poured from her. Her eyes were wide.

"I got a job in the X Hotel, near Leicester Square. What a place. Nothin' but a ——" (she used an obscene term for a

136

brothel). "Nothin' but that. That's what it was. All the actors an' actresses. It was a good place, mind ye. Plenty o' tips, an' that. But I had a row with the manager. He was a bastard—a real bastard. I called him everything. 'E gemme the sack. I didn't get no references."

I found her story and her language somewhat painfully at variance with the ideas I had formed of her from her fresh, happy appearance. I prepared to sympathise vaguely, but she rushed on :

"I'm waiting for the season. That's what I'm waiting for—the season. I think I'll be alright in the season, don't you?"

"What's the season?"

She simultaneously ignored and answered my query.

"In the season the hotels an' that are not so particular. They're so busy, they take on anybody. Won't matter much if I 'aven't got a reference." She was gazing in front of her, as one who gazes at some dearly desired object, half afraid that it will disappear ere she can possess it. "I'll get a job," she said softly—"get a job. Save up. And then I'll go away."

"Will you go home to Ireland?"

She looked towards me with a happy, insouciant smile. It was as though at first she did not see me. "Have a sweet?" she asked, and fumbled in her bag.

An idea had suddenly occurred to me. The poor kid was a bit drunk, that was what was the matter with her. I felt somehow disappointed. Should I take leave of her now? No. She was very attractive to me. Besides, it was interesting to be with her. She had a story to tell, and I would listen to it.

She gave me a sweet, but hurriedly closed her bag without taking one herself. Again she gazed before her, absorbed.

"I didn't have the price of a cup o' tea, an' when I met two girls I used to know, an' asked 'em to lend me a couple o' bob, they ses they never lends money to no one." Her face frowned with pain, and a sort of puzzled, childish anger. Her eyes were clouded and troubled. "There's bloody friends for you!—friends! Friends when you've got money, an' when you're on the stones, an' ask 'em to lend you—oh, only a bob, a coupla bob!—they can afford to do it; they won't miss it, an' to you it means everything—they turns round an' says they never lend anybody anything. There's friends for you!"

"Yes," I began, "people——"

Suddenly she shook with silent laughter. "Tell me," she giggled. "Why d'you go about without a hat?"

I was rather disconcerted. "Well——" I began.

"It's alright, dear," she said kindly, putting her arm through

137

mine and patting it. "We're nearly there. You don't mind, do you?"

"Mind what?" I asked. Her swift changes of mood and conversation were somewhat baffling. "She's real drunk, she is," I thought, and felt rather sorry for her. I was embarrassed by her arm being through mine. It placed us on a rather more intimate basis than I was prepared for at the moment.

She made no reply to my question, and for a time we walked on in silence. It occurred to me how odd it was that I should be walking about a strange neighbourhood with a young woman who a few minutes previously had been totally unknown to me. And here we were walking through the streets, her arm in mine, after eleven o'clock, towards an unknown destination. For a moment I felt that I was engaging in a rather silly, unreal enterprise, and wondered again whether I should leave her or not. She interrupted my thoughts.

"Are you Scotch?" she asked.

"No. I . . . er. . . ."

"I'm Irish," she giggled.

I wondered whether she realised that she had asked me the same question and given me the same information once before. But then, if she were drunk she wouldn't realise these details.

"I was out o' work for a very long time——" she began.

"How long?" I interrupted.

Once again she gave me the impression of ignoring my question, and yet replying to it quite incidentally, as it were.

"——A year an' three months. An' then I met a coupla girls I useter know and asked them to lend me a coupla shillin's. And do you know—the mean bastards—they wouldn't lend me a penny—not a penny. There's friends for you! An' me on the stones!"

"This is getting tedious," I thought.

"An' then one night I went for a walk in the park, an' a man stopped me an' asked me if I would go with 'im, an' 'e gave me a pound!" She shook with silent laughter. "There's easy money for you!"

"Yeh."

"D'you know Richmond at all?" she asked inconsequentially.

"I'm afraid I don't."

"D'you think I could get a job there in the summer? It's nice there in the summer, isn't it?"

I was about to say that I didn't know, then decided to say "yes", but she went on before I could reply:

"If I wouldn't'a' met a man, I don't know what I would'a' done. An' 'e gemme a pound. You could'a' knocked me over

138

with a feather. A pound!" She giggled. "An' them mean bastards wouldn't lend me a coupla shillin's. I don't know what my poor mother would be after thinkin' if she knew. But then," she added gaily, her eyes alight with amusement again, "they got plenty o' money. What's a pound to them?"

I had given up expecting any order or sequence to her remarks. The conversation at once irritated and interested me. It irritated me because I wanted a consecutive conversation. I also wanted someone to talk to, some stranger whom I could tell of my experiences and yet know that we would never meet again. But with this girl it was impossible to discuss anything. Her utterances flew from one tangent to another. I never had any indication of what she would say next.

"It's funny when you come to think of it," I said. "A pound's nothing to some people, and to others it's a fortune. Now I——"

She nudged me excitedly.

"We're nearly there," she whispered, and giggled. "Sure, an' I always get so nervous in case my landlady ever finds out."

Her whisper became softer and softer, until I could scarcely hear her words. "You won't make any noise going up the stairs, will you?"

I had not been sure all along whether I would actually accompany her to her room. Her tacit assumption that I would at once disquieted me and made me thrill with anticipation.

As we progressed along the quiet, empty street, her manner became more and more conspiratorial. Occasionally she glanced over her shoulder, as though on the look-out for unseen enemies. Then "Here we are," she whispered tensely, and then she giggled. "Be careful," she breathed; "don't make a noise."

She unlocked the door and then well-nigh tiptoed up the long, narrow lobby. On the left-hand side, doors led into mysterious rooms which seemed, on account of the secrecy of our movements, to hide goodness knows what dread and formidable beings, any one of whom might suddenly throw open the door and make outraged protestations. On the right-hand side were two or three hallstands. We negotiated the lobby in the midst of a threatening and hostile silence. She turned to look round at me, her gaze half fearful, half triumphant.

"Don't make any noise," she breathed, and with difficulty repressed a giggle.

I was by now repentant of the whole affair, and wished that I had not allowed myself to become involved in this somewhat melodramatic escapade. Moreover, each time she giggled I felt, for some obscure reason, less enamoured of her company. However, I was almost afraid to turn back now, though it occurred to

139

me that if I were seen when I left, later, it might be more awkward still to explain matters.

We entered her room—a typical bedsitting-room, with its table, two chairs, chest-of-drawers and bed. There was a faint musty odour about the room which struck me unpleasantly at first, but which I immediately forgot.

She crossed the room and lit a gasfire, and then took off her overcoat.

"Sit down, dear," she said. "Take your coat off."

I sat down, but without taking my coat off.

"Can I have the money now, dear?" she asked.

"This is where the trouble starts," I thought. "Why on earth did I have to come here, anyway?" Aloud I said very firmly, hiding the awkwardness I felt, "I told you before, I haven't got any money."

"Haven't you? Well, never mind, then. I've got plenty. But I can't lend *you* any. I'll never be after lendin' anybody any money. Never!"

"I don't want any," I said, but I wondered how she would have fared had I been a glib-tongued trickster.

Forthwith she took off her dress, and stood revealed before me. She seemed to me to be a vision of surpassing beauty. Her slender body was perfectly formed, and was clad in thin underwear of a faint rosy hue. Her gold-red hair, white face and scarlet lips were a matchless combination of colour.

The admiration and desire which overwhelmed me were somewhat damped by a feeling of guilt. It wasn't really fair that she should be like this before me. Whatever one thought of her vocation, she was really paid for this sort of thing. And I couldn't pay her anything. For a moment I wished violently that I had a lot of money to lay before her, whilst at the same time it was at once ridiculous and ignoble to reckon such an encounter in terms of money.

She came over and sat on my knee, suffusing me with ardent emotions.

Nevertheless, even as she sat on my knee, I was already fabricating reasons to myself as to why she was not desirable. Your youth or maiden who are the product of an over-moral upbringing often discover, when faced with the opportunity, that they want to retreat from the very situation for which they have longed. Moreover, at the back of my mind was the guilty feeling that all this was wrong, that these circumstances reeked of crude immorality.

So it was that I found myself noting carefully that she was not quite so pretty and unspoiled as she had first seemed. Her

140

face was too white, her lips too red. That which in the street had seemed a natural pallor enhancing her beauty proved at close quarters to be due to a somewhat liberal application of powder. Under the street lights her features had seemed the perfection of youthful freshness, but now I observed that they were a little sunken, and that there were slight wrinkles here and there that marred my earlier impressions. Nevertheless, I still thought her very beautiful, and her presence on my knee still filled me with ardour.

"What are you thinking about?" she asked thoughtfully, stroking my hair.

"I think," I murmured slowly, "that you——"

"You have nice hair," she said. "Are you Scotch?"

"Yes," I lied, in curiosity, "I'm a Scotsman."

"I come from Glasga," I went on, trying to neutralise my emotions through flippancy. "I come from Glasga, from the Gorr-r-bals. D'you know the Gorr-r-bals?"

Her insistent desire to know if I were a Scotsman seemed to have no foundation, however. "I think I'll wear green," she mused. "D'you like me in green?"

"I've never——"

"They say it's a lucky colour," she went on thoughtfully. "D'you think I'll get a job in Richmond? Oh, it'll be nice in the country in the summer!"

Suddenly she shook with silent laughter, clasping me about the neck. "What d'you think of that—of me—my photograph?"

I looked at the photograph on the mantel-piece. Her hair was long and piled richly down her back. She gazed at the photographer with all the questioning earnestness of noble adolescence.

"I think it's a very good photograph—very good."

"Oh, do you think so? You say such nice things, such kind things. You're very nice."

I was not aware that I had said anything very nice and kind to her as yet. Nevertheless, her gratitude made me feel as though in some way I was being nice and kind.

She seemed now desirous of securing my approval of everything. "What d'you think of me?" she asked. "Have I a nice figure? I have, haven't I?"

"Yes, you have. Very nice." I wanted to say more, but I felt that anything else I might add would be either too trite or too high-flown.

"Give me some more money," she coaxed. "Sure, an' you have some more. You're only kiddin' that you haven't any more."

This was a somewhat disagreeable admixture to the conversation. I hated her assumption that I had sought to win her favours with money, and still more I hated to have to confess yet again that I had none.

"I—have—no—money," I said, with irritated firmness.

"Haven't you? Never mind. You're only a working chap. I understand. I'd sooner have a working chap any day than one o' these swell toffs." She shook with silent laughter. "They're no good. No good at all."

"What d'you think of my room?" she went on. "I hate it." She giggled.

"Oh, it's not a bad room. I don't think you'd get anything better, unless you're willing to pay a high rent."

"I think it's awful," she smiled.

"All rooms are awful when you live in them by yourself."

"Isn't that right?" she smiled. "You go to bed, and you lie awake thinkin' of all your troubles, and you feel as if any minute you're goin' to go mad—mad."

Suddenly a suspicion which had been stirring vaguely at the back of my mind leapt up and came to the forefront. The girl was not drunk at all. She showed no signs of it. Simply—she was a little out of her mind.

"Is that—how you feel—sometimes?" I asked cautiously.

"I used to," she smiled. "But not now. Not so much as I used to."

"I see. . . ."

It was gruesome in that quiet room to think that this young girl who smiled at me was not quite in her right mind. I had no doubt of it now. In popular parlance she was "not all there". Her mind had been twisted askew by the relentless pressure of circumstances. I suddenly understood the meaning of the phrase. She was not all *there*. Had I not felt all along that what I said was not reaching Her, the real Her? The real Her was hidden away somewhere, hidden beneath a cloudy confusion of the mind. At first she had taken no notice of anything I had said. My remarks had simply not reached her. She had used me as a means of conversing with herself. It is not right that one should speak to oneself, alone. Therefore, she had spoken to herself through me.

I felt impelled to question her. "Do you—that is to say— have you any friends?"

She was smiling dreamily, gazing before her. At first I was not certain whether she had heard me. Then she slowly shook her head, and frowned. "No," she murmured distastefully, "no friends. I wouldn't be after lendin' money to anyone." She was silent for a few moments. "When I go to Richmond," she began again, smiling. Then she turned, and she saw my questioning gaze upon her. Her eyes suddenly grew wide with terror and rage. She slipped from my knee. She stood before me, her hands defensively over her breasts.

"What're ye after lookin' at me like that for?" she shouted. "What d'ye want?"

I was appalled. The silence, peace and intimacy of the room were shattered to fragments. There was this girl, a stranger but undressed, standing before me, shouting.

"It's alright," I said uncertainly. "Don't shout. There's nothing to get upset about."

"Leave me alone!" she shouted. Her eyes were wide with fear and hate. She turned from me and began weeping passionately. "Oh, Mother o' God, what am I doin'? What would my mother be after sayin' if she knew?"

"Now, now, don't get upset," I reiterated feebly.

"Leave me alone!" she sobbed. Her tears ran into the powder on her face. Her uniform of coquetry seemed now like fancy dress on a child who has been overtaken by tragedy at a party.

She turned on me, and there was a wild look in her eyes. An impenetrable silence brooded over the room, the house, the whole street.

"Go away," she said in a low intense voice. "I don't want ye here. What good are ye, anyway?"

I was sorry for her, but I could not see what I could do to help her. Moreover, I was excruciatingly nervous in case some people in the house might have been attracted by her shouts. They might come bursting into the room. . . .

"Why don't ye go *away*?"

I needed no further bidding. "Goodnight," I said hastily, and made for the door.

The house was still and undisturbed. Nevertheless, to my wrought-up imagination it seemed alive with dreadful possibilities. I hurried down the stairs and along the lobby, as in one of those nightmares in which one runs and runs, but never makes any progress. All around me were ghostly presences, gibbering and weeping, with faces that were masks of tragedy.

I gained the street door. I fumbled an eternity with the latch. The door opened. The cool night air came to me healingly. I closed the door behind me. It was still sanely raining.

I walked hurriedly along the pavement. How do I get to Hyde Park Corner? I was just another pedestrian now. I had a long walk in front of me. The street was very quiet.

END OF BOOK FOUR

BOOK FIVE

JOURNEYINGS IN THE WILDERNESS

CHAPTER I

THE P.A.C.

Towards the end of the year I received a printed letter from the Labour Exchange. The letter said that I was required to attend at the Exchange on a certain day and time for an interview with the manager.

The manager of a Labour Exchange is, in the official sense, like the King. Documents may be sent out in his name, but that does not necessarily imply that he himself is aware of the document or its contents. Consequently I found that my interview was not with the manager, but with a Labour Exchange clerk.

The clerk set himself to make a record of my periods of employment and unemployment. He asked me a number of questions relating to the places where I had worked, the time I had worked at them, whether or not I had been seriously ill in the past years, whether I had any disability, and so on.

Some time afterwards I received a further letter from the Labour Exchange. This letter was brief and to the point. It stated in so many words that my benefit was suspended as and from 21/12/32, pending the decision of a Court of Referees. As 21/12/32 was the day on which I received the letter, it meant that without notice of any kind I had had my whole source of income cut off.

It was an overwhelming blow. I did not even have the satisfaction of knowing when the Court of Referees was going to meet, or for what purpose my case was being brought before them.

After I had thought the matter over it seemed to me that there was only one way out, for the time being. I would have to apply for relief as soon as possible. As I would be getting a week's dole that week (I hoped), I would not be able to apply for relief just yet. Nevertheless, I would have to do so the following week.

I sat down on the bed to think matters over. On one thing I was determined. I was not going to repeat the disastrous experience of the previous New Year. I would get relief out of them somehow.

But how? Supposing the Relieving Officer refused? What could

144

I do? Murder him? If I did, that would hardly help me to get relief. I would be past needing it.

A week passed without further incident. On the Thursday of the following week I went to the offices of the Public Assistance Committee. It was the same authority before whom I went to be questioned in connection with my "Means Test". However, I was not going there now to have my means, or lack of them, assessed with a view to the amount of Unemployment Benefit I could get. I was applying for relief, and would have to go before a different group of officials.

The place was very cold and damp. The floor was of stone flags, and the walls of the narrow passage were also of bare stone and brick. There was the same shabby crowd lounging restlessly against the stone walls of the narrow passage. Draughts blew spasmodically, and everyone muttered with cold and impatience. Now and again the door of one of the offices opened. Someone came out, another went in.

There was the usual desultory conversation that sounds so melodramatic and propagandist in books, so prosaic in everyday life.

One man with a lean, grey face was saying to his neighbour:

"I bin out o' work three weeks. I put a —— claim in at the Labour Exchange the day arter I come out. I'm —— if I've 'eard a word since. I bin signin' on at the Supervisor's counter every day. I ses to 'im, "Ere! When am I goin' ter get some money?' 'E ses, 'It's alright. You needn't worry. We'll fix it up fer yer soon.' I ses, 'An what am I goin' to do in the meantime?' Believe me, mate, we ain't got a crust o' bread in the 'ouse, we 'aven't."

The man was trying to speak as disinterestedly as though he were describing some minor domestic incident. Only a certain tension in the low, hurried voice, and an imperfectly veiled glare of bitter hatred in his eyes, told of his real feelings.

The other, a burly, thick-set man, with a three days' beard, dressed in worn dungarees and a torn jacket, spat on the floor and said:

"Well, I'm —— if I'd wait three weeks, mate, an' that's a fact. If I didn't 'ave anything in the 'ouse, I'd go an' get it. That's honest, that is."

Whether by "honest" he was referring to what he would do, or to the sincerity of his feelings in the matter, I could not immediately determine.

I had come to P.A.C. in a mood of cynical distaste. I made ferocious remarks to those about me on the loathsome character of the Relieving System, on the methods of granting relief, on how the authorities spent a pound in order that an applicant for relief should not get a shilling more than was regarded as essential to keep him alive, on how cattle were better treated than applicants for relief, who were forced to hang about for hours in draughty corridors.

The morning passed slowly. At midday an official poked his head out of the office and said casually:

"You fellows come back this afternoon."

We dispersed with many muttered curses against officials who seemed to think that we had nothing better to do than wait in their corridors all day till they saw fit to see us.

At two o'clock we assembled again, with sarcastic inquiries amongst ourselves as to whether the officials would interview us before Christmas.

A little before four o'clock it was my turn to go before the Relieving Officer. I went in prepared for a stubborn struggle, determined not to go out again till I had secured relief of some kind. However, the interview proved to be somewhat of an anti-climax. When I explained that I was applying for relief because my Unemployment Benefit had been suspended, I was given a form to take to my box-clerk when I signed on at the Labour Exchange the next day. With this I had to be satisfied, after a day's futile waiting.

There was no money for me when I signed on the next morning. I gave the P.A.C. form to my box-clerk. Perspiring before the endless, unabating stream of signers-on, the box-clerk glanced hurriedly at the form, and told me to bring it back to him at twelve o'clock. With feelings of ever-growing fury I went out of the Exchange. Living, as I did, over two miles away, it was not worth while for me to go back to my lodgings and then return to the Labour Exchange. I would have to hang about here for an hour and a half. In the time that remained for me to secure relief before the week ended a valuable morning would be wasted.

I walked aimlessly up and down the busy main road, glanced in at the Public Library, and was repelled by the shabby, hungry crowds that swarmed round the meagre vacancy columns of the papers, or sat at the tables, gazing unseeingly at magazines that depicted the most exclusive sections of "society" being very exclusive and very "society" very expensively and very inanely.

At twelve o'clock I took the form back to my box-clerk, and on it he verified that my Unemployment Benefit had indeed been suspended and that I was not applying for relief in order to swindle the State.

A little after two o'clock I was again leaning against the stone walls of the corridor in the P.A.C. building and wondering whether my case would be attended to.

There were not so many waiting as there had been on the previous day, and at about three o'clock I was called into the office. This was a small, unpretentious room, occupied chiefly by two tables. At each of these tables an official dealt with an applicant for relief.

I was glad that I did not wear a hat, for those who did were required to take them off on entering the office. It was not left to the individual to remove his hat from custom or civility (or some might say, servility); he was definitely instructed (or some might say commanded):

"Take your hat off!"

The Relieving Officer asked me whether I'd applied for relief before. Ignoring the fact that I had applied for relief in Forgeton, I said, "No." That application had been in another town, and anyway, I had not been given anything.

The Relieving Officer drew before him a nice, new, clean file, and a number of lengthy forms. With a sort of sensuous enjoyment he prepared himself to fill in the forms.

One by one, with slow solemnity, he made his inquiries. There were the usual questions as to my name, age, and address and circumstances, how long I had lived at my present address, where I had been previously, and where I had been before that, why I left Forgeton. Finally came the crucial question:

"Are you single or married?"

I braced myself for trouble.

"I'm single."

"Oh. You're single? We don't give relief to single men."

"What do you mean—you don't give relief to single men?" I snapped. "The question of whether I'm single or married doesn't affect the question of whether you grant me relief or not. It only affects the amount of relief."

Outwardly I might have appeared angry, domineering, but inwardly I was filled with anxiety as to the effect my words would have on him. My heart sank, for he appeared unmoved.

"Have you no relatives who can help you in any way?"

"No."

I was damned if I was going to be parked on to relatives of mine who had not enough to maintain themselves.

"Well"—he shrugged his shoulders unconcernedly—"you won't get any relief from us. We're not allowed to give relief to single men."

"Don't tell me that!" I said derisively. "You know yourself you'se compelled by law to give relief to those who are without

147

means of support. It's a criminal offence," I went on wildly, determined to shake him somehow. "And if *I* can't get you to give me relief, I'll take the matter up with those who can."

Again he seemed unmoved. I felt as though I were expending my energies punching a large, well-stuffed cushion.

"Anyway," he said casually, "you're destitute. You'll have to go to the workhouse."

A pang of fear smote me. The workhouse? A yawning gap seemed to open beneath my feet.

"You don't know what you're talking about," I said desperately. "Destitute? A destitute person is someone who has nowhere to live. I have a definite place of abode. Therefore how can I be destitute?"

I had no idea whether this definition and other statements I had made that afternoon were correct. I had a vague idea that what I was saying might be correct, but I was not sure.

"Maybe you have a fixed place of abode," he said sardonically. "But how are you going to pay the rent if you have no means of support?"

"That's my business!" I snapped.

"No," he said, shaking his head slowly, "I'm afraid you'll have to go to the workhouse."

He seemed quite definitely to enjoy this prospect of my future. Once again I felt appalled. Nevertheless I could not give up. I must get relief out of him somehow. How? Somehow.

"I tell you," I exclaimed, very nearly shouting, "that you're acting contrary to the law by refusing me relief. You're satisfied yourself that I'm in need of relief, and yet you refuse it. You won't get away with it. I'll get the matter taken up."

"Well, anyway," he said in a manner half casual, half weary, "I'm not going to give you any relief. That's final. If you want to, you can fill up this form. I don't know that it'll do you any good. Here." He tossed a form towards me. "Fill it up outside."

I grabbed the form, and, as in a fever, hurried outside with it. I had had numerous forms to fill up before now, but they were all pygmies compared with this one. It was a giant, a Colossus of forms. It probed into every conceivable detail of a man's history. It ranged from his name, age, address and relatives, to illnesses and disabilities, pensions, and each separate section of the armed forces to which he might or might not have been attached. I was, however, accustomed to filling up forms, and even this form did not daunt me. I filled it up in record time. Then I re-entered the room. I found that my somewhat hectic encounter with the Relieving Officer appeared to have had an effect on the man applying for relief at the next table. He had started out by being very timid and propitiatory, even servile. Now, however, he was banging his fist on the table, and shouting:

"What the hell! Suppose I was earning three pounds a week! How much do you suppose a man with a wife and three kids can save on that money?"

My Relieving Officer was already dealing with another applicant. I was, however, in no mood for further waiting. I went up to the table and shoved the form under his nose.

He took the form, but did not even glance at it. Then from under the papers on his desk he took a small piece of paper, about the size of a postcard. He tossed it negligently towards me.

"Here," he said carelessly, "that's all the relief you'll get."

I was astounded and overwhelmed with sensations of victory. I almost staggered from the room in my excess of joy. So I had won! After his obdurate, careless and negligent insistence that he was not going to give me any relief, the fact that he had given me at least something almost overpowered me after the tension and feverish anxiety of the interview. Then I glanced at the form and discovered that it was for six shillings. Even this as an amount to live on for a whole week in no way damped my ardour. I went out drunk with victory.

CHAPTER II

THE COURT OF REFEREES

I HAD NOT been given relief in cash, but had been given a form entitling me to get groceries to the value of six shillings. This form has on it a list of various groceries and household commodities. The grocer who takes such a form has to write against each item the amount spent. Goods can, of course, be taken only to the amount of the value on the form.

I explained my position to the people with whom I was lodging, and they cheerfully waived the question of the rent for the time being, although I knew that they were very hard up and depended on the rent I paid them. I wondered what would happen supposing I lost my case at the Court of Referees.

Meantime I "spent" the relief ticket at a nearby grocery shop, and tried to pretend to myself that things were just the same as usual with me. I spent a very nice Christmas that year, thanks to the combined efforts of the Ministry of Labour and the P.A.C.

During that week I received a form from the Labour Exchange telling me that the Court of Referees would be considering my case on the 3rd of January. There was also enclosed for my perusal a copy of the data which would be before the Court of Referees in connection with my case.

I discovered from this, somewhat to my astonishment, that the matter which the Court of Referees would be deciding was "whether from and including 21/12/32 the claimant is normally employed in and will normally seek to obtain his livelihood by means of insurable employment."

Apparently, at a time when there were approximately 3,000,000 unemployed, and there were no jobs to be got, the machinery of the Labour Exchange had nothing better to occupy itself with than surmisals as to whether I would ever again be employed in an insurable occupation. Surely the answer to this was obvious. As soon as trade allowed, I *would* re-enter insurable work. Until I had the opportunity, and either took it or refused it, what was the use of guessing? After all, the Labour Exchange itself had so far failed to find one single job to send me after.

As evidence that I was prepared to take any job going were three stamps on my cards for a period of three weeks I had spent on a miserable canvassing job in which I had earned barely the equal of my unemployment benefit. I imagined that most un-employed who had been out of work since the beginning of the crisis would have had difficulty in getting even such a "job" as this.

I was not very hopeful about the outcome of the Court of Referees. I had had previous experience of such a Court. In my nineteenth year I worked for a sweating employer. The effects of weeks of working from eight in the morning till eight or nine at night entirely alone in a slum workshop (whilst the boss rested himself in front of the fire in his house round the corner) were aggravated by the increasingly insulting attitude my boss took up towards me. Finally, after a couple of weeks' sullen silence on my part, we quarrelled furiously. Afterwards I reached the con-clusion that probably he engineered the situation in which I had to have a quarrel with him or lose my self-respect. The quarrel took place in the slack season, and when it was time for him to redeem his long overdue promise of giving me a rise. In his own words, he gave me "Paddy's rise"—*i.e.*, the sack. In the quarrel, however, I told him off very efficiently, to such an extent that I left him smarting with rage.

The result was that he wrote to the Labour Exchange inform-ing them that I was "the most insolent fellow" he had ever had working for him. This flattering estimate was based on about four and a half months' employment of me; during most of this time we had said barely anything to each other apart from purely technical and financial questions.

"Oh, Forgeton!" exclaimed one. "I myself come from Forgeton."

He said this in a tone that made me think he felt that I and Forgeton ought to be flattered by this fact. The man on the right-hand side of the Chairman also interposed.

"I came from Bradford once," he said, and there was a proud note in his voice too, as one who would say, "See how I have advanced in life. I once came from Bradford, and look at me now."

There were interchanges of sentimental remarks about the Old Town, remarks such as:

"You can't beat the folks up North, I say."

"What Forgeton thinks today, London thinks tomorrow, you know."

Then finally, the one who had said he originally came from Forgeton, turned to me and said:

"Why did you come to London?"

"Why did you?" I thought. Aloud I said, "Trade was bad in Forgeton, and I thought I could get a job in London quicker."

"Why not try to go back to Forgeton?" he asked.

I wanted to ask him why he didn't do the same, but of course, he had a job of some kind here, one supposed, and I hadn't. Therefore he possessed the right to ask me such a question, whereas I had none to ask him a similar question.

"It would be too expensive," I said briefly.

"Don't you think perhaps you might be able to get a job in Forgeton?"

"I don't know," I replied. "From what I've heard from friends, trade is very bad up there just now—if possible, worse than in London. And in the long run I might be worse off by going back there. Now that I'm down here I might as well stay here."

There appeared to be nothing more to be said on this subject, and so they began to devote themselves to the more technical aspects of my case, such as when and where I had worked in the past, and the fact that I had three stamps in the last twelve months. Then inevitably they seized upon the phrase in the "remarks" on my form which, for some peculiar reason, said "Efforts during the last week or so appear restricted". Suddenly one of them asked:

"Where have you been looking for work? Where did you go, for instance, a week ago today?"

It was impossible for me to remember. However, I was familiar by now with almost every firm in the areas in which I sought work, and could practically have recited them backwards. I reeled off a list of names at hazard.

"Where were you a month ago? To what firms did you apply?" another one asked.

I was rather surprised at these questions. I had not thought that these "decent fellows" would ask such types of questions—questions so inane that it was remarkable that anybody at a Court of Referees should ask them. But maybe the Government preferred to choose the kind of person who was sufficiently naïve to attach importance to this type of question.

"I seem to remember," I thought ironically, "that constant protest forced the Government to withdraw the 'Not-Genuinely Seeking Work' clause. However, it apparently doesn't matter what the laws of the land are as far as Courts of Referees are concerned. If you can make a man lose his presence of mind and stammer and stutter and suddenly become at a loss, and unable to tell you where he sought work a month ago—well then, that's all in the game, I suppose."

However, I felt in no way disposed to challenge them on these questions. For a moment I looked vague, as though I were seriously trying to remember where I had sought work a month ago—as though in the grey monotony of days, when one day was just like another, it was possible to tell what one had done a month ago. I reeled off another route for their edification. They seemed to be quite satisfied with my reply; at any rate, they were in no way suspicious. That, however, did not elate me. I did not even feel contemptuous of them. I merely didn't care about them.

"Have you ever tried to get work at another occupation?" the Forgeton man asked me.

"From a strictly legal point of view," I thought, "I should imagine that that question, also, is *ultra vires*, as they say in legal jargon. If I made any attempts to secure a job in another trade, then I did so entirely voluntarily, of my own accord. I doubt whether you, as a Court of Referees, are entitled to regard me with favour or disfavour on this question of whether I sought work or did not seek work outside the occupation for which I am registered."

However, I did not feel like debating this point either. Aloud I said:

"Yes, once I tried to get a job as a secretary to a synagogue, and on another occasion I very nearly got a job hawking bananas. I tried to get various other jobs," I ended vaguely.

"And none of them came off?"

"No."

"How was that?"

"There were different reasons. Somebody got the job before I did, and sometimes the job didn't exist."

"And how was that?"

"Well, I heard about these different jobs from people who did not understand that it is important to go after jobs early, soon after they are vacant. They generally told me about these jobs in a casual sort of way, some time, maybe even a week, after they heard that the job was going."

"I see. And have you ever applied to your local Rabbi to see if he could get you a job?"

"Since when has a Rabbi been an unpaid official of the Ministry of Labour?" I thought. Aloud I said, "Yes," although I had had no dealings with Rabbis for a number of years.

"And did he put you in touch with any jobs?"

"No."

"How was that? Didn't he know of any—a Rabbi?"

I suddenly felt sarcastic.

"A Rabbi gets so many people asking him for jobs," I answered quietly, but with a certain emphasis on various words. "He could hardly put all of us in touch with jobs."

"That's so." They looked at me suspiciously. They couldn't quite decide whether my tone was meant to be impertinent. I looked impassive.

They asked me a few more questions, and then told me to wait outside.

As I waited I made a mental survey of the Court's trial. Had anyone been able to read my thoughts they would think that I had been biassed and prejudiced against the members of the Court. But who can blame an unemployed man for being biassed and prejudiced against the machinery that dictates the terms of his existence? He knows that in many ways the machinery is biassed and prejudiced against him, despite a diplomatic appearance of courtesy, even of friendliness. In the present case, for instance, the members of the Court had asked quite a number of questions which they were not legally entitled to ask. And in any case, the whole purpose of the "trial" was, in my opinion, a futile farce.

I did not feel anxious about whether I would win the case or not. I did not care. Fifteen and threepence—no fifteen and three-pence—what did it matter? I could not feel that it mattered any more. After a time the clerk called me back. Once again I faced the Court.

"Well, Mr. Cohen," the Chairman said kindly, "we have decided to allow your claim. But you must try to get work, you know. You will only get benefit for another six months, and after that, whether we like it or not, we shall be compelled to refuse you any further benefit."

The clerk gave me a little green form that stated that my claim had been allowed by the Court. I said "Thank you, good afternoon," and went out.

I did not feel elated at the decision of the Court. It seemed to have made no difference at all to my circumstances. So they wanted me to get a job within six months, did they? A year ago such a remark would have made me smile. Get a job in six months?—that was easy. But now it made me smile for an altogether different reason. It seemed such futile advice—the sort of thing that Chairmen of Courts of Referees felt it incumbent upon them to say. What did he think I'd been trying to do for the last year? Did he think I could get work any quicker because he asked me to?

CHAPTER III

NERVES

MANY PEOPLE CANNOT understand why so many unemployed become, if not out-and-out nervous wrecks, then at least gloomy shadows of their former selves, walking phantoms of worry and dejection. Some people take it upon themselves to "cheer the unemployed up", "make them look on the bright side of life", and so on.

"Tut, tut, my dear fellow," they say, kindly and well-meaningly, "there is no need for you to get downhearted. Every cloud has a silver lining . . . the darkest hour is before the dawn", and similar amiable platitudes.

These people forget, do not know, cannot know, the multifarious sources of worry that can afflict an out-of-work. Unemployment brings into being many diverse sources of worry which become so intermingled and interlocked that their cumulative effect is well-nigh intolerable.

These worries are not merely financial—though of course financial worries are at the root of the whole problem. When a man has been out-of-work for any length of time, he begins to worry about his past, his present, and above all about his future. He worries about himself and about his wife and his children and his parents; in short, about himself and his dependants.

He worries about the Labour Exchange; about how long it will be before his present parlous financial condition gives way to a worse. He worries because he has too much time on his hands, and he worries because nearly all the more pleasant ways of passing his time are barred to him. He worries about his clothes.

158

because they are shabby; and he worries because soon, willy-nilly, he will have to get new ones for himself and his family, and he does not know where the money for them is coming from.

And above all, more bitter than gall is the fact that day after day, despite search after search, application after application, work is denied to him. In the vast edifice of our civilisation there is no useful work to be given to him—work that will at one and the same time enable him to be an equal with his fellow-men, and provide him with the necessities of life and peace of mind.

It may be thought that unemployed single men or women will not be so affected by worry as those unemployed who are married and have children. What must be kept clear, however, is that it is not the fact of marriage and children that is the basic cause of worry to the unemployed. The basic cause of worry is the fact of unemployment. Single men and women are just as much worried by unemployment as married people, with the additional fact that they are often living on their own and have no one with whom to share their more secret and agonising worries. Moreover, young people need that interchange of experience between the sexes known as "romance". Too often unemployment makes a romantic social life impossible; where it comes into being in spite of unemployment it is starved and stultified and poisoned, owing to the lack of the elementary material basis to keep it alive and healthy.

What is astonishing is not that there are some unemployed men and women who are nervous wrecks and psychopathic cases (the medical statistics on this question would surprise many people), but that there are not many more. It is, however, not the least crime of the present social system that there are today, at this very moment, thousands upon thousands of people who are suffering what can be literally described as excruciating mental tortures. They suffer in this way not because they are congenitally more neurotic than the average, but solely and simply because anarchic social forces have uprooted them, and undermined their social, economic, and therefore psychological stability.

Psychological suffering or instability does not necessarily reveal itself openly to the casual observer. There are far more cases of abnormal psychology signing on at the Labour Exchanges than are apparent on the surface, because relatively few are really noticeable. Nevertheless, those who, by reason of their more unbearable existence on the dole, combined with the lesser stability of the temperament, have become somewhat abnormal, are generally those who talk loudest and most vociferously in the queues. They argue vehemently about things that don't matter, and are often very aggrieved and angry over things that are not of very great importance.

Cases of people who have become abnormal because of the intolerable harshness of their economic existence are more noticeable among "down-and-outs" than among others—though whether it is psychological abnormality that has made them down-or-out, or the fact of being down-and-out that has created psychological instability, is a moot point. Neither conclusion reflects a very flattering light on the present social system.

These abnormal down-and-outs fall mainly into two categories, which correspond fairly closely to the two types so beloved of psychologists—the "extrovert" and the "introvert".

Your extrovert down-and-out is often fairly noticeable because of his volubility and passion for speech. You will see him, a shabby, unshaven figure, hanging on to the outskirts of crowds, and engaging in arguments on any subject under the sun with anybody who is sufficiently interested to argue with him. As a general rule, he has a "bee in his bonnet"—there is some special topic on which he constantly harps. He has—or he imagines he has—a specific grievance, and he will recite the particulars of this grievance in monotonously similar detail to anyone who will give him audience.

The defect of neat, scientific classification—as far as human beings, at any rate, are concerned—is that it often fails to take into account the many diverse characteristics that go to make the various types. Thus in this extrovert type there is also a fairly distinct type who is the opposite to the one described. He is cheerful—ludicrously and publicly cheerful. He walks along the street being loudly cheerful to everyone in general, and to no one in particular. He shouts out witticisms that are not witticisms. He stands at a street corner smiling vacantly and cheerfully at mankind in general.

I often saw one of these down-and-outs, near the place where I was lodging. He was clad in the most grotesque, and in the literal sense of the word awful, clothing. His short five-foot-two figure was clad in a ragged frock coat that no doubt had originally been made for some tall, lean aristocrat. The rest of his clothing was of a similar scale and size. His face was invariably covered with half an inch of ginger beard, and his most constant expression, which was one of vacant cheerfulness, disclosed a mouth that was toothless save for three or four blackened stumps. This example of *homo sapiens* often cavorted up and down the street arousing shrieks of laughter from passing girls and women by his fatuous attempts at public love-making.

Your introvert is more difficult to discern. You may see him shambling down the street, his hands shoved into his pockets, his shoulders round and bent. Possibly he mutters incoherently to himself. Generally he is wrapped up in his own thoughts. It is with difficulty that he is roused into the world of actuality. He may stand in a particular spot staring gloomily into vacancy. His features are careworn and sunken. His manner, when he is spoken to, is one of extreme nervousness. He is bashful and utterly lacking in self-confidence.

Life has battered him so that he has no trace of respect for himself before others. The rest of the world has become to him a world of superior, forceful beings, before whom he can but abase himself. He has forgotten what it is to live a social life. He drags himself about from morning till night, and sometimes from night until morning, enveloped in a nightmarish atmosphere of his own fancy and imagination. He is sunk in his own fantastic thoughts because the only things he can think about that have any practical application are too painful to be thought on. He has thought about these things a great deal in the past, and they merely worried and worried him, and now he has given up this painful occupation, and he is as you see him—shrinking, vacant, unhappy and brooding.

I often saw an old man who regularly took up his position outside the Hackney tram depot, near Hackney Station. He was a man with a long, patriarchal beard streaked with grey. His whole dress was extremely slovenly and unkempt. With his hands stuck deep in his pockets he would stand on the corner of the pavement talking loudly to himself in a deep, booming bass voice. Although I listened carefully on a number of occasions, and although I became certain that he was not speaking a foreign language, I could never make out what he was saying. He seemed to have a grievance about something, but what it was, it was impossible to discover. His glance at everybody and everything was at once troubled, impartial and absent-minded.

Then there was a man I sometimes saw pushing a barrel-organ. This was no ordinary barrel-organ, for it was covered with brown paper on which all kinds of phrases and appeals were scribbled. Apart from the usual phrases, such as those relating the fact that he got no dole or relief, there were others, such as "Kind friends, help to Take this Burden off me", "Oh God, why Should I suffer like This?" "What have I Done to Deserve such misery?" He had a face such as one would imagine a philosopher of Ancient Greece to have had. When one looked at that serene brow and noble face one was puzzled that this man should be pushing a barrel-organ. One day I passed him when he was writing further appeals of this kind on his barrel-organ. He was bending down as he wrote. He happened to glance up as I passed. It was then that I noticed that in this philosopher's face of his the eyes were exactly like those of a hurt animal.

I myself could not continue living alone for months under intolerable conditions without being affected not merely physically, but mentally. These mental effects could be divided into two kinds. The first was more or less gradual and cumulative in its results. The second was sudden in its onslaught, though more temporary in character.

The first of these effects has been more or less indicated, in passing, in what has been told previously. It consisted of the slow but sure change in my attitude to the world and to myself. It took the form of a lack of self-confidence and an absence of self-respect; a tacit assumption of inferiority to nearly everyone, and the innate certainty that I was not, and never would be, a useful member of society. These unspoken and unconsidered feelings increased and became part of my intellectual make-up in geometrical proportion to the length of my unemployment.

Distressing though these feelings were, particularly when they reached consciousness and were accompanied by depression and pessimism, they were as nothing compared to that which came later. Privation and frustration gave birth to a distress of mind which went beyond reasoning and control.

I had felt for some time vague moods of uneasiness and depression. Then an incident took place which at one stroke catapulted me into a state in which morbidness began to play an ever-increasing rôle.

One day as I stood waiting in the queue at the Labour Exchange, the thought came to me that it was fantastic to be standing waiting so long in a queue just in order to sign one's name. I agreed with myself that it was fantastic, though I felt too tired to reason why it should be more fantastic than anything else. The thought recurred to me: "It's fantastic!" Again the thought recurred, insistently: "It's fantastic!" Suddenly everything seemed fantastic—the whole complex of civilisation, with its underfed and underclothed unemployed, its idle, sybaritic upper strata, its teeming millions of earnest workers by hand and brain, so essentially naïve and innocent in the way they tolerated the drones in their beehive—it was all fantastic.

The feeling became more intense: "It's fantastic!", still more intense. "It's fantastic!" I began to be alarmed ("All right, no need to be excited about it! Calm down.") It was unreal—everything was unreal. I could not shake off a nightmarish sense that it was all unreal; everything was unreal: the Labour Exchange was unreal; the clerks were unreal; the notices were un-

162

"You don't want to worry about that, son," he said. "If you're smart, you can earn three pound ten a week, and more, in this place."

"What is it—piece-work?"

"Yes. But it's all right," he added—"the work's easy, and you've only to get down to it to earn a good wage. There's one lad 'ere—can't be as old as you, I don't think—knockin' out four pounds a week regular."

I hesitated. I had worked piece-work once before, and after three weeks of concentrated and baffled rage, disappointment and sweated labour, had thrown the job up, got myself into a tangle with the Labour Exchange authorities, and thereafter had sworn never to take a piece-work job again.

However, a lengthy period of unemployment is remarkable for the way in which it can make one forget the hardships of previous jobs, and can, indeed, transmute these very hardships into romantic memories of those glamorous times when one was actually working, for no matter how small a wage.

A few months previously I had refused a piece-work job. Many times I had repented that refusal. I had told myself that one unfortunate experience of working piece-work did not necessarily imply that all piece-work jobs were bad.

So it was that I was no longer predisposed to refuse this job hastily on the grounds that it was piece-work. After all, this was a large factory, and there would be no messing about; things would be well organised, I told myself.

In addition, however, I had to confess to myself that I would accept almost any job on almost any terms. I had already, by travelling here, gambled away nearly all the money which I would normally have spent on food for the ensuing week. By the time I returned to my lodgings in London it would have cost me close on six shillings to inquire about this job. A reckless, almost insane proceeding! In the circumstances I hardly dared to refuse the job, had to be grateful, indeed, that a job was held out to me.

I intimated that I would be willing to take the job, and the worried-looking man became affability itself. We agreed that I would start on Monday morning.

I walked away with my head in a whirl, what of the strange, peculiar sensation of actually having been accepted for a job, and the immediate, almost insoluble problems to which this gave rise.

NEW LODGINGS FOR OLD

How was I going to manage until I next got paid? I had to pay the rent of my lodgings in London. I could not afford to travel daily to my place of work (quite apart from the time that this would take). I had to find food for myself during the ensuing week. I would require another six or seven shillings, if only to travel back to Newslum again.

Obviously the best thing would be to get some lodgings in the town. On the other hand, supposing nobody would take me unless I paid a week's rent in advance?

The best thing was to try to tackle one problem at a time. With difficulty I sobered my whirling thoughts and walked along the main street of the overgrown village, and looked in shop windows for particulars of rooms to let. Soon I was walking amongst unfamiliar streets looking for a cheap lodging.

The first place at which I inquired was little more than a cottage. It was situated in the original village from which the present town had sprung.

After I had knocked at the cottage door for the third time and was about to go away, the door opened revealing a ruddy-faced, medium-sized man of about forty.

"Good morning," I said. "Have you a room to let?"

He scratched his head perplexedly.

"Well, it's like this, d'ye see. I'm only a lodger here. And she's gone out."

"Oh."

"But just a minute. Wait a minute, and I'll see."

He went up the lobby and knocked at the door of what was evidently the front room. He opened the door and scrutinised the inside of the room. Apparently he was satisfied by what he saw. He beckoned mysteriously to me.

"Go inside. Her mother'll speak to you about it."

I went into the room, and immediately there was wafted to me the stale air of a room that has been lived in unventilated for years. The walls were covered almost in their entirety with photographs of stern, bewhiskered men in frock coats, and glowering women in mushroom-shaped skirts. There were numerous religious texts, and oleographs of prayerful virgins. The floor space was crowded with furniture. Near the window was an iron bed, covered with soiled bed-clothing. In the bed was the shrivelled effigy of an old woman. She turned her drawn, bloodless face towards me and smiled hideously, revealing pale, toothless gums.

"Come in," she croaked discordantly. "Sit down." She patted the edge of the bed.

I entered reluctantly. I had already decided not to take the room. I could never live in the same house as This.

"Sit down," she croaked again, and I sat gingerly on the edge of the bed.

Then I noticed that near the bed was a basin which contained some pale-brownish liquid. I felt that it was the mouth-washing of the old lady, and I began to feel sick. The lodger had meanwhile entered the room, and stood surveying us both with a proprietary air.

"Me darter's gone out," the old woman quavered. "Would ye like to wait for about quarter'n hour?"

"I'm afraid not. I'm in rather a hurry."

"Speak up! I'm a bit deaf." She twisted the left side of her mummy-face towards me and smiled hideously again.

"He's in a 'urry! 'E's got ter go away!" the lodger bellowed suddenly from the door.

"I see. . . . I see. . . ." She breathed as one in the throes of a last illness, and pondered thoughtfully over this complicated statement.

"Are ye workin'?" she croaked suddenly.

"Yes," I said loudly.

"'Ow long 'ave ye bin workin'?"

"I'm just starting."

"Oh, is that all?" She paused. "Where are ye workin' at?"

"The YXZ Company."

"Oh, them. Where are ye livin' now?"

"In London."

"Oh, in Lunnon. An' why d'ye want to come 'ere?"

"Because I'm going to work here."

"Oh, he's goin' to work here." She pondered over this. "Are ye teetotal?" she piped sternly.

"Yes."

"D'ye smoke?"

"Yes."

The lodger hastily interceded for the virtues of my character.

"A man must do somethin' with his money!" he bellowed.

The old lady smiled in hideous leniency for the failings of mankind.

"You're a non-smoker an' teetotal, ain't yer, Richard?"

"Me? Naw! I smoke nah an' agen! A man mus' do somethin' with 'is money!" he bellowed.

"Ah," she murmured, "I was thinkin' of my son-in-law's brother-in-law. 'Is name's Richard." She became lost in

173

meditation on the saintliness of this relative, and when I was wondering how I could decently withdraw, she croaked again:

"Are ye walkin' out?"

"What?"

"Goin' out with a young woman?" the lodger bellowed.

"No."

"That's right," she leered. "Leave women alone, young man. I don't like lodgers goin' out courtin'. They comes in all hours of the night."

"I must say that you've got very definite ideas on the type of lodger you want," I thought. "Apparently a man has to be a devitalised saint in order to qualify for the inestimable privilege of paying to stay in your house."

"You don't go courtin', do you, Richard?"

"Me? Naw!" he bellowed. "I got more sense!"

I speculated on his sexual history, and then I again noticed the basin and the pale-brown liquid. Once more I felt sick.

"I've got to go somewhere," I shouted. "I'm in a hurry! Call back later! Good morning!" And with that I rose hastily. In a few minutes I was out in the sunshine again.

After this I applied at three more houses. At the only one that still had a room to let (the bugbear of people seeking lodgings are advertisers who let their rooms, and blissfully allow the advertisement to remain in the shop window for weeks, thus causing endless futile trouble), the landlady refused to consider me as a lodger after I had told her that I would not be able to pay a week's rent in advance.

I was now beginning to wonder whether my whole project of working in Newslum might not fail because of my inability to find lodgings.

The advertiser at the next house at which I inquired proved to be a young married woman. Obviously she and her husband were one of those young couples who listen eagerly to everything told them by the agent of a building society, ecstatically buy their own house on the assumption that it is only going to cost them twopence halfpenny a week, and then shortly afterwards find themselves burdened with worry because they discover that there is not only the repayment to the building society, but also such things as rates, electricity, gas, furniture repayments, etc., to cope with. Thus this couple were taking the usual step of many who buy their own house because they want complete privacy. That is to say, they were letting one of their best rooms to a complete stranger.

This young woman appeared to be so flustered by the fact that someone had actually responded to her advertisement that she seemed scarcely to know what to do about it. There had obviously not been the slightest arrangement made for receiving a lodger. Eventually I managed to hint that it would be just as well if she showed me the room she proposed to let. With many incoherent apologies she hastened upstairs and showed me the room. As yet it had no floor covering of any kind, was filled mostly with old lumber, and the sole indication that it was eventually meant for occupation was a new iron bedstead complete with wire mattress, but without any bedclothing on it.

This was not very encouraging. However, the young house-wife was so much on the defensive that it never occurred to her to ask whether I would pay a week's rent in advance. I therefore hastened to agree to move into the room as and from Sunday night. Then I returned to London as quickly as I could.

I managed to borrow ten shillings from my sister in the East End, and this gave me the certainty of being able to travel back to Newslum and of having money for a few days' food.

My departure from my lodgings in London was not altogether without incident. I was compelled to leave my landlord and landlady, with whom I had lived on the best of terms for fourteen months, without giving them any notice, or being able to pay them anything in lieu of notice. As they depended a good deal on the rent of my room as a source of income, my sudden departure was a blow, and they took it rather badly. My landlady quarrelled with me outright on the question, and my landlord kept his face gloomily averted from me. I was mortified, and promised faith-fully to pay them a week's notice as soon as I could, But it was of no avail. I left the house under a cloud.

CHAPTER VII

THE REWARD FOR SEEKING WORK

ANY UNEASINESS AND doubt I might have had about my new job were fulfilled in the most devastating way. My blackest thoughts about the piece-work system became wild optimism compared with the reality in this factory. My worst anticipations about the type of work to be done, the amount of wages I could earn, and the general circumstances in the factory became as dreams of Paradise.

When I first entered the YXZ factory and surveyed my new workmates, I thought that there must be some mistake, that I had been shown into the wrong department. Not only was there no sign of cabinet-making as I knew it, but the young workers sweating away at the various benches did not seem to bear any resemblance to cabinet-makers I had been familiar with in the past. None of them wore aprons, as cabinet-makers do, or seemed to possess any tools or any knowledge of woodwork. Not a single bench possessed a vice, and instead of the sound of planes and saw and mallets, all that could be heard was the sibilant hiss of sandpaper on wood.

Frail plywood boxes were scattered and piled in heaps on the floor. These boxes (*i.e.*, wireless cabinets) were covered with veneer and with paper glued to the veneer. The young men at the benches were engaged in scrubbing this paper off the veneer which covered the surface of the wireless cabinets. The term "sandpapering" or " 'papering" was unknown here. The work was known as "scrubbing", and indeed the work greatly resembled that of a charwoman incessantly scrubbing the same limited floor space.

It did not take me long to discover that scarcely any of my workmates were cabinet-makers by trade. They were young lads who had migrated south from all the various Distressed Areas of the country. The Government had sent them to institutions known as training centres,* where they had undergone a few months' farcical "training". From these centres they had been despatched as semi-slave labour to various factories. In this particular factory, for instance, they earned scarcely enough to keep body and soul together. They could not leave to go to a better factory, if such existed, because they had not sufficient confidence or technical knowledge. They could not leave of their own accord without another job because they knew that this would mean the loss of unemployment benefit. Attempts at revolt to secure more pay had been met by the employer's blackmail to the effect that he would sack them and get their dole stopped. He had actually done this on a number of occasions to many workers as an example to the rest. Those who remained in the factory were the most highly skilled in sweating, the most robust, the most desperate and the most degenerate of spirit.

The work seemed to me to be fairly simple. I felt that I ought to be able to earn about £2 a week at least, even though the price paid for sandpapering a wireless cabinet to mirror-like perfection was only one penny farthing. Nevertheless, I was soon disillusioned. Despite all my efforts, and what I imagined to be my superior skill, I seemed to get far less results than the other workers in the factory.

* The Government Training Centres established during this war for the training of munition workers were, whatever their faults, vastly superior to their pre-war equivalent.

The system by which work was paid for was as follows. Each worker took a number of cabinets to his bench. Then he sand-papered them as near as possible to a glossy smoothness. When he had finished them he took some more cabinets and went on sandpapering. In the meantime an inspector examined the finished cabinets, and if they were not flawlessly smooth and clean, he rejected them. It was possible that the same cabinet would be re-sandpapered, given to the inspector, and rejected time after time. It was indeed a heartbreaking process, for there seemed to be no definite standard by which a cabinet was passed or rejected. Some cabinets might be a hopeless proposition from the start, for the veneer might be badly damaged, and the unfortunate "cleaner" might waste a considerable amount of time before he discovered this fact. Again, sometimes the cheap plywood cases came from the presses all warped and undulated, yet the cleaner was supposed to be able to perform the impossible by at once sandpapering the cabinets absolutely flat, and at the same time not rubbing away any of the thin veneer that covered the surface.

As I have said, I seemed to make a very poor showing at my new job. This was very mysterious to me. My cabinets always seemed to be as well, if not better, finished than those of my workmates. Nevertheless, the cabinets were returned to me with unfailing regularity, covered all over with chalk marks which were supposed to reveal the flaws in my work. I soon gave up attempting to discover these flaws, for to me at any rate they seemed to be non-existent. I merely rubbed the chalk marks off with a piece of cloth, for our sandpaper was severely rationed. As likely as not a cabinet which had been repeatedly covered with chalk marks would eventually be accepted when all that I had done to it was to rub out the chalk marks.

I made inquiries amongst my workmates about how much they were earning. Their replies were evasive, but it was clear that although their earnings were very small, they were greater than mine. In my first day's work of nine and a half hours I earned less than four shillings.

I soon discovered, however, that bad as the factory was, it was not quite as bad as my first day's work made it appear. Apparently the management regarded it as necessary that a new-comer to the factory should earn as little as possible, for two reasons.

Firstly, the more independent workers generally threw up the job on the first or second day; only the most desperate remained. Secondly, because of the enormous difficulty which a beginner had in getting his work accepted, he took meticulous care to make his cabinets as perfect as possible. It took him some time to discover that the standard of acceptance of cabinets was not quite as high as he had first been led to believe—though, as payment was by piece-work rates, the management could afford to demand a far greater degree of perfection than would have been economical had they been paying hourly rates.

The inspectors of the cabinets, or "passers" as they were called, were in a position of great power. They could make things very difficult for a worker. Most of the broken-spirited youths who remained at the factory were therefore on terms of sickly friendship with the inspectors, and these latter did not hesitate to take advantage of their position.

On my second day of work the inspector who examined my cabinets approached me and began to make friendly conversation. I felt rather flattered—I had never worked in a factory where inspectors were employed, and these individuals with their white overcoats seemed to me to be very high and mighty personages indeed. After the inspector had asked me one or two questions, such as what part of the country I came from, whether I was lodging in Newslum, etc., he said with a fine air of unconcern, "By the way, could you lend me a couple of bob till Friday?"

I was astounded, astounded both at the idea that I had two shillings to lend anybody, and that this high and mighty individual should be trying to borrow two shillings from me, of all people.

"No, I'm sorry," I said. "I can't lend you anything. I haven't got any money to lend."

The inspector made no reply, but immediately went back to his bench. That afternoon I found it practically impossible to get any of my cabinets accepted. It was only when I was on my way home from work that it dawned on me that there might be some connection between my inability to lend money to the inspector and his reluctance to pass my cabinets. I fumed with impotent rage, as I remembered the afternoon's sweating.

On the third day matters began to brighten up a little. For one thing, I took care, as all the others did, to examine cabinets before I began work on them. With a certain amount of experience it was possible to tell which cabinets had no faults in them, and were thus fairly easy to clean. In theory everyone was supposed to take his cabinets as they came, but the initiated took care to leave the bad ones for beginners like me. By making this quick examination and rejecting faulty cabinets, I saved myself an enormous amount of wasted labour.

I also decided that I would give my cabinets to a different inspector, for it occurred to me that there was no definite rule that one had to give cabinets only to one particular inspector.

even more boring in Newslum than it was in London, I decided to leave the town at the end of the week.

So I returned to London.

CHAPTER VIII

POVERTY

I RETURNED TO London in a more or less desperate state of mind. I had spent most of my week's unemployment benefit on paying my landlady in Newslum and on my fare to London. There was no one I knew who could give me hospitality till I settled down, for neither of my sisters had any surplus rooms in her home. It was very difficult for me to find somewhere to stay without paying a week's rent in advance. In the end I had to take what lodgings I could get. Those I moved into were far worse than those I had abandoned to go to Newslum, and cost me sixpence a week more.

My new lodgings were, strangely enough, my first introduction to real poverty. I had known, of course, what it was to be absolutely penniless, to go without food for days on end, for my clothes to become shabby and worn in the extreme. But despite all this I had attempted, all along, to retain some last shreds of decency and self-respect. In my new lodgings, however, I saw poverty with the lid off.

I went to live in a street that was superficially quite unremarkable, if a trifle drab. It was only when one penetrated beyond the front doors of the houses that one detected the real character of the neighbourhood—that peculiarly crowded squalor which is hard to find outside London.

The people with whom I stayed were used to poverty. They accepted it and resigned themselves to it. There was about their poverty, however, none of that clean, spick-and-span abstemiousness, the clever calculations and the cheerfully-making-the-best-of-things that one reads of in novels and ingenuous stories of poverty-stricken childhood. With them poverty was something openly and shamelessly mean and slovenly, dirty and despicable. Poverty had long since crushed them, weighed them down like a heavy load.

They had forgotten the meaning—if, indeed, they had ever known it—of good food and clothes, space, air and light, of cleanliness, culture, of noble uses of the body and mind. They had to live crowded together in small rooms. What should have been kitchens were bedrooms and living-rooms, or bed-living rooms. Tiny sculleries were kitchens. Basements that admitted air and light only with tardy reluctance housed whole families. Beds that would have been comfortable for one person, slept two or three. Rooms that were big enough to contain comfortably a table and some chairs, held a large bed, table, chairs, and any other furniture that could possibly be crammed into them. And all the furniture was dirty and dilapidated, broken-down and ugly. Whatever could possibly be damaged and dilapidated and dirty in a house was damaged and dilapidated and dirty. There was no convenience for hygiene, and this lack of convenience itself bred into the inhabitants a lack of desire, a positive reluctance for the astringent effort demanded by the needs of hygiene. The food was paltry, coarse, and lacked real nourishment. But it was cheaper than the real thing—this latter qualification being of necessity a recommendation instead of a condemnation.

One heard everything of what went on among the three or four families that lived in the house, and also most of what went on in the adjoining houses. The idea of a private quarrel between people was something unknown. When families or individuals quarrelled, they were at pains to broadcast their version of the case with the utmost vehemence and exaggeration, in the loudest voice, and at the greatest possible length, to anyone within earshot. People had forgotten how to talk to each other in normal voices, even when they were on friendly terms. The normal speaking voice had become debased to a hoarse shout. Children never played without one incessant clamour of shrieks and yells.

During the week or two that I stayed at this lodging I almost forgot the meaning of the word quiet. Added to the ordinary bedlam of the place was the bedlam of vociferous and conflicting wireless sets. Although no one in the house possessed a wireless set, those in both the adjoining houses did. Their idea of getting the greatest possible satisfaction out of a wireless set was to turn it on to its loudest possible extent, so that the atmosphere of the whole neighbourhood vibrated in sympathy with gargantuan jazz bands and hollow-voiced young men who bellowed terrifically about the state of their hearts. There was no surcease from the clamour of the wireless sets from tea-time until midnight.

In the family downstairs, the husband would come home from work and after eleven hours in the sweat-shop he was greeted with the howling and shouting of kids, the banging of doors, the nagging of a nerve-wracked wife, the blaring of cheap, discordant wireless sets, the yapping of dogs, constant knocking and ringing at the door by other lodgers in the house or by their friends and callers, and the stamping and domestic noises of families overhead. And his nerves, further, would give way under

184

the strain. He found vent for his uncontrollable irritation in full-pitched, insane quarrels with his wife, by browbeating and bullying his wife and children, and by beating his children unmercifully because they behaved in the maddening way children will behave in circumstances such as these. All this added further to the maniac noise, what with the fearful howling, wailing and blubbering of the children, and the screaming recriminations of the wife.

There were quarrels with neighbours and lodgers and visitors, and a general brutal, unjust and domineering attitude towards anyone who, being weaker, was not able to retaliate to quite the same extent.

Thus there was set up a vicious circle of poverty and strife in which poverty and strife bred shattered nerves and ugly tempers, which in their turn still further poisoned the atmosphere, so that nerves were shattered and tempers were lost still further, and so ad infinitum.

It was no wonder that the family, that all the families, that the next-door neighbours, that the whole block of houses, that the whole district of dirty, festering, squalid, decaying slums resembled at times nothing so much as a disordered lunatic asylum overrun by shrieking, gibbering inhabitants, bereft of their reason and howling for one another's blood.

I sought desperately for some means of escape from circumstances such as these. But once again I was held captive by the chains of unemployment, for it happened that I could not find any place where I could lodge unless I paid a week's rent in advance. This, of course, I could not afford.

In the midst of all this, it seemed as though a marvellous opportunity of escape and regeneration presented itself. An acquaintance of my family, a young man who was fairly well off, moved to London. He happened to pay my mother a visit one day when I was also visiting her. During the course of the conversation it appeared that he was living temporarily in a furnished room, but was shortly to take an unfurnished flat. His original intention had been to buy the furniture at one of the large stores, but on learning of the lengthy period I had been out of work, it occurred to him to suggest that I should make his furniture instead.

It had occasionally happened in the past that people had approached me to make them small items of furniture. Unfortunately, these orders had never come simultaneously, but always singly, at times wide apart. Relatively insignificant though these orders were, they had required all the resources of a workshop. It had therefore been unprofitable for me to make

185

them because I had no place I could use for a workroom, and I would have spent more on renting the workshop, buying a vice, bench, cramp, gluepot, handscrews, etc., etc., than would have been worth while.

As circumstances were at present, however, I was in a reckless mood. This relatively large order fired me with exultation and enthusiasm. I decided to rent a small workshop and, with this order as a beginning, to start working for myself. Whilst I was working on this first order, I decided, I would go round to various people who had approached me in the past and try to get enough orders to keep me busy for as long as possible.

My acquaintance was as good as his word. I went to visit him one evening, and we spent an hour or two discussing designs and measurements. In my eagerness to get the order definitely and at once I submitted a rather recklessly low estimate for the order en bloc. My first customer agreed to my price and advanced me five pounds with which to proceed with the work. As I had scarcely seen a one-pound note for nearly two years, the receipt of this sum of money overwhelmed me with sensations of wealth and prosperity.

I felt that I was beginning a new life. I was intoxicated with hope for the future. With a sigh of relief I signed-off the Labour Exchange the next morning. As the sort of individual who receives five pounds in advance on an order, I took lodgings the next day for the sum of ten shillings a week, which I paid in advance—an incredibly expensive room, to my ideas. Then I paid ten shillings for the rent of a workshop, bought some essential workshop equipment, and laid in what seemed to me to be an enormous stock of timber. By the Saturday night I had only a few shillings left on which to exist until I had finished my first order and got paid for it. My enthusiasm was somewhat damped when I saw the difficulties ahead.

CHAPTER IX

THE MASTER CABINET-MAKER

To people who live ordered and secure lives, the step I had taken may seem sheer madness. To sign off the dole and start working for myself on the basis of one order, incurring at one and the same time the loss of fifteen and threepence a week unemployment benefit and the liability to pay ten shillings workshop rent, without the certainty of any future orders, and without any capital, this was the height of recklessness.

So it may have been, but nevertheless among people who are desperate such recklessness is quite common. Desperate people must seek some way out of the *impasse*, and even if the way out is often but an illusion, they will embrace this illusion eagerly rather than face the hard, intolerable facts any longer. The political history of the past few years would have been vastly different if this were not so. Similarly with me. I had very little idea how much profit I was going to make on the order I received, how long the job was going to take me, or indeed whether the whole project was worth while. Nevertheless, because it offered me a quick, if only a temporary, escape from intolerable circumstances, I seized it with enthusiasm, even though it might land me into even more desperate straits than before.

I soon discovered that the life of an artisan who is totally without any capital is difficult, if not impossible. For one thing, I had spent nearly all the initial five pounds deposit on the rent of the workshop and on some essential equipment and timber for the job. How was I going to manage to live until I finished the order and got paid for it? There was only one way out, and that was to approach my acquaintance constantly for more and more advances of money on the job. I hated doing this, but circumstances compelled me.

I had no machinery and could not afford to have any of my work done by machine at a saw-mill. The result was that I had to do it entirely by hand, even to the sawing up of many pieces of timber. Thus the work took me much longer than I had first anticipated. After six weeks of incredible toil, I had finished, polished and delivered my first order. A balance of exactly thirty shillings remained, and I considered myself lucky to have any balance at all.

I now began a feverish search for new orders. An exhaustive round-up of the people who at one time or another had approached me to make things for them produced disappointing results. Most of them had already bought what they wanted, and those who had not were not now in a position to do so. Nevertheless, I was more fortunate than I realised at the time, for I did get a few odd jobs, sufficient to last me for a few weeks after I had finished my first order. The jobs I did get, however, were not on the same scale as my first one.

I floundered from one difficulty to another, trying to exist on nothing until I finished jobs and got paid for them, wealthy one day and penniless the next because I spent what money I had for timber and fittings for the next job.

Nevertheless, when I had been working for about three months I came completely to an end of my orders. There were two or three people, it is true, who for some time had been promising me fairly substantial orders. They seemed to be quite in earnest that they would definitely give me these orders, but there was always some delay. It was always going to be "in a week or two". The result was that I was afraid to abandon my workshop and the bench (which I would be unable to take away, as I had nowhere to store it) because of these orders which I might receive. Besides this, I realised now that it would be rather difficult for me to obtain benefit immediately at the Labour Exchange, because I had been working for myself.

I was in a very tight corner. I had no orders, and even if I did not spend a penny on food, I still had to find a pound every week; ten shillings for my lodging, and ten shillings for the workshop. The first step I took in an effort to reduce expenditure was to give notice at my lodgings and to look for a cheaper one. However, once again I found myself in the position of not being able to afford to pay a week's rent in advance. The days of the week passed, I got no orders, neither was I able to find any place that would take me unless I paid a week's rent in advance.

Suddenly it was Saturday, and I realised that I had nowhere to stay. As hastily as possible I removed my belongings from my lodgings to the workshop. I set out on a hurried search for new lodgings. Although I found one or two places that might have been willing to accept me without a week's rent in advance, they were suspicious of the fact that I wanted to move in that very same night. They suspected some lightning removal from a lodging where I owed rent. The result was that my search failed.

For the next two or three hours I wandered aimlessly about the streets. I still had two or three shillings left. Every hour or so I went into a café, ostensibly for a cup of tea, but in reality for a rest. When it was about nine o'clock I came to the conclusion that there was only one thing for me to do: that was to try to get my sister Rosie to put me up for the night.

Hitherto I had been very reluctant to contemplate this idea. For one thing, there was really no room for me to sleep in the house; I would probably have to sleep on a few chairs. More than the actual discomfort, however, I disliked having to publish the acuteness of my position by having to resort to such measures to achieve a night's sleep.

In addition to this, however, I had all along been very reluctant to become in any way a burden on my brother-in-law. He already had pressing family responsibilities of his own. And in addition my mother lived in the house, and of late had been able to give only a nominal sum towards her support.

In view of these facts, and because of the morbid sensitivity with which I viewed any open manifestation of my state of poverty, I felt extremely reluctant to bring my difficulties before the notice of my brother-in-law.

However, there was nothing else I could do. I would have to stay somewhere for the night, and my sister's place was the only one I could think of. I therefore made my way to the East End. I came to my sister's house about nine-thirty. My mother opened the door, and was not unnaturally surprised that I should pay a visit at that time of day. I felt a bit chary of explaining the reason immediately, and wanted to break the news more gradually at a later stage. Moreover, a middle-aged housewife had dropped in to have a gossip with my mother, and it was impossible for me to explain the circumstances while she was present.

My sister and brother-in-law were out on a visit, and were not expected back till late. In the meantime the middle-aged visitor was keeping my mother company. I groaned inwardly, for it seemed as if the visitor would not make her departure for some time.

I waited with dreary doggedness till the visit would end, but the discourse of my mother and her visitor was unflagging. Time passed. I had already stayed far later than I usually did. Unemployed, and therefore without money for car-fares, I never left my sister's house later than ten o'clock at night, whilst the majority of my visits were during the day. It seemed to me that my continued presence at this late hour was very conspicuous. I sat there wordless and unmoving. I ought to get up and say "Goodnight". Would that I could afford that luxury and to be free from the necessity of waiting importunately till I could find the opportunity to beg a favour. I pictured the surprise I would cause when I asked to be allowed to stay the night, the awkward explanations I would make. I fidgeted under an exaggerated picture in my mind of the unspoken impatience of my brother-in-law, who I was certain would get the impression that I was trying to become yet another burden on his back.

Suddenly my mother looked at me in surprise.

"It's late. Why don't you go home? Soon you'll be too late to get a tram."

The presence of my mother's visitor effectually precluded me giving my true reasons. For a moment I was undecided as to whether I should make some excuse for staying a little longer, until the visitor left. But I could not think of an excuse on the spur of the moment. Impatience seized me. Enough of this! I would go, and would spend the night walking about. It was a warm summer's night. It would not be the first night I had spent out of doors. I rose with an air of indifference.

"Well, it's late now. I'll have to be going. Goodnight."

They both replied. After a moment, my mother, looking at me in a somewhat troubled fashion, as though she suspected that something was amiss, asked, "Will you be coming tomorrow?"

"Yes, I daresay I'll come tomorrow," I replied. "Goodnight." And I went out.

CHAPTER X

OUT ALL NIGHT

Outside, the night and the streets seemed different from other nights, from the usual streets. I was walking through the streets beneath the night, but I was not going anywhere. I was not bound for a comfortable home, a warm bed, supper before bed, something to eat on getting up after a night's sleep in bed. I was apart from that comfortable world of people who earned wages, had regular incomes, no matter how small, had homes and families.

I watched them coming from their Saturday night pleasures, and it seemed to me that they were the inhabitants of a delightful and luxurious world. They were going home. When they got home they would probably eat something quite casually, as though a meal were the most ordinary thing in the world. They would go to bed, they would have a roof over their heads all night. They would get up for breakfast, there would be a day of untroubled leisure before them.

I saw their lives in clear, glowing colours. There were in their lives no complications, no sorrows, no hardships, and no worries. For, having homes, beds, a roof over their heads and food and some money, what else could they worry about? I puzzled over this question. I remembered vaguely that even those people who had secure, permanent jobs, and whose incomes were above that which was necessary to keep them barely alive—such people were not necessarily filled with happiness, seemed often to have worries and tribulations. But as I walked along I could not understand why they should worry about anything at all.

After a time it suddenly occurred to me that maybe I was taking this matter of staying out all night a little too fatalistically. After all, there were such places as hostels for the down and out, places where, for a few coppers, a man could get a night's lodging. True, I did not look forward with any great pleasure to the prospect of a night in a hostel. That part within me that always clung to respectability in spite of everything shrank from the rude prospect of spending the night among those who were among the lowest levels of the dispossessed, among those who were the more obvious rejects of society. I felt that once having spent the night among such as these, I would never be quite the same again. I would have touched, for no matter how brief a time, one lower depth in the strata of society.

Nevertheless, I decided that I was merely being snobbish and stupid. Better men than me had used these places, and better men than me would use them again. A night in a hostel could do me no harm.

A few moments later I arrived at one of the hostels so plentiful in the East End of London. Groups of men lounged about the doorway and in the passage that led into the building. At the sight of them, all my former squeamishness reasserted itself more desperately than ever. On the faces of some of these men were written viciousness and depravity, desperation and cunning. Others bore all the hallmarks of prolonged privation and destitution. I shrank from the symbolical step of becoming one of these, for no matter how short a time. This was no adventure or temporary experience, as I had at first tried to picture it to myself. It was a step to which I was being driven by sheer necessity. Who could tell how long it would be before I would have need of one of these places again? Who could say but that in a few short weeks or months I myself would be transformed into one of these outcasts, would become reconciled and accustomed to this mode of life and these associates, as I had to become accustomed to those other modes of life and associates which I had first faced with shrinking and reluctance?

However, I had no other alternative for tonight. Tonight, and —come what may—tonight only, I would lodge there. Making my way with as unconcerned and hardened an air as I could assume, I approached a kiosk at the end of the corridor, where presumably one booked lodgings for the night.

The kiosk was like a small booking-office at a suburban railway station. Behind a glass window was a mild-mannered, bespectacled man of about sixty. I was reassured by his presence. I felt that no place could be really intolerable if people such as he held some kind of official position in it.

The man raised the lower half of the window and looked at me inquiringly. I made a rapid calculation. One could sleep with other men in a dormitory for fivepence a night, or one could hire a cubicle for ninepence. I was intimidated by the prospect of sleeping in the same dormitory with men of the type I had seen at the entrance to the hostel. Besides, I had heard many tales to the effect that any inexperienced young man who slept in the same room with men such as these was asking to be robbed of everything he had, no matter what precautions he took.

"I want to hire a cubicle," I said as casually as possible, as though I had done this many times before.

"'Ave yer booked a cubicle?" the bespectacled man asked.

I was surprised. I had never thought this would be necessary.

"No," I answered.

"Well, I'm sorry, we're full up. You should always book your cubicle a few hours beforehand if you want one," the man in the kiosk told me.

Full up? I somehow felt relieved at the news.

"We haven't any spare beds either," the man volunteered. "I'm sorry. You should have come earlier."

I felt even more relieved. I discovered that I preferred infinitely to walk about the streets all night rather than sleep in one of these places. There was no doubt that if I went to other hostels at this late hour there would still be difficulties about my getting somewhere to sleep. I would therefore walk about for an hour or two. No doubt I would eventually find a quiet place where I could doze for a few hours. Tomorrow I would definitely make a real attempt to get lodgings.

I began walking rather aimlessly along Aldgate. It was strange to me that the streets should still be so brightly lit and crowded. To me the long night had already begun, and I somehow expected the streets to be silent, hushed and deserted. The clock above Aldgate Tube Station showed three minutes to twelve. It was not very late yet.

I turned into Cornhill, where there were only occasional passers-by. Now and again a bus filled with home-going passengers rushed along the narrow, gleaming ribbon of macadam. The great blocks of insurance and steamer company offices stood massive but dead, towering but sightless, giant corpses that would be miraculously restored to life on Monday morning.

I strolled along aimlessly, gazing into windows that showed photographs and paintings and models of ships. You could travel here for the moderate sum of 60 guineas, go there for the trifling payment of £115 10s. It seemed well worth it. The accommodation was just so; a trifle overstuffed with luxury maybe, but people who spent £115 10s. for the fare alone presumably like it that way. The food; ah, the food! I had heard what the food was like on a mere second-class trip to Canada. What would the food be like on a luxury cruise? . . . Well, maybe I'll try one of these trips one of these days.

After a time I got impatient of dawdling, began walking towards Holborn. There were still a number of people about. The elder son of a family for which I had recently made a small article of furniture passed me, and as he did so, looked at me somewhat strangely. He was no doubt wondering why I was walking in this region at this time of the night.

To my annoyance and concern a slow, heavy rain began to fall. This would happen when I was out without an overcoat. The rain became increasingly swift and heavy. At the junction of Tottenham Court Road and Oxford Street I stopped to shelter within the doors of an ornate café. There was a motley group of late night stragglers sheltering there, apparently waiting for the last bus home. There were two fat, untidy women who seemed as though they had just finished work. There were one or two young men of unhappy, frustrated appearance, who looked as though they had been out for a night's pleasure, and had either not been able to experience any, or else had discovered that not all that seems pleasurable is pleasurable. A very smartly dressed young lady stood aloof and apart from the others, so that she was barely sheltered from the rain. Her appearance was exceedingly haughty, and she seemed to wish to make it quite clear to everybody that she was very high class. A young woman with a ravaged, painted face and a beautiful figure, clad in a thin black dress, was ostentatiously smoking a cigarette and looking at everyone else appraisingly and inquiringly, whilst trying to appear entirely indifferent. A tall, thin man with a long, hooked nose jutting out of a villainous lantern-jawed face was talking loudly to everyone in general.

"Ah!" he exclaimed, "Ah've got a brairn, Ah can tell ye." He peered at everybody with an expression of diabolical cunning. "Ye canna beat the guid auld Aber-r-dawnian brairn!"

He tapped his forehead significantly, with a very large, knobbly finger. His face was perspiring, and his eyes had the filmy glitter of one who is under the influence of drink.

At this moment a young man came running for shelter. He was good-looking in a flabby, greasy fashion, and he was very correctly dressed, with perfectly creased trousers, patent leather shoes, a pearl pin in his tie, and a white silk scarf round his neck. The Scotsman turned on him as a specific audience.

"Ye canna beat the guid auld Aber-r-dawnian brairn!" he challenged.

He tapped his forehead again, and his misty eyes seemed inspired, as though he spoke of divine things.

"Oh, who says you can't?" the young man asked in a cultured tone, which was so obviously unnatural that it should have deceived no one.

"Ah ses saw!" the Scotsman persisted lyrically. "Ah ses saw!
193

Ah've got a brairn ap hi-er-r! Ye canna beat it, mon. Ah defy ye to beat it."

"Alright," said the other, with his rapid, pseudo-cultured accent. "Like a game o' cawds? Nep? Pokah? What? Anything you like."

The Scotsman made a gesture of disgust. "Heh! Ye canna fool me, mon! Ah've got a brairn, Ah tell ye! *A guid awld Aber-r-dawnian brairn!*" he insisted. "Ah defy ye to beat it. Ah knaw you. Yids. Ye clever. Aye, Ah'll admit that. Ye clever, you Yids. *But ye canna beat the guid awld Aber-r-dawnian brairn!*" he repeated vociferously.

This sort of thing went on for some time, both the Scotsman and the flashy young man striving their utmost to shine before their impromptu audience. I felt irritated with the whole stupid conversation, and wished that the Scotsman would shut up, with his powerful Aberdonian brain, and that the excessively cultured young man would betake himself and his cheap talents elsewhere. As the Scotsman's eulogies of the Aberdonian brain in general and his own brain in particular did not cease, and as the flashy young man was monotonously insistent on challenging the Scotsman to some feat of petty skill, and as the rain had turned into a slight drizzle, I decided to move onwards.

I set off along Tottenham Court Road. I had often walked much greater distances than I had covered so far this night. I had often gone to bed later than ten minutes past one in the morning (which was the time now). Yet I seemed to feel more weary and sleepy than I had ever felt before.

One of the reasons why I had walked to the West End (apart from the fact that I might as well go there as anywhere else) was that I imagined that, even in the early hours of the morning, it would still be fairly wide-awake. Shortly after I came to London a daily newspaper printed a series of articles describing London. These articles were written in that lyrical and semi-religious style which it is one of the conventions of Fleet Street to adopt whenever the subject of London is mentioned. One of the articles had described Tottenham Court Road in melodramatic journalese. The article itself was headed by the title "The Never-Sleeping Tottenham Court Road". Since reading this article I had been curious to observe this street in the middle of the night.

Well, now I had the opportunity, and I had to confess myself tolerably disappointed. At a mere one o'clock on a Sunday morning the place was as dead as ditch-water. The centre of Forgeton could probably show more life at such a time. Instead of the picture I had conjured up of hard-bitten cosmopolitans (who regarded sleep as effeminate weakness) all being exceedingly cosmopolitan in a very cosmopolitan way, I beheld merely a blank, dreary vista of dead cinemas, forsaken amusement saloons and abandoned furniture shops. An occasional taxi purred mysteriously by; ever and again I passed someone who I imagined, rightly or wrongly, to be in the same homeless position as myself. Once three rather boisterous youths came out of a side street and with much loud conversation and laughter hailed a taxi and rode away into silence. But the general effect of the celebrated night-life of London, in so far as it was visible, was the reverse of exhilarating.

From Tottenham Court Road I turned into Euston Road. In spite of my fatigue, I had to keep reminding myself to go slow, for I was a naturally quick walker, and I did not want to exhaust myself before morning. Ever and again I pretended to appraise the possibilities of a place for a quiet rest or doze. But I found that these places were much fewer than I had imagined. Scarcely any were safe from the prying eyes of a passing policeman. I did not care to look for such a place in any of the side-streets, for I had an illogical but persistent feeling that this would be taking me out of my way. In any case, I realised that in practice I was not at all enamoured of the idea of sleeping out, or even resting, in some furtive hiding-place. Above everything, I preferred to keep walking.

Near King's Cross I paused to go into an all-night café. I went in as much to sit down as for the refreshment. Nevertheless, I was not sufficiently expert in the art of spinning out a cup of tea and a slice of cake to make them last me very long. Also, I must have been somewhat self-conscious, for, although I dawdled for what seemed to me an inordinate length of time, I discovered when I went out that I had been in the café little more than a quarter of an hour.

After a moment's indecision I set off up Pentonville Road towards the Angel. The brief respite in the café had seemed to make it harder than ever for me to keep going. I longed for rest and sleep. In addition to fatigue, however, a minor torture began to manifest itself; I was becoming obsessed about the time. The night already seemed endless. It was an eternity (about two hours) since I had first started out. It was eternity until the morning. I found myself looking at every clock, and the time on each of them was the same. "As you will insist on staring at us so rudely, we refuse to budge," the blank, haughty clock-faces seemed to say. If one clock showed a few minutes later than the last I felt that I had won a victory on the sly.

A long, slow toiling up steep Pentonville Road. The Angel. No roaring, milling traffic here now. City Road, blank and empty, a symmetrical double line of lamps curving into the distance, stretching to the east. A sense of desolation, and an awareness of humanity fast asleep. Islington High Street, going north. A sense of desolation, and an awareness of sleeping humanity. St. John's Street, leading to the south. Pentonville Road behind me. A still silence. Lamps that were somehow blind, in spite of the light they gave. And all the millions in London, recently so active, now unconscious in sleep.

Down City Road, between the long avenue of lights. Silence, solitariness and a brooding relaxation from the effort of day. Maybe the town will never wake up. Maybe it is in the grip of a spell. There's something sinister about this vast, unanimous sleeping.

City Road is endless. Also, it's no easier walking downhill than uphill when you're tired. Cafés, factories, cafés, offices. I pause to gaze sedulously into the display window of a firm which sells tractors. My head is humming a little with the need for sleep. Who wants tractors in City Road? A warm, voluptuous yearning for sleep. It is an outrage, a violation of nature to keep awake. Who wants to keep awake? Sleep is the warmest thing in the world. (That reminds me; it's darn cold. Should have brought my coat with me.) Sleep is the sleepiest thing in the world. There's nothing sleepier than sleep. Funny thing, last night (how long ago? *Last* night. Yes, *last* night)—last night I could have slept for as long as I'd wanted. But I'd gone to bed late, and got up earlier than usual this morning. (Well, in a way, yesterday morning. Strange. . . .)

I realise that a policeman is looking at me watchfully. I feel somehow apprehensive. It is borne upon me with sudden forcefulness that I am now a little beyond the pale of society. I have no address now. I can be arrested, very easily. For what? Oh, the policeman might decide that I am a "suspicious character", or something. My imagination presents a vivid scene of a court room, me in the dock, and the policeman informing an inimical magistrate that he found me at three o'clock in the morning "loitering with intent to commit a felony"—or whatever policemen usually arrest loitering young men for in the small hours of the morning.

I am galvanised into wakefulness and energy again. I move away from the window, trying to seem purposeful, yet not too hurried. I review my legal position. One of the first things a policeman would do if he were suspicious of me would be to ask my address. Of course, I had none. True, I had a shilling, even more. That was something. I remembered vaguely some information I had once heard about people found wandering with no place of abode. If they could show that they possessed at least a shilling, it proved something or other, and they were either let off lightly, or not arrested at all—I forgot which.

These thoughts remind me of an incident which took place some years before, when my pal and I were on a week-end cycling and camping tour. In our efforts to reach a certain farm before nightfall, we took a road which ought to have been a short cut. However, after we had ridden for a couple of hours we had to admit ourselves completely baffled, for the road had taken us through miles of desolate and unfamiliar country that did not seem to lead anywhere—least of all to the neighbourhood of the farm we were trying to reach. As it was already dusk, and we were both tired, we decided to call it a day. There were now wide stretches of grassland on either side of the road. Hauling ourselves and our bikes over the fence, we made off some distance into the interior, where we pitched our tent and settled down to sleep. But not for long. About three o'clock in the morning we were summarily awakened. "Come on! Open up! Get out of that tent!" a gruff voice shouted. A powerful torchlight was shining through the thin canvas, dazzling our eyes. We soon found that our discoverer was a roving country policeman equipped with a bicycle and a particularly vicious-looking Alsatian dog which had only one eye. With the air of one who had tracked a couple of obviously desperate criminals to their lair, the policeman asked us who we were, where we came from, what we did for a living, and so on. Then he told us, in tones in which horror and indignation fought for supremacy, that we were trespassing on the land of the local magistrate, and that we would "cop it" severely if we were hauled before that gentleman. This we could well believe. The policeman then asked if either of us had a shilling. The construction I placed on this question was that he was attempting to get us to bribe him. He had already reiterated several suspicious phrases, such as: "Why, two great, powerful, strapping young fellows like you could settle me in a minute, if you wanted to,"—despite the fact that he was about six inches taller than either of us, and had his dog. I therefore told him that neither of us had any money, that we had brought all our food with us, and so on. After further parleying, and after we had gathered our possessions in a rough-and-ready way, we followed the policeman to the road. Before we knew what had happened, he had disappeared into the dark night. We spent the rest of the night on a grass verge a little farther along the roadside. . . .

I am grateful for this memory. It has helped to pass the time splendidly. It is already five past three. I am in Old Street, walking towards Shoreditch. I do my best to remember, in as much detail as possible, other incidents that took place when my pal and I went camping and cycling. I become sentimental. I tell myself that those were the good old days.

In Shoreditch High Street I pause to consider which way I should go. It is sixteen minutes past three—the very depths of the night. The streets are silent and desolate with an almost terrifying silence and desolation. The buildings gaze at me with brooding distaste and seem to complain that I disturb the fast silence with my alien presence. Uneasily I ignore their baleful stare. On the one hand the road curves round under the gloomy railway bridge and leads a silent way to Dalston Junction. On the other hand it curves round between the dead warehouses and shops to reach eventually the City.

I wait for a long time, unable and unwilling to make up my mind, because of my fatigue. It is as though the direction I should take has become a matter of crucial importance. Whilst I hesitate, making my decision, I stand still, ceasing from the long, unending perambulation that leads nowhere. Suddenly I hear a vague, rumbling noise. Is it my imagination? The noise approaches nearer, becomes louder. Suddenly round the bend, beneath the railway bridge, a tramcar sways and lumbers, groans and grumbles. It is brightly lit and cheerful. As it turns to go down Old Street I see inside it authentic human beings. I notice an elderly, respectable workman filling his pipe, quite unconscious that he is performing a homely miracle for a bystander on the pavement. The tramcar disappears, its noises retreat into the distance.

I realise that I am, after all, not the only one alive and conscious at this hour. I decide to make my way towards Liverpool Street Station, near which I will probably find an all-night café open. I am now very near the streets where, aeons ago, I first started on this endless journey.

Slowly and reluctantly, with heavy effort, I begin walking again. Soon my movements are automatic and apparently effortless. I can keep walking like this for ever and ever. It would be more trouble to stop walking than to go on. I seem to have passed over some strange mystical bridge which now separates me from the world of fatigue. Nevertheless, at the back of my mind the longing for rest and sleep is even more intolerable than before. . . .

At about four o'clock I prevailed upon myself to enter an all-night café. I had already passed one or two since leaving Shoreditch, but it had seemed a pity and a waste of money to interrupt my new mood of strange effortlessness by sitting down in a café, and so I had passed them by.

I was soon sorry that I had not passed by this café, as I had passed the others. It was a dirty, smoky den, and its half a dozen or so inhabitants appeared to belong to the scum of London's slum life. All of them, including the man behind the counter, had that undersized body, that V-shaped countenance, that somehow sinister agility of movement which are among the physical characteristics of the product of the slum. They were dressed in clothes which had once been the height of loud and flashy fashion, but which were now greasy, worn and torn. Their voices were husky and savage, and when they talked and laughed they all displayed decayed, festering and broken teeth. The language was one long, dreary and monotonous oath.

When I entered they were all engaged in shouting obscene proposals to a girl or woman behind the counter. This set the whole degenerate and degraded tone of the place, for the creature behind the counter was as repulsive an example of malformed womanhood as I had ever seen. Eventually, when the object of these attentions had coyly disappeared into some room at the back of the place, the café proprietor served me with a cup of tea and a slice of cake. I was now even more sorry than before that I had come into this place. I had eaten poor-quality and near poisonous stuff in many of the cheap cafés, run by ignorant and greedy misfits, which are a feature of all large towns. Compared with what I now received, however, the worst I had previously come across was as manna. The tea was like the lukewarm essence of stewed leather, and the cake was the original piece of old leather from which the tea had been stewed.

I sat at the table bleary-eyed and filled with hate. I felt that I had been cheated, cheated into paying over some of my store of precious coins and getting worse than nothing in return. There ought to be a law against these places, I decided savagely, or at any rate a system of inspection that made certain that the food and drink sold conformed at least to a minimum standard. As things were, any filthy slattern could proclaim to the world that he sold food and drink, and you didn't find out about the quality of it until it was too late.

Suddenly the heavy emptiness before me materialised into a shape—the shape of a very weird human being. He was a fat and dumpy-looking individual, with a round, fat face that reminded me of a pudding. This resemblance to a pudding was made even more close by the fact that he wore a hat that bore a strong resemblance to an inverted pudding basin. He had a small, triangular nose that was tilted upwards at an angle of forty-five degrees, and two small, very bright twinkling and aggressive eyes. His mouth was merely a little hole in the lower half of his face.

Round his neck he wore a somewhat startling effeminate scarf of chiffon, or some other material affected by women. The rest of his corpulent frame that I could see above the table was enveloped in a loose overcoat which reminded me of a shepherd's smock.

He gazed at me meditatively for a time. Then he leaned forward and asked in a very confidential tone:

"Did ye 'ear what 'appened outside 'ere yesterday?"

"No," I replied, trying to indicate that I was not particularly interested.

As one who has a tale of eerie mystery to unfold, the fat one continued in low, portentous tones:

"There was a woman walking past 'ere—a charwoman she was—an' she fahn' five pahn'."

"Some people have all the luck," I mumbled, and wished excruciatingly that I, and not the charwoman, had been the discoverer of the "five pahn'."

"Five pahn' she fahn'," said the fat one, who was now apparently getting into his stride, for he in no way allowed the fact that he was taking huge bites of cake to interfere with his speech. "Five pahn' she fahn'. An' what d'you think 'appened?"

I didn't know, and intimated as much.

"She was jest goin' 'ome, thinkin' like that she would be able to go on the spree, when somebody comes up to 'er and taps 'er on the shoulder an' says, 'Wot was that you jest picked up? It was five pahn' notes in an envelope, wasn't it? I've jest lorst them. They're mine.' The charwoman gives 'im 'is money back—'e was a well-dressed feller, an' 'e proved that they were 'is. And wot d'you think she got?"

I remained silent. The story disappointed me.

"Tappence!" exploded the fat man, suddenly giving vent to all the outraged feelings which apparently he had been nursing for some hours. "Tappence! Now I ask yer, does it pay anyone to be honest?"

I did not see the point, or what honesty had to do with this particular tale, but I was too sleepy to argue.

"Tappence!" he bellowed. "An' they say honesty is the best policy! Caw! But that's nothing," he went on, as though aware that he had not succeeded in the all-important task of enthralling, amazing and astounding me. Apparently he had even more succulent items of information to impart. "I was 'elpin' a feller with a fish-stall las' Sat'day, an' I was sellin' some fish to an old lidy. I wraps up the fish—two nice pieces o' plaice they was, an' one piece o' cod—when she says to me, 'I ain't got no chinge. Could you chinge me a pahn' note?' Well, I didn't 'ave no chinge meself, really, neither did the guv'nor, so I ses to 'er, I ses, "Ere, lidy, you jest wait a minute and I'll go and get some chinge.' She gives me the pahn' note, an' when I was goin' for the chinge— Caw!" he bellowed suddenly, banging his hand on the table. "what d'you think it was?" He fixed me with his glittering eyes, leaned over the table, and spoke with sibilant intensity. "It was two pahn' notes stuck together that close you would have thought there was only one o' them. Well, I didn't know what to do, you might say. I goes back to the stall with the chinge for a pahn' note, an' jest gives 'er the chinge for one pahn'. A little bit later on, I sees 'er walkin' past cryin' an' sayin' she'd lorst a pahn' an' she wouldn't be able to pay 'er rent. Well, I thinks to meself, maybe I'd better let 'er 'ave the pahn', though I could 'ave done with it bad meself. So I goes up to 'er an' I says, 'Ere, lidy. Was it you bought the fish orf of me before, an' got chinge of a pahn' note?' She says, 'Yass, it was me.' I says, 'Well, I fahn' another pahn' note. It must 'ave dropped on the grahnd. Maybe it's the pahn' note you lorst, lidy.' So I gives 'er the pahn' note and— Caw!" he bellowed, "what d'you think she gimme?"

I shook my head mutely as a sign of ignorance.

"Naffink!" he shouted, "naffink! Not even a word o' thanks! Now I ask yer, does it pay a man to be honest?"

"No," I said.

However, apparently this did not conclude the fat man's repertoire of anecdotes.

"I once knew a feller," he went on determinedly. Then, with a sudden access of excitement, he raised his voice and announced loudly. "'E fahn' a thahsen pahn'! Wodye think o' that? 'E fahn' a thahsen pahn'!"

A man at another table turned round with interest.

"What!" he said. "'E fahn' a thahsen pahn'?"

"Yass! 'E fahn' a thahsen' pahn'!"

"Caw! Fahn' a thahsen' pahn'!" said the other, and dreamily took a sip of tea.

"Yass! 'E fahn' a thahsen' pahn'!"

The phrase began to fix itself in my brain—an intriguing phrase—"'E fahn' a thahsen' pahn!'"

"In an envelope it was, an' the envelope 'ad an address stamped on the back of it; an' this feller—caw! what a —— fool 'e was!—'e thinks, 'I'll take this back, an' maybe I'll get a reward for it.' So 'e takes it back, an' wodye think they give 'im?"

I did not know.

"They give 'im a shillin'!" he shouted wrathfully. "A shillin'!" He fixed me with his twinkling eyes. "Now wodye think o' that?" he demanded viciously, and there was a note in his voice, and a look in his eyes, which said, 'I have been expounding to you items of exceeding interest, and so far your responses have been disappointingly inadequate. Now come, if you are a man, show what stuff you are made of. Tell me what you really think of this last most intriguing matter.' "Wodye think o' that?" he repeated inexorably. "Does it pay a man to be honest?"

The fat man gave me the impression of being like one of those small but exceedingly spirited puppies which spend their time excessively worrying a bone. In this case I was the bone.

"He should have kept the thousand pounds for himself," I conceded heavily. "He was a fool to give it up."

One or two other men had come in, and had drifted to our table, and for some time there was an orgy of tales about people who had found things and when they had returned them had been treated with scurvy ingratitude by a harsh and ungrateful world. The general consensus of opinion was that it did not pay a man to be honest, that honesty was decidedly not the best policy, and that, on the whole, men who found a thousand pounds ought to keep same and say no more about it to anyone.

After a time the talk took a somewhat wider range, whilst I floundered deeper and deeper in the mire of sleepiness. My complete repose was somewhat marred by the fat man, who was engaged in recounting some horrific murder story.

"They fahn' it in a pon'," I heard him declaim with great insistence at regular intervals. "They fahn' it in a pon' ... Dahn' 'Emstead way it was ... wiv a scarf tied rahn' its neck...."

This phrase also began repeating itself in my mind—'They fahn' it in a pon'.' The children of the neighbourhood in which I had lived as a child had been fond of singing a certain old doggerel which began,

> "The farmer wants a wife, the farmer wants a wife,
> Ee—aye—ah-nee-o,
> The farmer wants a wife."

And the doggerel now repeated itself as:

> "They fahn' it in a pon', they fahn' it in a pon',
> Ee—aye—ah-nee-o,
> They fahn' it in a pon'."

Then the café proprietor came up to me and asked somewhat heavily and meaningly whether I wanted anything else. I deduced that this was a hint that if I was not going to have anything more he preferred my room to my company. I decided that, rather than have anything more in the café, I preferred to poison myself in an ordinary, orthodox fashion. I therefore got up and left, amidst an urgent incantation from the fat man and his associates of such remarks as:

"They fahn' it in a pon'. 'Ad a scarf tied rahn' its neck. Dahn' 'Emstead way it was."

"Yass! Stabbed 'er three times in the back, 'e did."

"Yass! Cut 'is throat!"

And other such dramatic and gory sentences.

I set off towards Shoreditch and Dalston. I was by now weary to extremity. I realised that whatever the effects of a night's continual walking might be on one who had been leading a comparatively normal existence, they could be little short of catastrophic on one who has been unemployed for a lengthy period. I was certain that but a couple of years ago I could have endured this experience with relative ease. I was shocked by the revelation that this night had given of the effects upon me of twenty months of starvation and worry. I had hitherto taken it for granted (in so far as I had considered the matter at all) that any unemployment was having no real, basic effect on me, that any malaise I might suffer was purely temporary and superficial. Yet, after walking about for five hours, with two intermediate rests, I was tired with a fatigue which made all previous fatigue insignificant by comparison. I had known what it was to cycle 120 miles and more in a day, to spend a day tramping the moors, and the effect of this was merely a pleasant tiredness. But now, after relatively trifling effort, it seemed as if I had not force of will enough to hold myself erect; as if I had only to relax for a moment to fall together into an ungainly heap of limbs, like a marionette that collapses when the strings are dropped.

An intense yearning for rest and sleep overcame me, a longing for some place where I could lie down and not have to move any more; where I could relax these limbs, relax my hold on consciousness and sink into sleep—endless, eternal sleep. The very pavement seemed inviting, even alluring. I had but to lie down on it, and I would drift into profound and satisfying sleep.

Somewhere a clock was chiming the hour in thin, flat tones. Ere it had finished, another clock echoed it in a solemn, sonorous bass. Then silence brooding everywhere. Five o'clock.

The sky was somehow strangely different from that of a quarter of an hour ago, ten minutes, five minutes ago. I gazed about me. Overhead it was a heavy purple, but in the east it was a dark blue. A gradual, subtle change was taking place. I thrilled with hope of I knew not what. The dawn was beginning. . . .

The street-lights did not seem as strong as before. The long lines of shops and houses brooded stark and black. A raw, chill breeze was blowing; astringent, freshening, whipping the blood to the face, driving away the desire for sleep. I shrank from the brisk whip of the breeze, reluctant to lose the desire for sleep; it was warm and comforting. The chill wind tore away this warming and comforting blanket and ruthlessly exposed me to the rigours of the early morning. I clung tenaciously to the tattered rags of sleep and tried to surround and envelope myself in them. But the penetrating wind seemed to strip my very skin from me, leaving me naked and defenceless. And whilst my body was whipped into wakefulness, my mind became increasingly numb, dazed and soporific.

I was at Dalston Junction. I paused, uncertain where to go. I felt now definitely at the end of my tether. The mere prospect of walking any farther was torture. I was ready to drop in my tracks. It would be hours yet before I could unsensationally present myself at my sister's house in the East End (I realised that this was what I had been planning to do). But what was I going to do for the next four, five, six hours?

I had been standing in the doorway of a shop and resting my body against the shop-door. I was not going to walk any farther, I decided. Here I would stay until it was time for me to go to the East End. Suddenly I was aware of a policeman standing on the opposite pavement. Was he looking at me watchfully, or was it my imagination? I made up my mind that he had not seen me, and if he had, was in no way concerned with me. Then, with a stab of alarm, I saw that the policeman was crossing the road, was walking directly towards me.

It did not occur to me that my night out might have had the effect of making me unusually nervy and jumpy. I only knew that on a sudden I was filled with a tense fear. Hurriedly I set off again, in what direction I neither knew nor cared. I was aware that my hurried retreat might make a suspicious policeman all the more suspicious. Nevertheless I could not slacken my pace. My heart pounding, I hurried on. Every moment I expected a heavy hand to fall on my shoulder, a stern voice to sound in my ears. Only by the greatest effort did I prevent myself from looking backwards to see if I were being pursued.

I was some distance along Kingsland Road, walking towards Shoreditch, before I knew with relief that I was not being pursued. I slowed my pace. What now? What now?

The purple sky in the east before me was split by bands of morning's first white light. The streets were devoid of witnesses of this miracle. I had thought that with the coming of light would come life. But nothing stirred, nor did any sound mar the complete and all-pervading silence. Awe-inspiring cosmic changes were mysteriously unfolding themselves, but humanity ignored them. And the cosmic changes underwent their ancient ritual in utter independence of man's regard.

The growing light was an irritation and an offence to my reddened eyes. Every step I took involved heavy effort. Vainly I strove to think of some place where I could rest and sleep for a few hours. But any place which, in my present desperation, I might have been willing to rest in—such as a convenient doorway or alleyway—was no longer feasible now that it was morning.

I had turned off the main road and was walking in the neighbourhood of my workshop. My workshop!—I thought of it sardonically. A master artisan with no place to sleep, no money to pay the rent, no orders, using his workshop as a place to keep his household goods. Suddenly the idea came to me. Of course—what a fool I was! Why had I not used the workshop to stay in during the night? It was a room in a filthy broken-down house in the centre of a slum so decayed that nearly all its houses were long since unoccupied, and had been left to rot where they stood. It had made me feel creepy to work late, as I had done on occasion, in this festering and abandoned neighbourhood. The idea of using my workshop as a place in which to stay during the night was certainly not one that would normally occur to me. But now the workshop seemed a very haven of rest. I reviled myself for not having thought of it before.

I had somewhere to go now, and I hastened purposefully, with renewed energy, through the deserted and silent streets to the workshop. I soon reached the house in which were mine and four other workshops. Now came the most nerve-racking part of the affair. My nerves were on edge, and so I anticipated a thousand and one catastrophes. A decrepit iron gate stood in front of the house which contained the workshops. After working hours this gate was always secured with a heavy chain and padlock. Supposing a policeman interrupted me whilst I was unlocking the chain at this hour of the morning? Supposing he demanded to know who I was, where was my private address, why was I here so early? It seemed to me that of necessity I would be unable to give any satisfactory answers to such questions, and that therefore I would be immediately incarcerated in jail.

With all the sensations of one breaking into a house for the first time in his life, I unlocked the gate. Then I had what seemed to be a brilliant idea. I carefully put the chain back on the gate, and locked it again (the usual procedure was that the first tenant who entered the place in the morning took the chain and padlock inside with him). Thus, no passing policeman would be made suspicious by the absence of the chain. Then I unlocked the padlock on the front door—the decrepit old building, with its tumbledown workshops, was locked and bolted like a fortress—and left the padlock in such a position that it would seem, at a cursory glance, to be locking the door. Finally, I unlocked the door itself and shut it behind me.

Everything inside was gloomy, mysterious, silent and sinister. I walked along the lobby with fear and trepidation. I crept up the explosively cracking stairs on tiptoe. Menacing shadows lurked around every corner. At any moment something might jump out at me, make a sudden noise, do something terrible, I knew not what. My heart pounded. I was sorry I came here, sorry I had closed the dark, heavy front door, sorry I had locked the front gate. Supposing I wanted to run out of here on a sudden, and was held up by the difficulty of immediately opening the front door? Supposing I was held up at the gate? Panic kept surging up within me again the moment I suppressed it with reason, like a fire which insists on flaring up despite attempts to put it out.

At last I entered my workshop. It looked dead and unfamiliar in the grey half-light. Now that I was here—what? I had thought of lying on the bench, but now I saw that, having been constructed as economically as possible, it was far too short and narrow. I would sit on it, rest my back against the wall, and doze for a few hours.

I got on the bench, reclined against the wall, and closed my eyes. Vague noises seemed to sound in my ears, strange shapes to float before my eyes. The sinister silence of the house and the neighbourhood held me in thrall. The bench was hard and uncomfortable. It was too narrow, and so my legs dangled too much, giving me pins and needles. Neither could I recline properly against the wall, for if I tried to do so I was within an ace of slipping off the bench. I opened my eyes again. Everything was a shade lighter and clearer and—what was that?—a dark, evil shape scurried across the floor. I jumped off the bench overcome with panic at the sudden obscene apparition of the rat which had darted across the floor.

Eventually I once more seated myself on the bench. Once again soporific noises zoomed in my ears, shapeless masses floated before my eyes. An intolerably sweet fatigue overpowered me. In spite of my cramped position, in spite of the cold, in spite of nervous fear, I fell asleep.

CHAPTER XI

A FRESH START

AFTER A FEW hours of uncomfortable and restless dozing I climbed wearily off the bench, made my way down the silent stairs and successfully negotiated the formidable front door and iron gate. I was not sure how long a period I had slept. I felt that it had been only for two or three hours, but, on the other hand, would not have been surprised if someone had told me that ten years had passed since I conspiratorially entered the workshop. In the bright sunshine of the morning the happenings of the early dawn seemed to belong to another age, whilst the events of the previous night seemed as the feverish dreams of an interminable nightmare. There was an air of vague unreality about time and space.

The streets were still fairly empty and inactive. I was relieved to discover from the clock of Shoreditch Church that it was after ten o'clock. Half an hour later I arrived at my sister's house. My sister and my brother-in-law were both serving in the shop, and I passed through it without causing any comment. My mother was still in bed, for although she was relatively well, she was still a semi-invalid, and did not usually get up before midday.

I tried with a long and furious wash in cold water to wash off the evidence on my face of my night out, but it was like trying to wash off the marks of indelible sin. I knew that I would have to explain to my mother why I looked worn out, so I thought of an excuse which would serve a double purpose. I would say that I was living in intolerably noisy lodgings—could get no sleep—was going to move soon—was absolutely weary from lack of sleep—and could I in the meantime go to sleep for a few hours in one of the beds? I would also ask that, in view of these circumstances, I be allowed to sleep on the sofa this coming night. Tomorrow, Monday, I would definitely find lodgings somehow.

My story was accepted without much remark, and matters worked out according to plan. I slept heavily and brutishly till three o'clock in the afternoon, and arose feeling considerably the worse for it. During the night I slept on the sofa (which proved to be too small), and arose feeling better, but not well.

On the Monday morning I set out to look for lodgings. I was not now so confident as before that I would be able to find any, without first paying a week's rent in advance. There was only one real solution to my immediate problems—an order, together with a cash deposit.

The thought kept teasing me that even now, whilst I was trudging aimlessly through the streets, a letter containing an order, or a request to discuss a possible order, or even a definite cash deposit, might be waiting neglected on the floor of my workshop. Someone might have called to see me; and I was not there. Perhaps if I had been in the workshop I might have been able to get a cash deposit, there and then. Maybe it was dangerous for me to be wasting my time walking about, when someone might call at the workshop.

I tried to dismiss these tantalising thoughts. They were a commonplace, born of desperate need. They had no foundation in reality. I had often dreamed such dreams before, and they had inexorably proved to be dreams. The possibility of any of these occurrences was slight at the best of times.

Nevertheless, I decided, I would at least go to the workshop and make sure. It would be tragic if I spent the day walking about, and missed an order which might actually be waiting for me.

Monday was rent day at the workshop, but I had no rent today. Because of this I made my way through the now open gate and front door of the workshop as furtively as on the previous morning. As I crept up the stairs I expected to hear at any moment the owner of the place (who used the ground-floor as his own workshop) call after me to remind me about paying the rent. Nothing happened, and I passed through unnoticed.

There was no envelope projecting beneath my workshop door. Perhaps it was inside (but I had already resigned myself to disappointment). Trying to stifle a feeling of expectation, I unlocked the door. The floor was bare. No letters. Well, had I really expected any? I felt the numb indifference of despair. I was sorry only that I had come here, and so exposed myself to the unpleasant risk of an awkward interview with my landlord.

For some time I sat on the bench, indifferent and weary. I thought of once more taking up the search for lodgings; but now it seemed to me that the afternoon would be a more suitable time for this purpose. Meanwhile I might as well stay here as walk about the streets.

My dull reverie was suddenly interrupted. I heard the landlord shout my name. Filled with a sudden dismay, I jumped off the bench. Now it was too late. I should have left the workshop while I was as yet unnoticed—though how the landlord knew I was in puzzled me.

I did not answer immediately. I had some desperate idea of lying low until he thought I was out. In the nervy state to which I had descended, and in the morbid attitude I had acquired about money matters, it was an excruciating ordeal to have to face the landlord and tell him that I could not pay the rent. "In any case, if he wants his rent, let him come up for it," I thought inconsequentially. Then I heard his footsteps thudding up the stairs, as though in telepathic agreement with my thoughts.

He paused outside the door and knocked threateningly. I gave up the idea of further concealment; it was futile. Also, I could not stand the nervous tension this would have involved. Pretending to busy myself rummaging amongst the few sticks of timber in the workshop, I shouted for him to come in.

The landlord opened the door. "Oh, you're in, are you? I wasn't sure. There's a woman downstairs. She says she wants to see you about some furniture. Shall I send her up?"

My heart leapt. I felt myself turn pale.

"Yes. Send her up. By all means," I said, with a ghastly attempt at nonchalance.

"You ought to fix up a notice-board downstairs telling 'em you're on the third floor," he said, a hint of irritation in his voice.

He disappeared hastily; he had his own affairs to attend to. It did not seem to have occurred to him that he could have given "them" this same information instead of wasting his time.

For a moment I hesitated, transfixed between a paralysing hope and a paralysing fear. If this was going to be a disappointment (for not every inquiry about furniture would necessarily result in an order), I did not know how I would survive it. The next moment I had thrown off my jacket and donned my apron. I just managed to be taking a quite unnecessary shaving off the first piece of timber I could get hold of when there was a light step outside the door, and a timid knock on it.

I had meant to call "Come in!"—and present to the visitor an imposing picture of an artisan thoughtfully absorbed in his exacting craft. However, I was too excited to delay an instant. I hurried to the door and opened it.

A small, worried-looking lady of about fifty greeted me. I had no idea who she was, and she seemed to be considerably disillusioned by the surroundings in which she found herself. She asked me if I were Mr. Cohen who made furniture, and her tone seemed to express the hope that I would tell her she was making a mistake.

After replying to her, I asked her to come in. For a moment we stood nervously surveying one another. I was not very glib with customers at the best of times, and on this occasion I was too tense to attempt to be. I was acutely conscious of my small, bare and dingy workshop. Finally I stammered:

"I understand you've come to see me about having some furniture made."

"Ye-es," she said hesitatingly, as though doubtful of finally committing herself.

Having said this, she seemed to come to a reluctant decision. She told me what furniture she wanted making, and I realised with joy, not unmixed with a fearful anxiety, that this was no petty two-days-work order, but something fairly considerable.

After I had made one or two rough sketches, and shown her one or two of my finished drawings of furniture I had made, and after we had agreed on the sizes, the timber and the finish of the pieces of furniture, I told her my price—fifteen pounds. It was far lower than she would have paid elsewhere, even for shoddy mass-produced stuff, but I still could not realise that people who wanted to buy furniture for ready cash were presumably prepared to pay the (to me) enormous sums of money involved. The result was that I could never summon up the hardihood to demand a fair price for myself. Only prosperity and becoming accustomed to dealing in fairly large sums would have enabled me to do this.

The woman appeared to think, quite justifiably, that my price was reasonable. It seemed as though this undreamed-of thing was now settled and I had secured this utterly unlooked-for order. But here a new complexity obtruded itself.

"But how will you make it?" she asked.

I was nonplussed. "How do you mean?"

She kept on repeating in a worried, almost frightened tone, "But how will you make it?"

Clearly she was doubtful if I could make the furniture for her. I tried, clumsily and awkwardly, to tell her the main details of what I would do. But it seemed impossible to reassure her, let alone make her understand. She appeared to imagine that for the production of a few pieces of furniture monstrous machines and vast and complex organisms were necessary.

I was in an agony of apprehension. Was this order, which would mean so much to me, to slip through my fingers merely because of a misunderstanding? Ironically enough, my trouble with other customers had been precisely the reverse of this. Far from worrying as to whether I had sufficient means of production, they had all blandly assumed that I could produce anything, of any shape and size whatsoever, at a moment's notice, out of thin air. And now this lady wanted to know exactly how I was going to make her furniture, was incapable of really understanding, even if I explained for a couple of hours, and apparently refused to be convinced. Was ever a more atrocious situation? I turned hot and cold.

I was completely baffled. It in no way comforted me to realise, as I did by this time, that I was not dealing with a completely reasonable being, but with one of those people who become models of insensate obstinacy once an idea has entered their head. Nevertheless, I had to get the order. Even if she would give no deposit, there would be all the difference in the world if I got her order. With it I had hope, and a new start; without it, only blank despair remained.

In spite of my acute need for the order, I could not argue with her, or haggle, or attempt overmuch persuasion. She had made it quite clear that she did not doubt my honesty or my capacity. It was merely that she had the notion that, in these days at any rate, commodities are produced only in large modern factories, and are impossible to produce elsewhere. After I had tried to show her that the manufacture of her furniture would present no insurmountable obstacles for me, we both lapsed into an awkward silence.

The silence seemed to last for a long time. Finally, as much to dispel the awkward situation as to satisfy my curiosity, I asked:

"Did anyone recommend you to me?"

I was puzzled as to how she knew of me and had discovered my whereabouts, for I could not afford to advertise.

She told me that one of my previous customers, hearing of her intention to buy some furniture, had recommended her to me.

The question I had asked merely as a conversational move became suddenly my salvation.

"Surely if they recommended you to me they must have been satisfied with the furniture?" I asked.

"Oh, they are, of course," she replied ingenuously.

In my eagerness I took on the manner of a prosecuting counsel.

"And if they are satisfied, surely that ought to convince you that I make good furniture?" I pursued.

"Oh, I'm not denying that," she answered naïvely. "I was just wondering how you would manage it."

"Did you see the furniture I made for them?"

"Oh, yes."

"Was there anything wrong with it?"

"Oh, no. Not that I know of. It looked very nice."

In view of this latter admission I was still nonplussed as to how to dispel her final reluctance. She was already visibly more disposed than before to give me the order. It needed one final touch to convince her completely. I turned to the various papers fixed on a nail near my bench. On these papers were numerous drawings and sketches, measurements, calculations of quantities of timber required, and so on. I soon found the papers which referred to the furniture I had made for her acquaintance.

I was about to show her these papers as further proof or persuasion when she interrupted me.

"It's alright. It doesn't matter about showing me those papers. When do you think you could have the furniture ready?"

An overwhelming relief flooded me. It was as though I had just been acquitted from a possible sentence of death. With difficulty I managed to concentrate my thoughts on the matter in hand.

We soon arranged a suitable date for the furniture to be delivered, and my customer turned to go. Now that she had taken the decision to give me the order, her nervous suspicion had given way to affability and kindness. Smilingly she bade me "Good morning," and made for the door.

For a moment I struggled with the longing to allow the exhausting interview to finish here and now, in this pleasant and kindly way. At least I had the order. But there was one more task yet. Quick. She's already going through the door.

Gathering all my faculties for one supreme effort, I stepped forward.

"Excuse me. . . ."

She hadn't even heard me. She was closing the door. Too late?

"Excuse me!"

She opened the door again inquiringly. "Did you call me?" she asked.

She was looking at me in a puzzled way. Her suspicion is returning. Desperately I pulled myself together. I cleared my throat.

"Customers who order hand-made furniture usually pay a deposit." I realised that now my voice sounded harsh and threatening. "Of course, you understand," I continued more slowly and normally, in spite of my acute embarrassment, "that the maker has to protect himself, in case. . . ."

"Of course! Of course!" she interrupted. "How stupid of me! I brought a deposit with me. I forgot all about it."

She brought a deposit! She forgot about it! Hosannahs are singing in my ears. So it's alright. Everything's alright.

She opened her purse. (Of course, my other customer must have told her about the deposit, even if she hadn't already known.) She counted out five pound notes. To her they were money. To me they were the certificates of my acquittal from the sentence of death.

"There!" she said with a smile. "I *thought* I forgot something."

Her smile made it easy for me to pretend that I was not a beggar, and she a beneficent dispenser of charity. I gave her a receipt, exactly as though this were a commonplace, everyday transaction as far as I was concerned. She examined the receipt carefully and smiled as she put it in her purse.

"Well, good morning," she beamed, "and mind you make a good job of my things, won't you?"

I murmured something deliriously, and showed her very carefully out of the workshop. When she had gone I stood for some time in a daze. So the incredible had really happened! A dream I had dreamt had amazingly become reality. I conquered the desire to rush downstairs, triumphantly pay the rent, and go out and experience the delicious sensation of having a meal without anxiously wondering at every moment whether I could pay for it.

I soon reckoned out the approximate amount of timber I would need to go on with. I intended to make only one of the pieces of furniture first, and then invite my customer to inspect it. I would then be able to ask for the inevitable further advance of money with a better grace than if I could show only an inchoate mass of uncompleted furniture.

At the timber yard I was told that they would not be able to deliver my timber until next morning. I could have gone back to the workshop to work out further details of the job, and even to begin work on some of the minor parts. I was, however, in no mood for these prosaic beginnings. I was not only very tired, but in the grip of a feeling of holiday. With difficulty I conquered the desire to go out and about. There was one very obvious and necessary way to spend the afternoon—to find lodgings.

I found them fairly quickly in the home of a fat, breathless woman with three chins and an air of resigned tolerance of the ways of lodgers. When she showed me the room her expression was that of one who would not in the least blame me if I decided that it was unsuitable. It was a dreary enough lodging, and had I been in critical mood I might have refused it. But there was one object in the room that redeemed it, that was beautiful to my eyes with a beauty surpassing that of women. It was a bed, and moreover a bed that was fittingly the property of the fat landlady. It was broad and high and visibly comfortable. The counterpane was turned back, and I could see clean white sheets and two fat and complacent pillows. It was only two nights since I had slept in a bed, but it seemed a long age since I had last had a bed to sleep in and a roof over my head.

I told her I would take the room. Her expression said, "Well, these young fellows don't know what they're doing, anyway. However, I don't mind."

"When from?" she asked.

"Tonight, if that's alright."

"Very well." She turned to go. "Let me know if you're short of any crockery," she added.

I realised that she had not even asked me for a week's rent in advance.

I sat down with relief. Well, now everything was alright. I had a new start in life.

CHAPTER XII

UP AND DOWN

During the time that I was working on the order which had so providentially saved me, I kept my eyes on the future. I paid visits once again to the people who had promised me orders "in a week or two". Also, by scraping together every penny I could spare, I was able to insert a small display advertisement in a local paper. The results of both these efforts were nil.

I secured orders, however, from a source which I had hitherto been inclined to regard as purely accidental, and of little permanent value, though now I began to appreciate it at its true worth. When I visited my relatives in the East End, my sister and my brother-in-law would often mention casually to a customer as I passed through the shop that I was a cabinet-maker, working for myself. This occasionally led to further inquiries, and a few people who wanted furniture, and could pay cash for it, would ask that I be sent to discuss the matter with them.

It was from this source that I now got whatever work I had. Before Christmas I was quite busy, and indeed for a couple of weeks scarcely knew where to turn. My average earnings, after deducting expenditure on workshop equipment, began to creep up from fifteen shillings a week when I first started working for myself, towards the thirty shillings a week mark. I began to feel a new-born sense of security and self-confidence. I reckoned on being able soon to fulfil my long-felt ambition of being able to re-clothe myself. I hoped that I would even be able to instal a small-power circular saw of some kind, or at least be able to get some of my work done at a saw-mill, and so save myself from needless drudgery. I began to picture a future in which gradually, but with increasing momentum, I became known to more and more people and received orders, not haltingly and singly, but almost daily and in a steady stream.

However, once again events failed to fulfil my optimistic expectations. At the very time when it seemed that at last I was consolidating my position and gaining a measure of security as the fruit of months of anxiety and hard work, orders for work began to dry up. Christmas came, and in the New Year the bottom fell out of the market.

For a few weeks I managed to keep myself going. I was able to obtain a few odd jobs that were scarcely worth-while doing, but which paid my rent. Three or four pounds which I had managed to accumulate from my work before Christmas, and which I had intended to use either as a much-needed reserve of capital or as the means of buying myself some clothes, was slowly but inevitably used up for food.

Finally even the odd jobs ceased, and my three to four pounds had imperceptibly disappeared. I was back exactly where I had started. I had no income, but still had to find the rent of both my lodgings and my workshop. I could not get any unemployment benefit because I had been working for myself. Even assuming my claim was eventually granted, I would have to wait a period of six weeks before I got anything. Six weeks was an aeon away. I needed help now, immediately.

Now followed two or three of the blackest months of my existence —months that were unrelieved by any gleam of hope.

There had been warnings and presagings of such a time as this. There had been weeks and fortnights since I started working for myself when I had been in a desperate position, when, if circumstances did not change for the better, I would be in a horrible predicament. But somehow, at the last possible moment, matters had always improved.

Nevertheless, the basis of my existence had been insecure. Whenever I had obtained some work there had always seemed to be a certain element of "luck" about matters. I had striven and striven to obtain work in one direction, but without success. And whilst I was chasing about trying to get orders from that direction, behold! someone slinked up behind me and gave me an order that saved me for the time being. And the thought had often come to me: "Supposing a time arrives when all my efforts to get orders come to nil, and none of these accidental and fortuitous orders come to save me from disaster?"

The months I now experienced were months of such disaster. It was one of those periods of an individual's existence upon which he afterwards looks back in astonishment and wonders how he managed to exist through it all.

So it is with me on looking back on those two or three months. My memory discloses only brief incidents of unrelieved gloom. I am penniless and without food. I have been in this condition for some time. As far as I can ascertain, I will continue in this same condition for an indefinite period; there is not the slightest prospect which gives me any ground for hope in the future. My face is unshaven, and I have not the money for a razor-blade. My socks cling damply to my feet, and I have no others, and no money to buy others. I have not had a proper bath for weeks, for there is none in my lodging, and I cannot afford to have one in the public baths. I am reading in my room (which is, of course, empty of any food) when suddenly the gas goes out. The room is plunged in darkness. I cannot tell my landlady that the gas has

H (Unemployed)

gone out, for I owe several weeks' rent. There is only one thing to do: to go to bed and try to forget the voracious gnawing at my stomach.

I am sneaking guiltily down the stairs to go out on my daily aimless prowl through the streets. Suddenly my landlady appears, and I have all the sensations of a criminal caught in the act of breaking the law.

"When am I going to get some rent, Mr. Cohen?" my landlady demands.

She is fat and good-natured. Nevertheless, she wants some rent. What can I say? I mumble something.

"This can't go on for ever, you know," she informs me.

I can only hope that in the better sense she is right. But sometimes circumstances have a way of remaining obdurately the same, no matter what frenzied efforts one may make to change them.

I am creeping furtively, like a pariah dog, up the worn wooden stairs to my workshop. I am breathless with fear lest I meet my landlord, who had already addressed stern and implacable words to me on the question of the rent I owe. Why do I go to my workshop? To rest, because I am tired of walking aimlessly about the streets. To indulge, as one indulges in a childish whim, my secret hope that perhaps someone may have written to me, or perhaps someone will call and save me from further torture, as someone did before; to cast eyes on the workshop and see that all is still well with it, and to yearn over the different things I might fashion there if I had the timber and the money and the orders.

I am walking about the streets. I pause before a large mirror in a shop window. I observe this grey-faced youth with long hair growing in a thick mane down the back of his neck; with his face torturingly shaved that very morning looking now unshaven and dirty; with the heels of his shoes worn down, and all his clothes shabby beyond repair. I notice how he has dropped into the unemployed habit of dawdling aimlessly along the streets, hands deep in pocket, back bowed, brow furrowed; he who once prided himself on walking upright like a man, walking energetically, with strength and purpose in his walk, he who once was possessed of ideals and strivings. The iron machine has moulded him to the same pattern as the others.

I am physically sick of my condition. I yearn to be rid of my old and filthy clothes, as a prisoner longs to escape from his cell. I long for a cool, clean bath. I want to have a shave that will clean and freshen my face without the torture of using a blunt and worn-out razor-blade. I long for a clean, whole pair of socks, and cool, clean shoes not impregnated with sweat. I want a bath, and clean, fresh clothes. But I have to go on as I am. . . .

These are some of the memories of that time which recur to me. Relying on my memory only, it would seem that for weeks and months I never possessed a penny, never ate anything, never did anything except wander around seeking more and more indifferently some way out of the *impasse*.

However, there were undeniably times when I ate, and times when I even possessed coins. Now and again I went up to my sister's in the East End, and I suppose I had meals there. I have vague memories of borrowing sixpences and shillings from her whenever I could summon up the hardihood to pretend that I meant to return these amounts. The financial position at my sister's house was now worse than ever, for my mother's condition had worsened again. This meant a constant drain of money in doctor's fees, medicine and appliances, and even in specialists' fees. The knowledge of these circumstances probably made me even more awkward at borrowing money than I would normally have been.

Sadie and Ted had long since moved to an outer suburb of London. Sadie had never secured her old job back, nor been able to get another. Therefore the family managed as best as they could on Ted's wage. Occasionally I walked to their house and back—a distance of round about a dozen miles; rather a heavy price to pay for the offchance of finding them at home and getting a meal.

In this manner I existed during the first months of 1934.

CHAPTER XIII

THE ABYSS

I THOUGHT UP all kinds of schemes in the desperate hope of extricating myself from my predicament.

I knew that many of the people who had vaguely promised to order furniture from me in some dim and distant future would have no hesitation in buying the furniture immediately if they were given the opportunity to pay for it by a series of small monthly sums. It says much for the desperation I felt at that time that I really considered this matter quite seriously on many occasions, despite the fact that it was obviously impossible for me to make the smallest attempt towards putting it into practice. I toyed with the idea of somehow raising the money with which to make one order, beginning to receive a series of monthly payments when I had delivered the furniture, then starting on another order, and getting monthly payments for that, and so on.

It was a blissful dream of an ever-rising, assured income, and it was only with the greatest of reluctance that I would allow myself to realise that even if I could raise the finance, which I could not, the many other difficulties, such as book-keeping, postage and correspondence, debt collecting and possible legal proceedings, made the scheme utterly untenable for a one-man, handicraft business. Hire-purchase marches hand in hand with mass-production.

Turning aside from such visionary schemes, I would force myself to become intensely practical. I resurrected my old notion of canvassing house to house for furniture repairs. This, as in the past, yielded no results. I went farther, and, as it was the re-decorating season, canvassed shops with a view to repainting the frontages and doing small shop-fitting jobs. Here again I met with failure. I showed, however, no very great persistence. I was by now so nervous and lacking in self-confidence, and my vitality was so low, that it was as much as I could do to screw up my courage to enter one or two of the more shabby shops, make a humble and stammering inquiry, and slink out like a beggar to whom alms have been refused.

The situation was intolerable in its utter hopelessness. I knew not what to do. I would have to abandon the workshop—that was clear. I would have abandoned it long since but for the fact that the landlord would want his arrears of rent before I did so, and he knew my private address. But if I abandoned the work-shop, what then? There was no hope from any side. The thought of suicide occurred to me many times, not as a sudden neurotic impulse, but as a stark necessity, the only outlet from circum-stances which had become too much for me. It was an abyss towards which I was being resistingly but implacably impelled.

Sometimes I toyed with the idea of getting myself injured in an accident. It seemed to me that nothing could be more delightful than being a patient in a hospital, even at the cost of broken limbs. Or I hoped that I would become seriously ill, so that I would be taken to hospital. But my health perversely refused to break down; my vitality sank lower and lower, but technically I was not ill.

At the very depths of this period it seemed as though once again my luck were about to change. It appeared that some mysterious agency, of which I was not aware, was advertising me. One day, when I paid a furtive visit to my workshop, I discovered there an illiterately scrawled postcard asking me to call at an address with a view to "doing business". The address on the postcard was that of a furniture shop in Homerton. A small flame of hope lit up within me. I hurried off there and then to the address given. The postcard had been lying on my workshop floor for two or three days, but this was just as well, I thought. The delay would make me seem somewhat independent. I would explain that I had been very busy.

When I arrived at the place I was seeking, I discovered it to be a very small and dingy shop which still bore many signs that showed it to have lately belonged to a boot-repairer. The window was graced with two shabby armchairs and a notice informing a public which was apparently yearning to have its furniture re-upholstered that this was the place which would do it for them, and the public could rest tranquil in this knowledge.

The proprietor of the place was somewhat of an anti-climax by comparison with his stirring and eloquent statement, for he seemed to be in some considerable need of a good re-upholstering himself. He was a weedy and shabby young man in the early thirties, and he appeared to have only the vaguest ideas on existence in general, and why he had asked me to call in particular. One's ideas of the grandeur of re-upholstering evaporated when one held converse with him.

Finally, when I had begun to despair of getting him to utter anything at all coherent, he suddenly asked me if I could make a dozen chairs. I had been on the point of departure, but, filled with the hope that from this man, of all people, I might actually be enabled to make a new start, I hastily replied that I could. I had made some chairs for one of my customers, and it had taught me that chairmaking is completely unprofitable when the chairs are made entirely by hand, and by one who does not specialise in chairs alone (for chair-making is a specialised craft). Nevertheless, in my desperation I was prepared to do anything, and I told myself that at any rate I ought to make a little profit on a dozen chairs. Moreover, this first order might lead to others, and I might gradually be able to make chair-making pay.

The bottom fell out of the interview for me, however, when I learned that, firstly, he wanted the chairs on credit, and secondly, the price he offered for them was one which would scarcely have paid for the timber. The re-upholsterer, meanwhile, seemed to have repented of his recklessness in impulsively ordering a dozen chairs at one fell swoop, even on credit. He seemed quite relieved when I said that I could not let him have the chairs on credit, and he agreed with me fervently when I told him that the price he offered for them was far too low.

I no longer had sufficient energy to feel very much anger or even despair. I left the shop, vaguely inclined to shake my head at the weird types one comes across on occasion.

A few days after this I received a letter from a shop in Stratford, in the east of London. The printed letterhead was quite imposing and informed me that I was dealing with So-and-So's Celebrated Mart. The phraseology of the letter was very business-like in a quiet and assured way. It stated that possibly I was interested in selling my furniture on hire-payments, and, if so, would I care to call on the following Monday afternoon to discuss the matter? The final sentence hit me with a shock of joy. It said, "Any financial questions which might arise could easily be dealt with from this end".

I was stunned. To think of So-and-So's Celebrated Mart wanting to enter into negotiations with me! It was true, the Mart was so celebrated that I had never heard of it before; but, then, many of these shops which were unknown outside their own locality were not to be despised on that account. What a piece of luck it was that I had not given up my workshop! My mind soared to visions of making half a dozen bedroom suites at a time. I would be able to get all my stuff cut up by machine, could perhaps even hire one or two machines on hire-purchase. I thought of the thousand and one ways I would be able to save time and labour in these circumstances; how if I became connected with So-and-So's Celebrated Mart (who could "easily deal with all financial questions") all hurry and flurry and worry were over. I would be able to plan, to work to a schedule, to have regular hours of work, and rest and recreation during my leisure.

It may seem that I was too easily inspired with hope. But it has to be remembered that on the whole I was not allowed even to hope, had no reason for hope, and so when an opportunity came it was small wonder that I seized it with avidity.

I smartened myself up as best I could for the forthcoming interview, hiding from myself the uneasy fear that my shabby clothes, and pencil drawings instead of photographs, would scarcely make much of an impression on the plutocratic So-and-So's Mart. I had to succeed. Mere superficialities, such as shabby clothes, broken-down shoes, and drawings instead of glossy photographs, were not to be allowed to stop me. I borrowed some money from my sister for the fare to Stratford and set off in the mood of a conqueror of circumstance.

It was a wet and gloomy day. At Stratford Broadway I dismounted from the bus and sought directions to the street I was trying to find. To my astonishment I discovered that no one seemed to have heard of it. Eventually someone told me, not very certainly, that he thought the street was in a certain neighbourhood, and with this I had to be content. I set off to find So-and-So's Celebrated Mart in the neighbourhood concerned.

The rain poured down ceaselessly. It was as though the leaden heavens were filled with an implacable bitterness against the insensate streets, with their shops and traffic and Broadways. Endless torrents of rain were necessary in order to chasten the complacency of the streets, the traffic, the Broadways.

And indeed everything had a deserted and chastened appearance. The streets were empty. A few passers-by, their faces mournful and punished, took shelter wherever and whenever they could. It was with difficulty that I found someone to direct me on my way.

Through the water-logged streets I squelched and splashed, my feet as wet as if I were walking barefooted. Indeed, I should have preferred to walk barefoot rather than in soggy, squelching shoes, and socks like wet sponges.

For about half an hour I walked down long, endless streets; drab streets of dull, blank houses which on that leaden afternoon looked like one of the more dreary parts of hell.

At last I came to the street I was seeking. It looked exactly the same as the other long streets of houses I had passed through. Certainly it was not the busy centre of commerce I had anticipated. In the distance I could discern a shop. It was not quite as imposing as I would have expected a shop to be, the owner of which spoke carelessly of "arranging" finance. Nevertheless, one never knew what the exterior of apparently small, uninteresting shops might conceal. I tried to smarten myself up, both mentally and physically. This was difficult, as the rain was now soaking down my back and down my chest, and I was beginning to feel mortally chilled and wet.

However, I tried to wear a reckless and hail-fellow-well-met attitude which was the one which I believed most commercial travellers adopted. I pictured myself talking in suave, careless phrases about different things—about "overhead", for instance. "But, my dear sir," I would protest genially, "I couldn't possibly do it for that amount. There's my overhead to take into account." That would impress him. To be able to talk about "overhead" was somehow a sort of unofficial diploma of commercial ability. Anybody who uttered the mystic word was forthwith considered to be a business man of the most profound and hard-headed character. After I'd impressed him that way I would probably climb down gracefully and do it for that amount—oh, for any amount if it would mean that I would return that night with some money in my pocket, with the prospect of work and food before me, with the freedom to be able to retreat, if only for a short time, from the edge of the abyss.

The shop proved to be even more shabby and mean in character than it had appeared from a distance. The windows were filled with all kinds of worthless, second-hand rubbish. The small shop was crowded to the doors with more rubbish, and one customer, and a seedy, pimply-faced young shop assistant. With difficulty I insinuated myself into the shop, very nearly upsetting a box filled with an enormous number of rusty keys.

"Maybe I've made a mistake," I thought hopefully.

The customer edged past me after I had squeezed myself between an overmantel consisting of a spotty mirror and two representations of stags variously at bay, and a large picture of British Cavalry charging exultantly into battle, miraculously slaughtering with their swords the enemy who was still half a mile away from them.

"What can I do for you?" the assistant asked wearily.

"Can I see Mr. So-and-So?" I asked, and presented the letter I had received.

The assistant looked rather grieved. "I'm sorry, Mr. So-and-So is away."

My heart, which I had not noticed before, fell suddenly inside me.

"Oh. When will he be in?"

"Couldn't say, really. Two or three days, maybe. He goes away for days at a time buying things."

This latter intelligence depressed me more than the news of the man's absence. I felt that, after filling his shop with worthless junk like this, a man who, in addition, stayed away from his shop for days "buying things" was more of a crank than anything else.

My pose of commercial traveller, which had in any case been wilting under the strain ever since I had come into the shop, suddenly fell away from me.

"Does this guv'nor of yours sell any furniture?" I demanded desperately.

"Furniture?" he asked, astonished. "No."

"None at all?"

"Not that I know of."

"Has he ever said anything to you about starting anything like that?"

"He never tells me none of his business."

"He hasn't got another shop, has he?"

"No." He leaned towards me confidentially. "And anyway, I wouldn't start anything wiv 'im if I was you," he whispered darkly.

He winked with great significance, and tapped his forehead meaningly.

"Oh," I breathed. "Like that, is he?"

"Touched," he affirmed briefly, "but mark my words, 'e knows which side '*is* bread's buttered on. You won't get much loose change out of '*im*."

There was a pause.

"Well, I'm very glad you told me that," I said very carefully.

I tried to imply by my bearing that but for this warning I might have allowed myself to become involved with Mr. So-and-So to the extent of giving him a very considerable amount of credit.

The assistant nodded with a certain reticence in his manner.

"All the same," he added cautiously, "you understand that I've told you nothing. I've never seen you, see?"

He winked again.

"Oh, yes, of course. Well, thanks. Good afternoon."

"Afternoon."

Through the seething streets I made my way back to Stratford Broadway. My soaking clothes and feet did not matter any more. I went on my way, hiding from myself that my last hopes had tumbled into the dust. It was necessary almost physically to prevent my spirits from grovelling in the depths of despair.

In the bus on the way back to the East End my position rose before me stark and clear. Although during the past months I had been weighed down by the difficulties of my circumstances, I had taken care not to examine my position too closely. But now I was forced to make a reckoning.

I owed eight weeks rent at my lodging and my workshop; that made a total of eight pounds. Then, during the past months I had borrowed regularly from my sister; true, only a sixpence here and a shilling there—the barest minimum to keep me alive. Yet the total must already be reckoned in terms of pounds. I was in debt to the extent of about ten pounds. Thus, what was to some people a trifling sum could clear me of all my debts, yet this trifling sum was beyond my wildest dreams. It was utopian to hope to get this ten pounds. What could I do to get it?

However, the debts themselves were of relative unimportance. They were of dire significance only when placed beside the fact that I had no income, and no hope of obtaining an income. One can get into debt, and the position will still not be very serious if one has an income and the prospect of discharging the debt. But there is a limit to the amount one can get into debt, and I had reached that limit. I had no more prospect of ever being able to repay anything I might be able to borrow in the future than that which I had borrowed in the past. What could I do about this?

Then there were my more personal circumstances. My clothes had been worn till they could be worn no longer. I could do nothing about this either.

A job? A job had passed beyond my line of vision. Although a job would have seemed like a gift from heaven, in my heart of hearts I had become afraid of a job, I knew not why. A job was something too formidable for me, physically and nervously, in my present state. Working for myself, despite all the worry and the handicaps I had had to struggle against, could at times inspire me with a sensuous satisfaction, but working under the iron discipline of the sweated cabinet-making trade filled me with a nameless dread. Moreover, I had sought for a job for so long without success that now I accepted it as an axiom that I would never again be given a job. No, it was utopian to expect that, miraculously, I would get a job and be saved.

What then? The Labour Exchange? But if I signed-on to-morrow, and all went without a hitch, I would certainly get nothing for at least six weeks. Six weeks? It was an endless stretch into the future. I needed something now, and could not bear to have to wait six weeks for a vague possibility of fifteen and threepence a week. Besides, had they not at the Court of Referees, over a year ago, told me that in six months they would cut me off benefit altogether? My job, such as it was, in Newslum, had prevented them from doing that before I started working for myself.

No, there was no practical hope of help from the Labour Exchange. (Besides, although I did not realise it consciously, the Labour Exchange filled me with that powerful mixture of dread and abhorrence which is familiar to many who have been unemployed for a long time. To starve to death, or to become entangled in red tape at the Labour Exchange were twin evils to my mind.) At the best they would send me to the P.A.C. The P.A.C. would lift up their hands in simulated horror when they heard that I had been working for myself. It was a kind of fixed axiom with these people to believe, or pretend to believe, that anyone who had been working for himself was of necessity a kind of plutocrat, with untold hoards of gold hidden away somewhere. The P.A.C. would, for one reason or another, refuse to give anything to the ex-business plutocrat, who was moreover single. They would probably once again invite me to go to the work-house.

No. There was no way out. I could not see any way out. And for that matter I did not particularly want a way out. Any way out that offered itself would involve effort and worry on my part, and I had no energy left for that. A job, or the Labour Exchange, or the P.A.C. meant worry and the expenditure of energy, and I was tired of worry and had no energy. I wanted to rest and do nothing and worry about nothing for a long time to come. What I wanted, though I did not realise it, was not an ordinary opportunity, but a miracle. The thought of all my debts being wiped out, and all my urgent needs being satisfied through some miraculous intervention, was like the thought of heaven. But I did not believe in the miracle I unconsciously desired.

No, there was no way out. There was only the abyss opening before me. I was at the edge of the precipice now. Sooner or later I would be impelled over its edge.

CHAPTER XIV

TRIAL BY ORDEAL

Two or three days passed, without any prospects of improvement in my situation. I was for the most part resigned and apathetic, content to let things take their own course. I had given up striving and worrying. Sooner or later all this would come to an end; in what manner I neither knew nor cared.

One day I was walking along the street. On a sudden the mist which already was beginning to gather around my consciousness was abruptly dispelled. There, undeniable and unephemeral, was a notice:

WANTED CABINET-MAKERS. APPLY WITHIN.

I stared, astounded. If the notice had been removed at that very instant I should have been in no way surprised. But although time was passing, the notice was not removed, neither did hordes of cabinet-makers suddenly rush up from the four corners of the street and invade the workshop. No one seemed to be aware of this terrifically exciting notice, despite the fact that it was written in large letters and was publicly exhibited.

In the grip of a feverish excitement, I entered the workshop. I soon learned that the employer was out, but that he might be back before work ended for the day.

I waited in a state of tension that was almost physically painful. And all the time that notice was bellowing aloud for cabinet-makers. Luckily for me, it was towards the end of the day, and there were probably few work-seekers about. Finally, the boss came.

He proved to be a pompous and conceited little man who was determined to extract the last ounce of satisfaction from interviewing a prospective employee. He called me "my laird" very condescendingly whenever he spoke (which was often), and showed me an enormous number of different photographs of bedroom suites. Despite the fact that from the point of view of the maker there was merely a superficial difference between each bedroom suite, and if you could make one you could make all, he insisted on asking me every time he showed me a photograph, "Well, my laird, could you make this?" "Can you make that, my laird?"

I scarcely glanced at the photographs. Each time he asked his question I answered yes. The interrogation seemed to go on for an eternity. Finally, when I felt I could scarcely stand the suspense any longer, he appeared to be satisfied that he could employ me without undue risk to the financial, technical and moral stability of his enterprise. With a grave and ecclesiastical air he told me that I could start work the next morning at eight o'clock.

Once again the incredible had happened, and I was saved at the last moment. I was bewildered by the sudden change of my outlook from one of dull and resigned despair to that of hope and striving.

Nevertheless, when the first excitement had worn off, I found myself facing the prospect of work with profound disquiet. I had sought a job, found a job, and now I was going to start work. Yet the prospect of starting work filled me with heavy foreboding. Supposing I should make mistakes, be dismissed in ridicule? It was one thing to work for myself, to do things in my own way and in my own time, but in workshops they expected you to conform to their ways, to do the job in the minimum time they considered necessary, otherwise you were accounted no good. With two slight exceptions I had not worked for another man for over two years. I had been away from workshop practice for the whole of that time—more than a quarter of the whole of my workshop life since I had left school. I had been out of the trade from just that very time when I was beginning to become accomplished in it, to make a complete job on my own, to handle my tools with easy skill, to gain confidence in my ability to solve the more complicated aspects of the trade. For over two years I had been away from the iron discipline of the workshop, and for over two years circumstances had combined to produce in me a morbid feeling of inferiority, a morbid lack of self-confidence. Now I had to re-enter the trade as one who by reason of age alone was experienced and able to compete with those of his own age who had worked more or less uninterruptedly all along.

So it was that work now loomed before me, not as a heaven-sent opportunity to rehabilitate myself, but as an enterprise of formidable magnitude and aspect.

To write down experiences is often to clarify them for oneself, and to over-simplify them for others. For instance, it is somewhat of an over-simplification for me to catalogue the various reasons why I felt as I did on various occasions, and on this occasion when I was about to start work. The reasons were there; they were the cause of why I felt as I did at the time. Nevertheless, it would be wrong to give the impression that I was conscious at the time of the reasons why I felt as I did. I did not say to myself, "Over two years of unemployment have given me a feeling of inferiority, have robbed me of self-confidence." On the contrary, those very causes, which, properly understood, might have enabled me to overcome such feelings, were in themselves transformed into accusing voices.

"You've been out of work two years!" "You've lost touch with the way they work in a workshop!" "You haven't much real knowledge of the trade!"

It did not occur to me, for instance, how much my physical condition might have had to do with my reluctance and fear of starting work. It did not occur to me that, as I had managed to solve my own workshop difficulties fairly satisfactorily on the basis of my previous experience in the trade, I might not be such a hopeless case as I thought.

However, like all unemployed men who have the chance of a job, I was compelled to accept it, whatever my feelings in the matter might be. The idea of any real choice was mere illusion.

That night I crept furtively up to my workshop, packed my tool-box, and left the workshop for the last time. I owed nine weeks rent, and could only hope vaguely that I would be able to pay it in the future. I left behind a bench and vice, a cramp, glue-pot, handscrews, timber, nails and screws, french polish, sandpaper, nail-boxes and tool-racks, and all the other various aspects of workshop organisation which I had so slowly and painfully built up. In their aggregate these may not have been worth very much, but to me it was as though I were abandoning a child.

After a well-nigh sleepless night, during which I felt much as a condemned man might feel as he awaits the morning of his execution, I arrived about half-an-hour too early at my place of work. I spent the half-hour making myself feel as uncomfortable and apprehensive as possible.

My place of work in no way helped to cure me of my defeatist attitude. Although I tacitly accepted the atmosphere of the workshop, did not think of criticising it, and, in spite of everything, regarded myself as the most fortunate of beings to have a job at last, I could not help but feel more oppressed than ever by the fact that I had stumbled across the worst kind of sweatshop in which to start work again after my long spell of unemployment.

The discipline was more strict than any I had ever known. No one was allowed to speak to anyone else, even on technical matters, and all addressed the boss as "Sir". There was a repulsive air of servility about all the workers there.

In this atmosphere time refused to pass, and my first day was as an eternity. It was impossible for me to relax from nervous tension. I was completing a half-finished job which, like most jobs which are left for someone else to complete, had so many things wrong with it that I thought I would become grey-haired over putting it right. Moreover, although I was working as quickly as I knew how, I could not tell whether the guv'nor or his foreman thought I was being too slow, and I was excessively worried on this point.

I began the second day still with the load of the unfinished job on my mind. I did not calculate how long it ought to take me to finish it, I merely decided that because I had not long since got the job off my hands I was a failure, and that it would not take the boss long to find this out.

In this state of mind I gave up the struggle, though I did not know it. I had always been somewhat independent in my dealings with employers, and so I decided that I was not going to tolerate the slavish atmosphere of the workshop. Others might be servile and silent, but I would not. I began to refuse to submit to the various rules of the place. I spoke to a fellow-worker rather ostentatiously, if I considered it necessary. I did not call the boss "Sir" (I had not done so all along), neither did I kowtow to him as the others did.

The boss spent most of his time in the office, from which he emerged occasionally to indulge himself in his favourite sport of finding fault with his employees. He had a way of strutting importantly from one bench to another (keeping the next worker in suspense as to his approaching fate) and pointing out to the worker how much better, quicker and cleverer he (the boss) would have been if he had been doing the work. Somehow he never did the work, preferring to leave it to the incompetent workers. He was, however, quite safe in criticising, for he was never called upon to justify his criticisms. He had the worker at a double disadvantage, for he had him in his power, yet at the
228

same time both he and the worker kept up a sedulous pretence that the carping criticisms were made purely in a spirit of impartial truth. If a worker had the temerity to attempt a humble self-justification, the boss had a very effective reply. He interrupted the worker before the latter had really begun to speak, and exclaimed in loud, sardonic tones, "You ought to be an actor, my laird. You ought to be on the stage."

This actually was the strongest impression I got of the employer himself: that he was an actor strutting self-importantly about the stage of his petty workshop.

On the second afternoon the boss approached me. On the whole, he had left me alone. He had apparently decided, however, that it was time to find fault with me as well as with the others. I, on the contrary, had decided otherwise. When he came to my bench I was ready for him—somewhat too aggressively ready, perhaps.

"Well, my laird," he began, "have you nearly finished that job, eh? Don't you think it's about time to start work, eh?"

It was his way of talk. He would have said the same if I had been finishing the job at record-breaking speed (and I was working quickly enough, in all conscience). The correct thing was to reply to such sallies with a few words of humble and apologetic explanation. I, however, broke the rules. I looked at him contemptuously and in a very distinct voice replied:

"*You* may think you're very clever, but I don't."

There was a sudden silence. Averted heads watched the scene furtively. The boss coloured to a brick red. He walked over to the foreman.

"Give that man his cards," he ordered thickly.

The foreman, a thin, pasty-faced helot, obediently shuffled over towards me. If he felt any drama in the situation he gave no sign of it. His expression was as always, dreamy, abstract, slightly weary.

"Sorry, boy," he mumbled in his high, tired voice. "You'll 'ave to finish with uzz. Pack yer tools. The guv'nor 'll pay you in the office."

So I'd got the sack. A nice, short, sharp job. If I'd have held my tongue I'd have still been working at the bench, the same as the others. But I'd chosen to be different—ridiculously different—from the others. I had tried to live up to some pitiful, purely mythical idea of my independence and incorruptible self-integrity.

Oh, I didn't blame myself. I was not going to fly into panic and self-reproach because I'd lost my job. Such jobs were not worth while fretting over for one moment. A man was a mixture of a craven and a cretin to keep himself enchained to such a job.

But it appeared that many people regarded it as right and normal to strive their utmost to keep such a job. The rest of my workmates, for instance. They lived according to the idea that one must keep a job, no matter what kind of a job; that one must work, no matter how hard or how long; that one must be thankful to receive wages, no matter how small.

But these ideas seemed to me now no better than mere superstitions. I had been too long out of the shackles to fret because the shackles had been loosened from me. Shackles might mean a certain amount of security, but they were still shackles.

Besides, two days ago I'd had nothing and the hope of nothing. Now at least I had a couple of days' wages.

I packed my tools and went to the office for my wages. The boss tried to re-assert his dignity over me by attempting a long, accusing harangue on the insolence and wickedness of modern working youth, and what things had been like when he was a boy. I made it clear, however, that I was not particularly interested, and the sooner I got my wages the better.

As, still haranguing me, he paid me for my two days' work, the idea stole upon me that he really seemed quite chagrined at the fact that I had put myself in the position where he had had to give me the sack. He seemed to be angling for a servile apology from me, so that, with a great show of magnanimity, he could reinstate me. And it dawned on me that perhaps I had been too defeatist, and too certain that I was not good enough. After all, I had only been getting a shilling an hour, and though this sum had seemed the height of fortune after my months of starvation, I saw now that it was very good value for him. He might have to search for some time before he found someone to do the work I had been doing for that sum. If I apologised, and managed to keep going over these first few harrowing days, I might gradually be able to reinstate myself in the ranks of the wage-earners.

But, quite apart from the fact that it was impossible for me to apologise, I felt that I could not keep going in such a sweatshop as this. I was at the end of my nervous and physical tether. I wanted above all to go away and do nothing for a long time. Also, after the past months, and after eking out my existence these last two days on borrowed pence, I was eager to know what it would be like now, immediately, to have nearly a pound in my pocket. To have to postpone affluence and complete rest till the end of the week (still three days away) was an appalling prospect.

I took the money and left the place. An immense relaxation stole over me.

I spent the next few days in a luxury of idleness and freedom from worry. I had not been really idle ever since I had been unemployed, for true idleness is a state of relaxation, and no one who is haunted and hunted by the worries of hunger and penniless-ness can know real idleness. Like a convict in a cell, he knows only the misery of enforced withdrawal from occupation, but he is ignorant of the beneficial delights of true idleness.

I had not much money left out of my two days' wages, for I paid a week's rent at my lodgings and returned a few shillings to my sister. The money I had earned was so preciously significant to me that it was like having my teeth out to part with almost all of it in these righteous but unexciting ways. Nevertheless, by paying a week's rent I secured a partial freedom from guilt in staying at my lodging at all, and for these few days was enabled to go in and out without feeling like a criminal. A landlady who has allowed herself to get into the position of being owed nine weeks rent feels more pleased when she unexpectedly receives rent for one week than she does when the rent is paid soberly and regularly as clockwork. There is a moral in this, of which not a few of the world's scoundrels have been cognizant.

During the period in which I had been working for myself I had never known what it was to be able to call a penny my own. Any money I had was either an advance on work which had not yet been begun, and had to be spent on materials with which to start the job, or else was borrowed in order to buy materials with which to finish a job, or else would be needed for the next job, and so on. At the best of times any money I had was needed in a dozen and one ways for the workshop. I could only spend the barest minimum on myself, and then with much misgiving and much calculation. But now these few shillings I possessed were my own. I did not have to buy any timber with them, or any glue, or nails, or polish, or pay the rent of the workshop with them. So it was that for two or three days I knew a delightful sense of easiness of the mind.

At the end of this time I again began to look for work. I had a couple of shillings left, but no other money to look forward to. Once more the future was menacing with the prospect of blank, empty days of hunger and want. By contrast with the last two or three days, the prospect seemed more unendurable than ever.

I happened to be walking in Shoreditch when I saw a number of unemployed men reading the vacancy columns of the news-papers which were pasted on the notice-board outside the Public Library. It occurred to me to stop and have a look also. I did not expect to find any suitable job, when suddenly I did. There was a job going for skilled woodworkers in a small town on the outskirts of London. If I walked to and from the Green Line bus terminus, I could just about manage the fare. I went to the nearest telephone box and 'phoned up the firm which was advertising. Yes, they still wanted woodworkers. Yes, it would be all right if I applied there in two or three hours' time. I hurried towards the Green Line terminus.

The experience at my last job had had the opposite effect to that which I might have supposed. In spite of the fact that I could not afford to choose, I had decided that from now on I was not going to work in sweatshops at low wages. I was going to get the Union rate, or something very near it. Therefore when I arrived at the works I asked for one and sixpence per hour, and to my astonishment the foreman agreed to this amount without any argument. I was not very hopeful that I would be able to keep the job at this rate of pay, but I felt that I might as well try to keep a good job as a bad one.

Once again I went along to my sister, once again to impress her with the fact that the few shillings I wanted to borrow meant all the difference to my future prospects. How fed-up I was with this endless borrowing, and how feverishly I hoped that this would indeed be the last time I would have need of it!

I had enough money for fares and food until the end of the week, if I did not spend a superfluous penny in any direction, and if I lived at little better than starvation level. It would be necessary to rise each morning at five o'clock, leave my lodging at half-past five, and travel by tram, tube and workman's train to my place of work. I would not get back to my lodging before eight o'clock at night. There would be nearly a week of this, together with the tense effort of work and the lack of anything to make the whole thing tolerable until the week ended. Would I be able to last out, or would I again feel impelled to throw up the job after I had earned enough to pay my week's rent and to buy food for a few days?

I was, however, determined this time to hold on to the job for as long as I could. Not only was the rate of pay very good to my ideas, and not only was I attracted to my place of work (a clean and airy modern factory) and to the work itself, but I felt dimly that this chance, worthwhile as it was, was a kind of test. If I failed now, I might never want to try again. So every night, in spite of my alarm-clock, I slept in my clothes for fear that otherwise I might oversleep. All my waking thoughts were concentrated on one thing—keeping this job, at all costs.

The week finished, and still I kept my job. After this I moved into the town of my place of work.

CHAPTER XV

AFTERMATH

Day followed day, week succeeded week, and still, to my inward astonishment, I kept my job. In actual fact the job lasted for nearly two years—quite the longest job I had held since my eighteenth year. Nevertheless, matters did not work out quite as simply as these bare facts might imply.

I had, after all, not known regular employment for two and a half years. Such a circumstance, with all that it implies, is one which is bound to have profound repercussions on the physical, nervous and mental state. The effects of the privations endured by those who have been unemployed for a long period are not easily overcome, neither are the fears, phobias, shocks and other wounds of the mind lightly forgotten.

At first I could not believe that I would be able to keep my job. Every day I waited for the hour before we finished work, waited for the foreman or charge-hand to approach me and give me an hour's notice. There was no special reason why this should happen. Nevertheless, the anticipation that this would come about haunted me, not for days or weeks after I started work, but for months. It was a long time before I forgot to anticipate such an eventuality. I was able to forget it only when I had been working for such a length of time that it would no longer have been such a very terrible thing for me if this had actually occurred.

The first day or so after I started work I reckoned breathlessly hour after hour, even minute after minute, the amount I had earned. I breathed a sigh of relief when I realised that taking this job would no longer have caused me any actual loss—that is to say, I had earned enough to pay for fares, meals, deductions for insurance stamps, etc. After this very early stage had passed I calculated many times every day the money I had earned so far. By now I had earned enough to pay back the money I had just borrowed from my sister, whilst at the same time still being able to use this money for the purpose for which I had borrowed it. By now I had earned enough to pay a week's rent at my lodging. By now I had earned enough to pay these immediate debts, and also to have some shillings left over. And so on, and so on. My attitude now was: "If I get the sack now, at any rate I will have so much money in hand."

All the money I owed, and all my urgent needs, pressed upon me with a new and more intense insistence than ever before. I could not wait for the time when I would no longer owe anybody anything and would have reclothed myself from top to toe. I was tormented between on the one hand the desire to be philosophical and realise that whatever money I earned, no matter how small, would at any rate be a net gain over the desperate position in which I would have been if I had not found this job; and on the other hand the feverish, excruciating passion to be at once, now, immediately in the position where all my debts were paid and all my burning needs satisfied.

The first few months of work also found me in the grip of a very profound sense of inferiority. I was nervous and propitiatory to everyone. I endowed all my workmates with a superiority not merely of experience in work at the factory, but also in age, brains, character, morale and in every other kind of attribute. Without any conscious desire to cringe, my conduct towards them was nevertheless marked by an excessive fear of offending them, and a somewhat exaggerated desire to please and be amiable to these Olympian beings. It took some months, maybe even a year, before it gradually dawned on me that my workmates were quite human, that a goodly number of those with whom I consorted in the canteen at dinner-time were actually some two or three years younger than myself, and because of their training entirely in highly mechanised factories, lacking in a good deal of the skill and experience that I myself possessed.

Because of this nervousness, I sneaked about the factory at first as though I were some kind of trespasser, or at best someone who was permitted there on sufferance. There came a day, however, when at last I was able to begin to overcome this feeling. It was a glowing day in autumn, and we were pouring through the factory gates towards the canteen. I was looking about me at my fellow-workers, and realising that the majority of them were young men and women, and that middle-aged workers were few and rare. I was reckoning in my mind how these girls were expected to live on a mere twenty-five to thirty shillings a week, and how these lads were doing well if they got anywhere near the two-pounds-a-week mark. I contrasted my own wage with theirs, and wondered why it had been tolerated so long that, for a week of hard and monotonous work, a woman must of necessity get a mere pittance by comparison with the wage of a man. I put myself in the position of these factory women, and wondered how on earth I would be able to manage on the wage they received. Suddenly, in spite of these thoughts, I felt a surge of pride. I was earning the wage of a skilled worker, and was getting very nearly the Union rate, would in the course of time certainly reach "the rate". And suddenly my sheepishness and timidity fell away from me. I felt proud that among all these, my fellow-workers, my wage and skill stood high.

Nevertheless, in spite of this momentary awakening, it was long before I became accustomed to think of myself as being at least an equal with my fellow-workers.

In money matters my thoughts followed a parallel course. The fear that I might be thrown out of work haunted me for a long time. I dreaded being entrapped—this time once and for all—in a blind alley of hopelessness, with no prospects of ever being able to keep myself in a reasonably secure state by work at my trade. I could not banish the unbearable thought that once again I would know what it was to be without money, without food, without security and without hope.

Poverty can become a habit, but security can be like a drug. That is why I had been able more or less recklessly to throw up my previous job in the first day or two. I had not yet been sufficiently drugged by security to be very alarmed at the prospect of this drug being withheld from me. But in this job (quite apart from the fact that I liked the job and the place of work as much as I had feared and detested the other) the opposite process began to take place. The longer I worked there, the more fearsome and awful did the prospect of unemployment seem. This may appear to be a paradoxical circumstance. Nevertheless, it was true, not merely of myself, but of the overwhelming majority of those in the factory. It seemed to me that the longer anyone had been at work, the more nervous was his attitude towards unemployment. Because of the vagaries of production in the factory, it occasionally happened that we would have "a day out". It always seemed to me that those who had been longest and most regularly in employment were those most concerned about these days out. They tended to regard them as major calamities, whilst those who, like myself, had not been working very long, took the loss of a day's wages fairly philosophically.

In the first weeks of work I was, as I have indicated, obsessed by the need to remain in work, to have the opportunity of achieving security. Nevertheless, simultaneously with this attitude, I prepared to resign myself as philosophically as might be to my condition if I were thrown out of work. As in my former job, so here also: it would not have needed much provocation or petty tyranny for me to have thrown up this job likewise. Nevertheless, as weeks went by and my position became more and more secure, so in proportion I became more and more reluctant to be torn away from security and be again plunged into need and want.

Because of this I made almost fantastic efforts to secure myself against a repetition of my former days of dire poverty. I spent scarcely any money on myself, certainly none on mere amusements and relaxations. My one thought was to keep by as much

235

money as possible for the inevitable day, which I believed to be near, when I would get the sack and again be out of work.

But indeed, added to this fanatical desire to save every penny, there was also the fact that I had forgotten how to spend. At any rate, whatever occurred to me as being something I might buy, also occurred to me as being something that it was not really necessary to buy. Now that I had the money with which to re-clothe myself, for instance, I was reluctant to do so, in spite of all my former yearnings and vows. My jacket was merely a soiled rag. But buy a new jacket? This was not really necessary. One could always at a pinch live with an old jacket, but one could not live without food and shelter. A new pair of trousers? Those I had might have been patched over and over again, might be very nearly falling to pieces, but at any rate they would "do". I had worn them for so long; I could still wear them for a little longer. Similarly with many other things I had thought at times of buy-ing. They were not entirely, absolutely essential. They were very much subordinate in importance to the primary questions of food and shelter. I must secure these things first, for now and for the future, no matter what eventualities might arise. Until I was secure for the future, everything else must wait.

There were times when this attitude of mine towards spending caused me much unhappiness. Spending was a problem. I had the money, why should I not get the things I needed? But two and a half years of unemployment had altered my sense of values very radically. Raggedness and shabbiness were not so important that I could easily bring myself to spend money on reclothing myself. I did not look upon my clothes and my external appear-ance from the viewpoint of one who has constantly presented a neat and decent appearance. I was inured and accustomed to walking about looking like a tramp. When I wore my overalls my clothes were just barely good enough for the factory. So it was that in the first three or four months, at any rate, I was reluctant to spend money on things which at the time seemed mere sops to convention and respectability, money thrown away on mere externals.

It was only when the August holidays came that I felt myself to be sufficiently wealthy to spend money on clothes. I well remember that evening when I walked back to my lodging loaded with many parcels, each of which contained new articles of clothing. On that walk home I knew the supreme satisfaction of one who has been unemployed and penniless for a long time, and now has the good fortune to be able to buy things with his own money—money earned by himself. I remember how I undressed, and the removal of the ragged, out-at-elbow jacket, the oft-repaired, shabby shirt, the torn and badly patched trousers, the shapeless, down-at-heel shoes—clothes that I had worn so long and so often that they were loathsome to me by their mere monotony; clothes that I had worn so long and so often that they were impregnated with my body-sweat—the removal of these was as the removal of a soiled and dirty bandage.

Then the putting on of the fresh new clothes, after I had had a luxurious, satisfying bath. How cool and clean the clothes were! I looked at the tumbled heap of clothes that I had worn so long, and wondered how I had tolerated them. How degenerate and dilapidated they seemed by comparison with those neat and new clothes I now had on. These new clothes were one of the changes that a mere few months opportunity to work and earn wages could effect in a man. Nor were they merely a surface change; for they were a symbol of the vast process of regeneration that could take place once a hopeless and well-nigh defeated out-of-work had the chance to recover his lost self-confidence and self-respect.

So far I have mentioned what might be termed the emotional and psychological after-effects of a lengthy period of unemployment. But the worst after-effects were physical. Many people are under the naïve illusion that a person can be unemployed for any length of time and then go back merrily to work, and the previous unemployment is from henceforth a mere memory. This would be highly satisfying to all concerned if it were true, but unfortunately, as much for the employing class as for the workers affected, it is not true.

There are many at work today who have been unemployed for a lengthy period, and who are still feeling the effects of those years of unemployment. Loss of former vigour which has never returned to the same pitch as before, various ailments and debilities still remain, tragic legacy of those years. The after-effects are, however, not only merely physical; mental wounds and scars still leave their ineradicable trace. There are many men, and especially youths, who might have been skilled and useful craftsmen, but who have degenerated into tramps, criminals, unskilled labourers, physical wrecks and neurotics.

There is no need for me to quote here many statistics or examples. Any medical man in an industrial district that is or was hard hit by unemployment must verify such a statement. The following example, chosen at random from many others of a similar nature, is merely typical of the authoritative statements which have been made on this question:

A group of men in a Sheffield rolling-mill had been out of work. Then orders came again, the men were given their old jobs, but not one was physically strong enough to hold his job for a fortnight.—A. S. Field, Secretary, Workers' Educational Society, at a conference of the British Institution of Adult Education.

Also I have heard of cases of young lads from Distressed Areas who were sent to Training Centres, and were physically so weak that some of them, whilst at work, fell down from exhaustion.

I, too, found the physical and nervous after-effects of unemployment to be far worse than I had imagined, the truth being that I doubt whether I have fully recovered from them to this day.

It seems to me a very strong probability that I might never again have re-entered industry except, possibly, for very brief periods. On each of these occasions I would have been rejected after a longer or shorter time, with a consequence of a mounting conviction of inferiority and uselessness on my part, and finally—what?

Circumstances were, however, extraordinarily favourable to me. The firm I joined was one which had a bonus system that came into operation three weeks after a man or woman started work there. Consequently, for no less a period than three weeks the result of the worker's labour was regarded as relatively unimportant by those whose job it was to check up on individual or departmental production.

In addition to this, my own work was of a relatively skilled character, and was not part of the general mass-production methods of the firm. I did not have to work on the conveyor belt, neither was I part of a "gang" of workers, whose labour was mutually inter-dependent. Consequently the fact that I might be lacking in self-confidence, or in experience of the work, had no immediate repercussions on any of my fellow-workers. Therefore, at first nobody cared two hoots whether I did or did not fulfil the recognised quota of work. The result of this was that I had a certain amount of time in which to gain confidence, and to overcome the difficulties of that first period which is so critical to one who has begun work after a lengthy spell of unemployment.

Fortune smiled on me even more benevolently than this. The fact that my work was not part of the general mass-production routine of the factory brought with it a number of tacitly recognised privileges. Had I been doing my type of work in common with a large number of other workers, I would no doubt have found that, in common with theirs, it had been studied down to the last detail, and that we all had to do our work in the minimum time possible for such work to be done. However, owing to the fact that my work was an exception to the general run, and was a mere tiny by-product to the enormous mass-production output of the department, it was on the whole ignored by that part of the factory apparatus which regarded it as its sacred duty to investigate every movement of the workers, with a view to eliminating anything not directly profitable. The result was that any time-limits placed on jobs I was given were merely nominal. In my first days at the factory, when I might have failed at too strict a test, the work made merely sufficient demands upon me so that by a concentration of all my efforts I was able to do satisfactorily what was required of me. By the time I became really accustomed to the work I was able to do it with little or no undue effort.

Added to this was the fact that I was overloaded with kindness by my fellow-workers. In the midst of every crisis there is always a rock-bottom base of people who are very little if at all affected by it. For instance, in this factory a large number had been sacked, but quite a number had remained and kept their jobs throughout the depths of the depression. I, apparently, was one of the first of the vanguard heralding the re-employment of workers in the factory when trade began to brighten up a bit.

I must have seemed rather a weird object to these people who had been sheltered from the worst effects of the years of 1930–1934. They regarded with astonishment my ragged and shabby clothes, my worn shoes, the unmistakable air I had of one who had gone hungry for a long time. Their astonishment soon gave way to practical sympathy, and I began to find their attentions almost embarrassing.

On my first morning of work, when hour seemed to stretch eternally into hour, with no end and no beginning, and when dinner-time seemed aeons away, and when I felt as though I might faint at any moment, suddenly there was placed on my bench a cup of tea and some sandwiches. Looking up in astonishment, I beheld a plump, kindly woman worker, who whispered with that hurried, conspiratorial air with which workers in a factory speak of that which is forbidden:

"Here, mate, have this cup of tea and these sandwiches. Keep your eyes open for the foreman. The charge-hand doesn't mind so much. He shuts his eyes to a lot of things."

With this she made off.

I was overwhelmed, if withal embarrassed, by this kindly act. That cup of tea and those sandwiches seemed, and I have no doubt were, the best I had ever had. Thereafter for some time, until I was shifted to another part of the department, this same woman worker, or some other, invariably brought me a cup of tea, and maybe a sandwich or a piece of cake, with the same surreptitious air and the same warnings, no doubt given merely in order to forestall any thanks on my part. The recollection of this typically selfless act of working-class help is one of the few incidents of this period of my existence that I remember with pride and gratitude.

Everyone seemed very concerned about me—a concern which came naturally to them as working people and needed no efforts on my part to rouse it, and which robustly refused to be side-tracked by any squeamishness on my part. They "showed me the ropes" of the place, and were concerned that I should know the quickest way of getting to and from the canteen, which cloakroom I ought to use, at which clock I clocked in and out, and the best way of getting from one part of the department to another, which was fairly large and complicated to a beginner.

After I had been working for a few days the same woman worker who gave me the tea and sandwiches asked me one dinner-time a number of questions in connection with the size of clothing and shoes I wore. I felt rather suspicious, and somewhat diffidently asked her the reason for her curiosity in this connection. Finally she divulged that a number of those in the department wanted to take a collection in order to buy me some clothes. Needless to say, I was embarrassed to the point of panic by this revelation. I urged her to do her best to get the plan scrapped, which it was.

Such recollection of inspiring and heartening comradeship of the workers in the factory, together with the relatively easy conditions under which I was able to work, make me wonder once again how I should have fared in a small workshop, under the eye of a worried employer, which was the condition in which I might normally have expected to have restarted work. For the truth is that, in spite of all these factors assisting me to re-enter the industrial field, I still found matters very difficult. The mere fact, for instance, of having to stand on my feet for eight and a half hours a day (ten hours when we worked overtime), was in itself quite sufficient to tire me unduly. Getting up at half-past six in the morning six times a week also required much effort on the part of one who, leading the kind of existence I had been leading for the past two and a half years, has drifted into a demoralised state of going to bed, and getting up, at any old time. (This kind of existence is almost forced on the average unemployed. During the cold winter days, when a man has no fire to warm him, only a fool will spend more time out of bed than he can help. Again, an unemployed man who has no breakfast to look forward to has no great incentive to get out of bed and make himself hungrier through activity.)

Added to these merely nominal aspects of work there was, of course, the fact that work, even under the best conditions, requires concentration of mind and will, requires training and discipline which come with difficulty to those who have been out of work for a long time. On top of that there is the physical fact that those whose energies have been wasted through a long period of consistent under-feeding find even the simplest work very much of an effort. My first days of re-introduction to work in the factory seemed intolerably long, and from the physical and nervous aspect almost unbearable. Many times it seemed that I would not be able to get through that day's work, or, if I could, that it was not worth the effort. I wondered why I did not give up the struggle there and then. It seemed to me, as I thought sardonically, that a wonderful lure indeed was the carrot held in front of the donkey's nose, that even a man who has been out of work for a long time will gladly go through the first tortures of getting himself once again accustomed to discipline, obedience and toil for the sake of the weekly wage packet beckoning from afar.

Every day my energies were used up to their utmost limits. I came home from work too tired to eat. My landlady generally had a hot meal ready for me, and during my first days of work I forced myself to eat it, partly from shyness, and partly because I could think of no alternative arrangement. Finally, however, my landlady herself noticed this fatigue. She altered matters so that when I came home from work I first had a cup of tea and a piece of home-made cake. Then I went upstairs and rested on my bed for an hour or two. Only after this did I feel sufficiently energetic to eat my dinner. I well remember the peculiar fatigue I endured on those evenings. I thought of it as a kind of thick black treacle seeping from my joints and limbs. It was as though after prolonged rest in an attitude of utter relaxation this thick black treacle became first diluted and eventually dissolved.

Just as spending was a problem, so was eating. For a very long time now I had been used, not so much to satisfy my appetite, as merely to dull its sharper edges. I was accustomed, for instance, to be satisfied if I could allay the pangs of hunger with one or two slices of cake and a cup of tea, taken surreptitiously whilst my sister was busy in the shop (for towards the end I reached such a peculiar and morbid stage in my attitude towards receiving food from others, even from my own sister, that I found it easier to steal furtively gobbled snacks behind her back rather than wait till she would appear and invite me to a full meal); or else with a cheese roll and a cup of tea bought with sparse coppers in a cheap café. I had got out of the habit of eating a reasonable amount of food. To such an extent was this so, that when I had been invited to partake of an ordinary meal, my patience and energy gave way before the meal had half-way run its course, and I had to declare myself no longer hungry. Similarly, I no longer had a breakfast in the morning before starting work. It seemed superfluous and unnecessary.

Starting work, far from improving matters, seemed to worsen them. I seemed to drift by a more or less natural—or unnatural—process into a habit of living mainly on tea and cigarettes. When the dinner hour came at the factory, my first thoughts were, not for dinner, but for a cigarette; not for something to eat, but for a cup of strong tea to drink. Food was of little or no interest to me. Such food as I ate was a mere sop flung to appease nature, or, in the case of the hot meal I had when I finished work, to avoid remonstrance from my somewhat maternal landlady. The dinner-hour at the factory was too precious to spend in the energy-wasting process of eating. I was too impatient to get out of the noisy canteen and into the fresh air and sunshine, where I might sit on a sunny pavement, resting against a wall, smoking, smoking.

I did not get this way without a struggle on my part, but the fact remained: I did not have the energy or patience to eat, and my stomach, having clamoured so long without having received any satisfactory answer, had resigned itself to being content with whatever scraps I might deign to fling it. Sometimes I wondered how I could keep going. I tried to reduce the amount of cigarettes I smoked and the tea I drank, and to concentrate a little more on food. But food was uninteresting to me now. If I did not eat very much I did not feel that I was depriving myself of anything, whilst I felt very much the need for my cups of tea and my cigarettes.

However, inevitably I discovered that Nature is not to be denied; that if I would not make the effort to treat myself properly, I would suffer drastically for it. Once or twice I found myself on the verge of fainting at my work, and one evening, whilst I was sitting reading alone in my room, I was suddenly overcome by severe symptoms of nervous breakdown, such as I had experienced during the time when I was unemployed. This latter incident, particularly, made me realise that I would have to change my ways now that I had the opportunity of doing so. A sort of slogan presented itself to my mind, "I must smoke less, eat more and take things easy".

I began to overcome the difficulties of eating by tackling the problem in a gradual fashion. Formerly when I had sat down to eat I had felt not merely fatigued, but a sense of tension in the nerves of the diaphragm and the stomach generally. Consequently I had been intimidated by the idea of eating an apparently enormous amount of food. Now, however, I limited the food to

242

an easily negotiable amount. Then I deliberately relaxed, and ate the food as slowly and carelessly as I wished.

The idea behind this was that sooner or later I would become accustomed to eating naturally, without a sense of either fatigue or tension, and that gradually, unnoticeably, I would be able to eat more food without discomfort or difficulty.

Apparently this plan succeeded in the end, though not to the extent that I had imagined it would. Gradually and imperceptibly I was able to eat larger amounts of food without discomfort, until ultimately my average meal was about three-quarters of the amount I had been accustomed to eat before this lengthy stretch of unemployment. At this amount it has remained more or less to this day—a none too satisfactory result, in view of the fact that at no period of my existence did I display any tendencies towards becoming a glutton.

. . . . .

So it was that, reluctantly and with difficulty, I struggled back into the ranks of the employed. I was to know seasonal unemployment in the future, and each of these periods of unemployment was to bring back in greater or lesser degree all the deprivations, humiliations and anguishes endured by those whom present-day society deprives of "the right to live".

These last lines are being written at a time when the storm-clouds of war have burst over Europe. The social implications of such experiences as have been here recounted may seem no longer relevant in the face of the more dramatic social danger. But there is a very definite link between unemployment and war. The anarchic social forces producing the one produce also, as a direct result, the other.

This same system of society which will not use its manpower and machinery to produce useful goods unless there is financial profit in doing so, willingly uses its productive apparatus to make the instruments of death, and all the expensive toys of war—because there is money to be made out of them.

Just as in times of peace a social order of "private enterprise" (*i.e.*, private selfishness and private greed) can find no way out of its endless complications but by condemning large masses of its population to living death through hunger and deprivation, so it seeks in a war a "solution" which, in addition, condemns huge numbers of people to death, hunger and misery.

The artificial scarcity which ruins the life of the unemployed is transformed into the real scarcity which characterises a country at war. The civilisation which "cannot afford" the most elementary standard of life for its unemployed and aged people, this society

243

takes millions of its citizens away from useful employment and feeds, clothes and houses them at the public expense without a qualm.

The road of unemployment leads directly to war. The latter is the former in an intensified state. The cause of the one is the cause of the other, and this cause is the production of the wealth of society not for the general benefit of society, but for the profit of the few. Thus in "peace-time" the mining and tin-plate towns of South Wales, and of the Distressed Areas generally, have been destroyed, literally, as if by artillery and bombs. Men and women and children in these areas have been destroyed as surely as if by weapons of war.

A "private enterprise" social order with unemployed people, unemployed machines and factories, unemployed resources—such a society wastes the wealth of the nation because a handful of anti-social egoists cannot make profit from the labour of others. Such a society finds profit, in the manner of a dog seeking its own vomit, in the criminal and lunatic waste of war. This fact find its reflection in the circumstance that every war, no matter what its immediate motive, has always resulted in enormously increased wealth for that same class whose insensate greed for profits is the cause of unemployment in times of peace. We see this process in advanced form in this country, already, in the first few months of war.

Only a social order which can solve the problem of employment and unemployment can solve the problem of war and peace. A social order of "private enterprise" cannot and does not wish to do this.

Wars are the result of a policy of "private enterprise" in the relationship between nations, just as unemployment is the result of "private enterprise" in the relationship between the lords of industry and the people as a whole.

Thus it is that there are those who, like myself, have come to the realisation that it is the task of our generation—a task which we will be compelled sooner or later to face—to do away with the system of society that breeds unemployment, and with it all the horrors of war.

In its place must be substituted another social order. In this new social system there will be only one criterion for the employment of the full man-power and the natural and industrial resources of the country; and that is, not private profit, but the general advantage of all working citizens and their dependants.